Dancing Unabashedly to Mariachi Music

A Woman's Year-Long Journey

into Living True

By Gail Grycel

Grycel, Gail
Dancing Unabashedly to Mariachi Music

p. 272
1. Biography & Autobiography / Women
2. Biography & Autobiography / Memoirs
I. Title

Softcover ISBN: 979-8-3302-8108-4
Ebook ISBN: 979-8-3303-7969-9

Published by

Rambling Dance Books
Westminister, VT
Printed in the United States of America

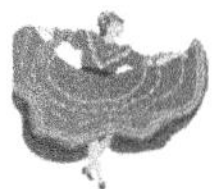

Dedication: In Memorium

I dedicate this book to my friend Bill Saari from Roanoke, Virginia, who taught me the meaning and importance of traveling through life saying "yes" to people, places, and experiences. After his passing in November of 2022, it is my greatest hope, and giddy expectation, that he is once again saying "yes" to the next great adventure of the soul, whatever that might be. I have changed the names of friends in this memoir to protect their privacy, but the reader will recognize Bill when he shows up along the journey. He has been loved. He will be missed.

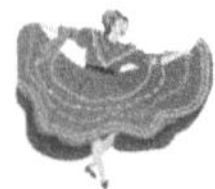

Table of Contents

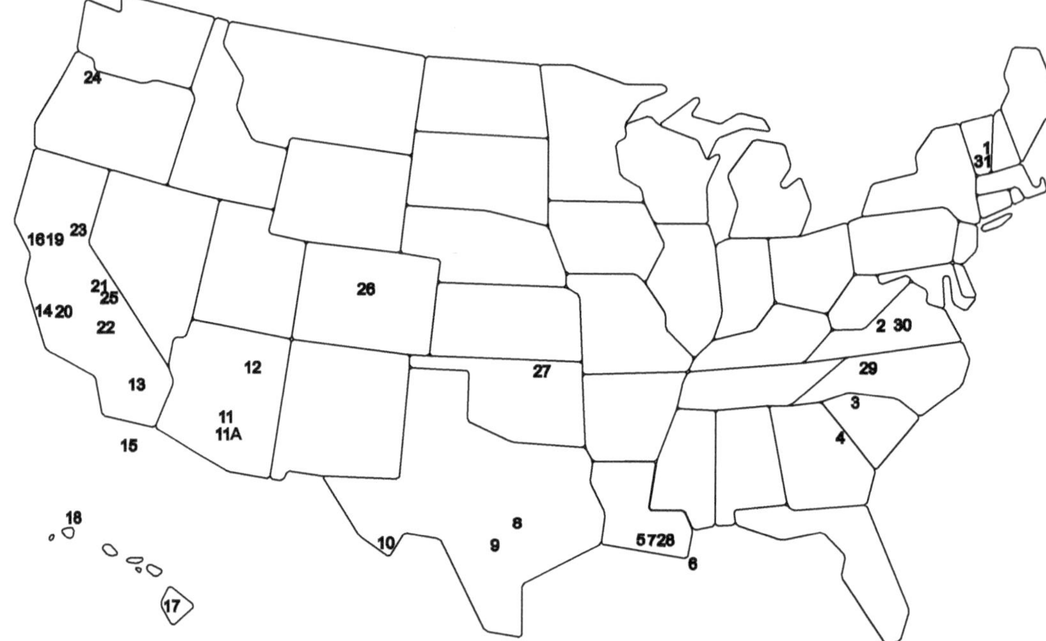

This is a map of my journey and locations are approximate.

1. Bellows Falls, Vermont
2. Roanoke, Virginia
3. Greenville, South Carolina
4. Augusta, Georgia
5. Lafayette, Louisiana
6. New Orleans, Louisiana
7. Lafayette, Louisiana
8. Austin, Texas
9. San Antonio, Texas
10. Big Bend National Park, Texas
11. Tempe, Arizona,
    11A Tucson, Arizona
12. Sedona, Arizona
13. Joshua Tree National Park, California
14. Los Osos, California
15. Channel Islands National Park, Calif.
16. Santa Cruz, California
17. Island of Hawaii, Hawaii
18. Kauai, Hawaii
19. Santa Cruz, California
20. San Luis Obispo, California
21. Yosemite National Park, California
22. Sequoia and Kings Canyon National Parks, California
23. Grass Valley, California
24. Portland, Oregon
25. Yosemite National Park, California
26. Conifer, Colorado
27. Bartlesville, Oklahoma
28. Lafayette, Louisiana
29. Wilkes County, North Carolina
30. Roanoke, Virginia
31. Westminster, Vermont

Introduction

Most names have been changed for the sake of privacy. Real names are used for those in the public view, just in case the publicity is helpful to them.

Each chapter is comprised of a series of vignettes about my adventures in a specific area and resembles a set of movements within a classical music composition.

In between geographical locations, transportation experiences have their own quirky encounters, movement, or lack thereof. I have based chapter transitions on the musical format of Mussorsky's *Pictures at an Exhibition* where the listener experiences the mood of a painting, then moves on to another painting and different mood through "promenade" music. My transportation vignettes are the "promenades" that link the book chapters together.

My best friend Nan and I sit outside a deli in Chester, Vermont to say goodbye pre-trip. We would often meet halfway between our homes at this fun deli.

Chapter 1
Forward Thrust

Bellows Falls, Vermont • September 2014

What have I done?

A sliver of morning sunlight illuminates a section of red brick on the small bus terminal's facade as I watch the building fade from view through the Greyhound bus window.

Am I just trying to prove something to myself?

The air conditioner blasts frigid air from its vents. As goosebumps quickly erupt on my arms, I dig out my jacket from one of my backpacks and pull it around my shoulders and chest. With my shallow breathing trapped between my dry lips, I force a deep breath and big sigh, then will my constricted chest to relax. While the bus hastens up the highway ramp heading south, I move my bags crowding my feet onto the aisle seat next to me.

I can always come back to Vermont early, I lie to myself. *Stay with friends if this trip doesn't work out.* The idea of changing my mind, at any time, comforts me. I always like having a safety net. Some kind plan B.

Vermont's open farm fields and views of lush green hills in the distance line the highway as the bus motors along the interstate. Some corn is still being harvested, and soon the pumpkins will start to be picked. A dairy farm's cows lounge in the shade of some maple trees across one of the smaller fields, and I flash back to similar sheep fields I saw in 2010 traveling around the South Island of New Zealand with my friend Bruce. A long-time nomadic traveler, he was wandering around Australia and New Zealand for six months that year. Being able to meet up with him in New Zealand for a month of travel allowed me to learn what he had to teach me about exploring on a budget: one doesn't have to spend a lot of money to embrace extraordinary experiences in new places.

We were two older people hitchhiking down deserted roads under the silhouettes of peaked crests sprinkled with new snow. We walked long days, scoped out sheep-grazing fields for setting up a tent in the dark if we didn't get picked up, listened for the hum of approaching vehicles while tired and hungry.

"You have to stay fluid in order to dance with what comes at you," he would say when having to change plans often. Like the time we hitched up to the Lake Gunn state-run campsite during a storm on our way to Milford Sound. In the middle of the night, while camped on the lakeshore beach, he woke me up saying, "Don't talk, we have to drag the tent to higher ground," as driving rains raised the lake's water level up to the tent. We could hear gravel slides, like thunder, eventually blocking the road in both directions as we dragged the tent to safety. He tied off the tent to an information kiosk's poles set in a concrete pad, left a light on so vehicles wouldn't back over us, and stayed up the rest of the night in case other actions were needed. By morning, no one could drive anywhere anyway, and once the road heading south was cleared of gravel, all campers were told to go back to the town of Te Anau, since hikers were getting helicoptered out of the mountains around Milford Sound. It took the better part of the next week to clear the road to the Sound, so we hitched to a different hiking trail instead. Bruce could switch gears without skipping a beat. I picture him free-form dancing, his legs turning in a new direction with a jerky motion, his long graying hair whipping around his face.

We ate a lot of crackers and cheese from small markets on our routes, and random packets of soup. We stayed in hostels and camped. We researched free things to do. He taught me to expect nothing and to try to stay open to life's surprises. It took a while for me to trust that all would work out okay at the end of each day. Once in a while, we took public transportation. That's the last time I was on a bus. Liberated by possibilities, I dreamed of my own solo journey someday.

I remove my shoes and lift my legs onto the bus seat cushion, wrap my arms around my shins, and pull them towards my chest, then give myself a tight hug. It's one thing to dream, but can I really pull this off?

Outside the scratched window pane, as vehicles yield onto the highway, a moving van accelerates along the side of the bus, the same company used by my house renters. I can still see their truck inching up my dirt driveway and me handing over the house keys to them.

It feels like yesterday, but really, it was early August when I lost hope about my property manager finding any renters. Not long after that, he called to tell me a family moving to the area needed housing fast, and he drew up the lease. Once I had an arrival date, my days became frantic with paying woodworking jobs still to be installed, furniture moved into my woodshop for storage, boxes filled with household items moved into the attic, scrubbing, vacuuming, weekly calls to the new internet company about running cable to the house . . .

Each morning, with a cup of tea in hand, I inhaled the sweet scent of the rugosa roses in my garden as they slowly turned into rose hips to calm myself down.

Each afternoon, while I pulled weeds, the sun stretched its rays farther over the other perennial beds, heading toward September faster than I could control.

Each night, I crawled into my sleeping bag in the middle of my empty bedroom floor. Exhausted, curled into a fetal position, I pulled the sleeping bag over my head to ward off the continuing fears and self doubts.

As August fled by, initial travel plans fell through and internet was still not installed for the renters. Close to one week before I needed to leave my house, an unexpected, expensive truck repair ruptured my fragile equilibrium, and all I could get out between sobs over the phone with Bruce was "just let me cry."

"If you wanna sing the blues, you have to pay the dues," he replied. *Always inviting life's mysteries, grit, and miracles*—his adopted attitude not only while traveling, but in life.

"I know . . . but everything seems to be blowing up around me," I whimpered while reaching for a box of tissues. "Maybe this trip was a bad idea. The renters are coming soon, there's too much to get done."

"You have to adapt as you go. I know that's hard for you." His voice softened, "I've learned the hard way that right before one leaves on a long trip, all kinds of happenings try to stop the momentum. I just expect it now. You have to do what needs doing, and then you have to let some things go."

"How do you go through this every year before you head off for your annual trip?"

He laughed, and said, "Keep breathing my friend. Once you step off, a new energy will thrust you forward. Trust."

I contemplate his words as the late-summer green of the trees blurs along the interstate within my window view. He was right—loss of control is really hard for me. Knowing what is coming next, and when, makes me feel secure and safe. I spend so much time planning for every option; maybe I overthink everything. Trust does not come easily.

The drone of the bus motor hums in my ears, masking the buzz of other passengers' conversations around me. Every now and then, I notice some random maple leaves quickening towards fall and the color red along the highway's edge, and sense the season's slow trek towards winter. The bus stops to pick up a few passengers along the route south into Massachusetts and no one chooses the open seat next to me. Better this way while my thoughts are swirling around my head, I'm not ready for small talk with anyone right now.

"What are you *thinking*?" my friend Nan asked last spring when I announced my developing plan about leaving Vermont for a year of travel. "You're just finishing building your house. How can you leave now?"

Since 1996, every extra moment, penny, burst of energy, drop of blood, and falling tear during the building of my straw bale house competed against the routines of my everyday life. Building the house felt like my one chance at security since I couldn't trust that a partner would be there with me to do it. I didn't even trust me. *Just start,* I had told myself, *then when you fail, you can at least say you tried.*

Old, tobacco-drying sheds dot the fields on the east side of the highway, and the bend in the Connecticut River flows past a small marina to the west, where my father once kept a small motorboat docked. A variety of moored boats crowd the piers, and I remember as a young adult, boating on the river with him one afternoon on a sunny day. Before he died, he finally found his way to Vermont to see my house in progress.

My stubbornness carried me through each of those years of house building. At the end of each workday, I soaked my aching muscles in the tub. Acknowledging the day's progress with pride, I would whisper into the steam, *I can do anything.* My security bubble, and my mantra, couldn't last—I didn't believe those words deep down. Still don't.

"I'm tired of trying to be what people expect of me," I told Nan. "And what I've come to expect of myself as I try to please everyone all the time."

"Well, you got that from your mother. I remember how important it was for her to look good to everyone, even when things were not so good. Sorry you had to endure that."

I look across the bus aisle at an older couple, maybe in their eighties: her reading a book, him napping, slightly snoring. A wooden cane leans against the window wall under the glass; I assume it is his. The woman looks up from her book in my direction and I nervously smile at her.

"Are you heading home?" she asks, putting her book down onto her lap and leaning onto her armrest towards me.

"No. Just leaving Vermont for a year of travel."

"A whole year? Alone?"

"A whole year if all goes well. Yes, alone. Life seems to go by faster and faster, and I feel the stretch of life ahead getting narrower. How long do I wait for someone else to do this kind of thing with me? I don't want to look back at my life not having done all that I want to do."

She looks over at her sleeping husband, then back at me, and says, "I wish I would have embarked on a trip like yours before I was married, when I was younger. You are so courageous. How exciting. Where are you headed?"

"Well, we will see how it goes. Starting out seeing old friends and family, then who knows . . . national parks for sure." I think about making new friends while dancing in other places than New England, free from any relationship history, and learning about writing to see what I might have to say that's actually worthwhile. Her husband stirs, she wishes me a safe journey, and as she picks up her book again, the bus rolls through the part of western Massachusetts where Nan and I both grew up. Exit signs announce the suburb where my family used to live during the 1960s before I even knew Nan.

I recall a younger version of myself cowering into the paneled corner of our living room after some childhood infraction that I didn't understand at the time. My father's outbursts of rage came often back then, "Sit down and shut up, you have nothing worthwhile to say." I would huddle next to our family dog, her licking tongue consoling me, and learned to repress my voice.

My mother had her own version of shutting me up, "You can't be doing that—what will the neighbors think?" I learned it was better not to speak at all and also not to *be* me. Even into my mid-twenties, I often froze in fear of not being accepted by others, not knowing if I had any value to offer my world. As an adult, I've tried to absorb any confidence, self-assurance, and resourcefulness that I could.

With the highway exit signs behind me, memories surface of Nan and I thrown together in the high school marching band, forging a lifelong friendship. Her voice returns in my head:

"I know you're exhausted, honey, by all that work on your house for eighteen years. But don't you just want to enjoy it for awhile?"

"I had to build it. I don't want to be chained to it," I responded. "If I stay, nothing will change."

I dig through my pack for my fleece pullover, another layer against the musty air conditioning blasting onto me. The older woman across the aisle has wrapped a fleece blanket around her shoulders, and her head bobs with each bump in the road. I think about Henry David Thoreau at Walden Pond and how he wrote that he left the pond for as good a reason as going to live there, and how he didn't want to get to the end of his life having lived only one life. Me too. I just want to let my life unfold for a change. Have no specific plan . . . just 'be'.

"I need a break from all of it—the house, the work, the dating failures," I said to Nan. "Who knows, maybe the man for me isn't here in Vermont. Maybe he's out there somewhere else." *Or maybe I'll learn that I don't need a man in my life at all.*

By last May, my short winter love relationship cracked apart. My boyfriend fled, protecting what he had hidden from me, and maybe hidden all of his life from himself. By spring, I wallowed in tears. While my heart ached, my garden swelled with burgeoning life, my tears mixing with each morning's dew. As I ripped new weeds from the dirt, my disillusionment sucked even more energy out of me, and I struggled not to let cynicism take me down further.

"I know you've had a lot of false starts. You gave the last one a second chance, clearly it wasn't meant to be," Nan said at the time. "I hope there *is* someone out there for you. I want you to be happy."

I remember her and I, even in early high school friendship, talking each other out of heartbreak. She's seen me through all the times I've walked through life shifts, each one a desire for additional healing and self-exploration: my classical music career as an oboist, my custom cabinetry business, woodworking classes I've taught to women, and then the building of my house. Over the decades, she's listened patiently—about my fears, old patterns, restlessness, exhaustion, overwhelm.

Sometimes I would imagine myself driving somewhere, anywhere, and not looking back. But I *always* turned back to avoid feeling like a coward running away from something.

I think about how Nan moved on and made her case: "Are you sure you want to do this? You're not twenty-two, you're fifty-seven. Usually, people take off for a year like this in their early twenties to go find themselves."

"I'm sure. I'm just tired of each day feeling like a variation of every other day."

"Well . . . know that I'm here for you . . . whatever you need. Just call. Call anyway so I know you are okay."

A warm rush through my body counteracts the bus AC chill. I close my eyes and lean my head back onto the headrest and pull loose strands of hair away from my cheeks, grateful for my friends.

Leading up to my departure, when I told other friends about the trip, they would light up, envious of the adventure. I would feign excitement while dread wrapped itself around my throat more often than not. Some days I could hardly breathe and choked out forced confidence about my plan. In my gut, I knew I had to face my fear of failing. *What if those visions of running away were not about cowardice, but the seeds of my future? What if I wouldn't be running away, but running toward something expansive and amazing? Maybe there's something important for me to find out about myself out there on the road while I explore this country. Just maybe . . .*

Having pulled off the highway into Springfield, the bus inches along potholed streets toward the transportation center, and my thoughts turn to the series of bus transfers that will eventually land me in Roanoke, Virginia, my first planned stop. At the terminal, the bus parks diagonally in line with another bus heading to Boston. Old, stained styrofoam coffee cups dot the cracked asphalt sidewalk under the dirty glass windows of the bus station. I rescue my larger backpack from the storage under the bus, rearrange the two smaller backpacks and over-the-shoulder purse onto my body, and follow other passengers inside. According to the departure and arrival screen hanging near the ticket counter, my next bus to New York was delayed. Settling in for the wait, I wonder what it is that I really want in my life going forward? Security with familiar routines and expectations? Or freedom from a life that has come to feel like a choreographed rut?

I scan the departure screen for an update on my next bus, but no details show up, so I shift my larger pack, filled with backpacking gear and dancing shoes, onto the sticky floor and straighten out my legs to rest on it. Other waiting passengers fidget in their seats near me, conversing in hushed mumblings. Bruce's words ring around in my head, ". . . you have to adapt as you go." I know he meant emotionally as well as literally. I pull up New Zealand snapshots from my memory again—the thrill of exotic adventures that arose daily while there: the neon sulphuric colors of the Tongariro Crossing, yellow-eyed penguins climbing up a hill to nest near the viewing boardwalk where I was standing, all giddy from watching them, and the guided hike on the stone-dusted blue ice of Franz Joseph glacier, ice pick in hand following closely behind the guide to avoid the danger of crevasses. Sure, there were mundane days, too, like hours waiting for rides that never seemed to come, while the sky darkened with the threat of rain, and then Bruce would start running through options and resources. But, each day, after the rain and hard decisions, there were the rainbows and diverse scenery. We had interesting conversations with drivers who eventually picked us up—like the Maori sheep-shearing brother and sisters, the helicopter pilot telling us about the rounding up of invasive red deer on the island, and the pig farmer who had recently gotten out of prison. We never knew what surprises each day might bring.

For a long time now, I've dreamed about Zydeco dancing in Louisiana. Hiking in the Sierra mountains of California, looking over at Half Dome within the backcountry in Yosemite National Park. Walking on a pebbled beach along California's Pacific Ocean. Exploring the deserts of the Southwest. Following my wanderlust wherever it wants to take me.

This is my time, I tell myself . . . *before I can't do it anymore.* I close my eyes, smile, and feel tingling racing throughout my body. *This is my time . . . to be free. I can do this.*

I did everything I could before I left home—research bus routes, couch-surfing and hostel stays, hikes, dances, money transfers. With nothing more I can try to control, the rest is up to chance . . . or, maybe, according to Bruce, *adaptation.*

My bus number finally lights up on the screen to arrive shortly, so I gather up my bags and ticket, then position myself into the line forming at the door.

The woman in front of me turns and looks at all my bags while we wait in line, then catches my eye.

I just grin. "Heading out into a year-long road trip," I say to her as I step into my future, and wonder—over this next year, how will I change?

Who will I become?

No Evil Oil

Greyhound Bus Terminal • Richmond, Virginia

Once again wrapping my jacket around my shoulders to stay warm, I wriggle on the wire seat that has been digging into the backs of my thighs. The clock's hands rendezvous at midnight above the ticket counter, but I'm not willing to attempt to sleep. Instead, with five hours of layover to go, I observe passengers departing buses and boarding other ones. Not sure who can be trusted, I worry if one of them might try to steal bags from someone sleeping on a chair.

Some bus riders carry fleece blankets to ward off the air conditioner's chilling blasts. Pillows allow them to catnap through the overnight hours while cushioned against their own irritating seats, or snuggled in a protected corner along the dingy floor edge.

While shifting around in my chair, hoping to find comfort, I invite distraction by staring at the television hanging from the ceiling. Once my TV fried several years ago, I elected not to replace it, but chose to isolate myself from that kind of pop culture instead.

After a series of reality shows broadcasting who's having sex with whom, I suffer through a couple of talk shows whose guests spew insults at friends and family.

Then, at four in the morning.:

"Be *ONE*. Be one of the first three hundred and twenty to call," he declares into the camera. "You can be one of those to receive your free, blessed *No Evil Oil*."

A huge phone number flashes across the screen under the well-dressed televangelist's smiling face looking directly at me. My eyes narrow as I glance around the terminal to see if anyone else is watching this, or worse, watching me watching this.

Intrigued by this idea of *No Evil Oil,* though, I run through just how often the oil could come in handy.

What kind of oil is used? Is it a special blend of many scents, or collected grease from a local burger joint? The announcer doesn't say so, but could I self-bless any oil that has significance to me?

I picture the oil in a convenient spray bottle, liquid rich and clear, to spray rapists and murderers on the street. Could some be dripped into bar drinks to avoid annoying pick-up lines? Or from a beautifully sculpted pear-shaped vessel with a cap, could drops be dabbed on creepy people in bus terminals or on trains? It could come in ready-to-use individual foil packets, under the TSA ounce limit for carry-on plane travel, to use against terrorists.

I speculate whether the oil might work in the wilderness against grizzly bears and poisonous snakes. Maybe old boyfriends?

While I'm lost in conjecture, a middle-aged man sitting two seats from me, agitated, squirms. "They take this stuff too far."

Suddenly released from the spell, I turn and agree with him. After all, I'm from Vermont; we don't get traveling snake oil salesmen coming through very often.

Before my bus leaves for Roanoke, I allow myself to envision many more ways it could be practical. And, I would *definitely* want the oil to be blessed—why take any chances.

I brave the wind on McAfee's Knob ledge along the Appalachian Trail outside of Roanoke, Virginia, during my visit with two couchsurfing friends in Roanoke.

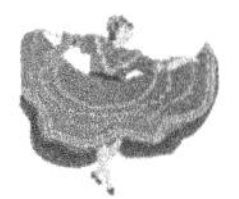

Chapter 2
Star Dust Over the City

Roanoke, Virginia • September 2014

After all my bus transfers, I've arrived at the beginning—of what I do not yet know. I may not know for a long time. Vermont memories fade behind me, and my year ahead seems both surreal AND destined, lost AND found. Doubts lingering from my pre-trip anxiety pale under the two thousand feet of the Mill Mountain Star's neon tubing shining down on Roanoke and now lighting my way.

Through the bus window, I see Ellen standing on the nearby sidewalk, her coffee cup grasped in one hand and her eyes scanning the windows for me. It has been over three years since I've seen her, but my time playing music with her in my living room travels with me. We opened her binder of song charts and my keyboard chords slid under the bowed melodies of her violin. And there was the homemade lasagna she transported all the way from Virginia to warm in my oven.

Many of my couchsurfing guests have become lasting friends like this. I'm grateful to Bruce for introducing the online network to me as a travel resource years ago. Since I joined the hospitality community, I've housed travelers at my home in Vermont: young, old, single, coupled, not only from the United States, but as far away as Spain and Qatar.

One from the state of Georgia stayed with me for a week while in my area for an art workshop, and each evening, we would share stories about our lives. Another from Arizona spent time in my home twice while attending nearby acro-yoga classes, and wants me to visit her in the Southwest during my trip. It will be my turn to send requests and ask for free housing. If it works out, it'll be fun to see both of them again during my travels.

Ellen weaves through the group of passengers waiting for the driver to pull their luggage out from the storage compartment. Perhaps travelers waiting to be swept back into a routined life I no longer want for myself, with day jobs and set schedules and . . .

She holds her cup in the air as she folds her other arm around me, and I melt into her embrace, relieved to have finally arrived. "So happy you made it," she says, releasing the hug. "Just in time for the house concert I have planned for tomorrow afternoon. You will love it."

The next afternoon, I pick up a paper plate and napkin and peruse the veggies, cheese selection, and sweets crammed onto Ellen's kitchen table. A variety of small plant pots sit on the nearby windowsill, allowing different cuttings of ivy to cascade down along the brick wall.

"Do you live here in Roanoke?" Joe asks as he slices a piece of cheddar and places it on a wheat cracker.

"No," I answer, "I just arrived from Vermont by bus. Starting out on a one-year travel journey around the United States. Ellen is a couchsurfing friend, and since I've never been to Roanoke, I decided to stop here for a few days on my way south."

"Hmmm . . . a wanderer. I have a lot of respect for those taking the risk to live *true*." He puffs on his electronic cigarette and swigs from his bottle of beer. Conversations murmur around the table as other plates pile up with olives and carrots, salads and cookies.

Before I can continue the conversation, Ellen herds everyone out the back door to their seats and Joe continues across the grass to pick up his guitar by the microphone. Beneath the drooping tree branches that form a canopy over the performer, blankets fan out over Ellen's lawn in front of randomly placed chairs. Patches of clouds temper the hot sun as I settle down on one of the blankets with my plate of fruit, chips, and cheese.

Coyote Joe—the stage name he goes by in the music world—strums his guitar and sings songs of internal struggle. During an instrument shift, his wandering gaze lingers on mine, and with a nod in my direction, he switches from guitar to banjo. A thin beard braid hangs from his chin, and he rips open his confession of leaving his past behind—those who could not understand his prison of feeling like a man within his biological woman's body.

His eyes soften and I see what I can only hope for our humanity: total acceptance for all of us finding our way to living *true*. I try to see past the facial hair made possible by introduced hormones, and see both the female and the male, the conjoined person building a new identity. Feeling we all have both female and male attributes inside, I've often thought about how to balance out gender within myself. I can't even imagine the internal debate Joe went through.

Within my periphery, Ellen's long brown hair spreads out on the blanket as she lays back to watch the sky, and I lose myself into the lyrics reminding me I am not alone excavating new parts of my own self.

A strained breath involuntarily erupts in me. Something deep frees up and a warm rush travels through my whole body, now relaxed, content, validated. Cicadas balconied in the trees chirp rhythmically with the vibrating instrument strings and coat each voiced syllable. Behind the backyard chain link fence, the afternoon light settles onto clusters of gravestones in a small cemetery, generations moving through from here to somewhere else. It seems that some things in our culture want us to stay the same throughout our lives, staying safe and secure. Joe's words about taking the risk to live true settle deeper into me, because we're always moving from here to somewhere else, aren't we? Maybe, if we pay attention to opportunities, find the courage to take the risks, transformation just might hasten within our dreams. Or at least, I hope it does for me.

THE ARTIST'S PALETTE

Brian gathers blueberries, yellow peaches, and green spinach from his fridge and tosses them into the blender with vanilla yogurt. A kaleidoscope of hues swirls inside the plastic. We met when he accompanied Ellen to my house in Vermont as they passed through en route to and from Montreal, Canada. Ellen had told me she didn't want to travel alone and knew that Brian usually said yes to random requests around trips like hers.

Bold yellow and red walls wrap the living room in Brian's apartment where his paintings, collages, and sculptures adorn the room, covering every flat surface.

I pick up his mummy-wrapped Barbie dolls in a row lying flat against a black wooden backer board and wonder what inspired him to make this art piece. Bound hands stick out of cloth wrappings. An eye, or a mouth, or two feet, unveiled, beg for leniency from their imprisonment. I have my own memories of these dolls—feeling that they were cultural implications of contained womanhood. I've struggled along my own personal journey of what *female* means to me in all her archetypal forms: maiden, expected mother, career woman, mystic, lover, earth goddess . . .

Yes, women succumb to being wrapped by these labels, but I feel we also wrap ourselves, leaving exposed only what is safe to show to those around us. I learned to bind myself early on, to keep private anything that exposure could humiliate, break down, or hurt, so I bound my emotions in the doings of a busy and full life. I've been binding myself to what I think others will approve of, what I am expected to be, even who I think I am. My body tenses as I remember how I thought my mother might have wanted a live Barbie doll to dress up when I was a child, rather than me.

I didn't consider myself a tomboy growing up, but I would rather have been a Boy Scout, like my brother was, than a Girl Scout like some of my friends from school. I wanted to build fires at campsites in the woods. I wanted to tinker with building things rather than playing house with dolls. Instead, I endured home perms and sewing classes. No wonder I traded my Barbie, along with all the handmade clothes my mother sewed for it, to a neighborhood girl across the street.

Brian breaks my gaze from the dolls and sits me down at the kitchen table, releasing my agitation with a new direction of thought. "A lot of people talk about taking off to travel," he says. "But you, you're actually doing it." He places a glass in front of me. I sip some of the thick smoothie and look at him across the table as he pulls back his gray ponytail with a hair tie.

"I don't really know what I am doing," I confess. "I just knew I needed to start."

As I begin to tense up again, he reaches over to touch my arm. "I always say *yes* when people ask me to do things," he tells me. "One never knows what will come of an experience. Take the risk. Keep that in mind as you go."

I place my hand over his, give it a squeeze in thanks for the support, and picture him couchsurfing at my house. While Ellen and I played some tunes, he found his way into my woodshop and returned with a plastic five-gallon bucket and two thin kindling sticks. Then he turned the bucket over and drummed a beat behind us. By saying *yes* to offering my spare couchsurfing room to him and Ellen a few years back, two strangers found their way into my future, into my now, into my heart.

Brian is filled with "yes" stories from around the world and the stories swirl around the table like the blended fruit we are sipping. African low-flying planes being shot at. Free trips to Asia. Russian soldiers with guns when he and his brother wandered into the wrong zone while visiting the country. I lean back into the kitchen chair, listening to his every word.

"I had some cigarettes and gestured them as a gift. Neither of us spoke the language. Somehow, the guards let us go."

MCAFEE'S KNOB

Within a couple of trail miles, an A/T thru-hiker scuttles around some large rocks in my direction. The Appalachian Trail, known as the A/T, connects Georgia to Maine, squirming over mountain spines and flat valleys for about 2,200 miles of length. McAfee's Knob is one of the trail's photography icons near Roanoke.

"Hey there, how's it going?" the hiker asks, coming to a halt.

"Great," I respond. "Hiking through?" Everyone makes the A/T their own hike—some hike all the way through from Georgia to Maine in one trek, others piece it together.

"Section-hiking between Pennsylvania and Georgia. And you?" He eyes my full pack.

"Visiting friends in Roanoke. Just out for an overnight at the Knob," I say. "But I've done some sections up in the Northeast: Vermont, New Hampshire Whites, and a bit in Maine."

"Wow," he says, his eyes widening. "I'm a bit nervous to do that northern section. I've heard it's grueling."

"Yeah, it won't be twenty mile days anymore. A lot of rock scrambling which slows you down. But once up on the ridge lines, you can make good time."

"What's your trail name?" he asks.

This is the norm for long trail "thru-hikers," having a trail name that will be their main identity for the duration. I don't know when that custom started. Maybe it was a privacy thing, or the giving of humorous nicknames just for the fun of it. I tell him that I don't have one, but if I could choose one myself (not the norm), it would be *Mountaindancer* for my two passions of being in the mountains and dancing.

We talk trail talk and gear for a few minutes, then wish each other well on the trail. As I start to walk away, he says, "By the way, I'm Detox."

I like that we give each other the gift of our names. Either name, it doesn't matter. I hope he finds what he's looking for on the A/T and that he, too, is living *true*.

At the Knob, the flat iconic rock ledge overhangs the mountain side where the Blue Ridges of western Virginia ripple across the lush Catawba Valley. Winds come up strong, calm, and then blow over the mountaintop again, and I find a protected tenting spot behind a tree line set back from the ledge. After thirty years of solo backpacking trips, I've learned not to need much: a small lightweight tent, sleeping bag and pad, tiny trail stove and pot, rain gear, boots, headlamp. I was able to cram all of my gear into my larger backpack before leaving Vermont. Camping allows me another low-budget way to offset housing costs while I travel. A few hikers set up camp near me below the Knob lookout and we all settle in for the night.

In the morning, my neighbors show little respect for quiet while making their hearty breakfast: pots clank, their conversation echoes around the site, and their dog yips at some rodent foraging the area for leftover crumbs from yesterday. As I try to ignore them, I'm reminded of why I like to get off the beaten path and camp where people typically don't. Once fed and packed, they finally meander onto the trail again.

Hungry for my own breakfast of oatmeal, dried fruit, and nuts, I quickly get dressed and walk the path toward where I hung my bag of food, toiletries, and other scented items. My method has been to put everything in odor-free plastic Ziplock bags, then stuff them into a metal mesh bag with a strong Velcro closure. I then bungee cord the whole deal as high on a tree trunk as I can, and nowhere near my tent. This method has served me in the Northeast for years. I scan down the path, look at every tree. Nothing—the bag is gone.

Across the path from the perfect tree, one bungee cord dangles on a low bush. I wade through the underbrush looking for the bag, but clearly it has been dragged off somewhere out of sight, most likely by a bear. Defeated, I pack up my gear, swig some remaining water in my bottle, and retrace my steps downhill towards the trailhead. A forced fast accompanies my growling stomach over the several miles to the road, where I dig out my cell phone to call Brian for the pick up. *Of course . . . no service.*

The paved road winds a couple of miles more downhill along Route 311 toward an intersection. Grateful for gravity pulling at my shuffling boots, I keep checking for service and stick out my thumb when cars drive by, but no one stops to offer a ride. Without calories to burn, my calves start to cramp, and I slow down to a shuffle along the road's gravel edge, berating myself for my misguided confidence about hanging my food. I shift my focus to each step forward.

The Orange Market at the intersection comes into view, and I remove my phone from my pocket to successfully call Brian, relieved to still have some charge left on it. Once I know he's on the way, I pull out some cash. I drop my pack under the sign saying "no packs allowed in store" and will my strained legs inside to buy several small bags of nuts, a few granola bars, and a sketchy-looking apple. Leaning against my pack that I left outside, I rip open the bags of nuts with my teeth and dig in to my breakfast until I see Brian's old silver Mercedes pull into the lot.

Consequences force me to re-think my routines, and I start to plan for new resources. *Adaptation ?* I can almost feel Bruce smiling at me from some faraway place.

With some research, I eventually order a half-size bear canister from one of my gear companies and have it shipped via General Delivery to Georgia, where I'll arrive in a few weeks. Several online trail blogs wrote about hikers shipping food and other supplies ahead to post offices that will hold their boxes for them for up to a month. It's about time I give it a try. This option could come in handy during my travels.

School for Myopic Native American Orphans

Roanoke, Virginia, to Greenville, South Carolina

The green hills of Jefferson National Forest flank Virginia's Interstate 81 to the west as the bus picks up speed onto the highway, taking me away from Roanoke. I lean my head onto the seat back, deep in thought about my friend Keith, and stare out the window at the mountains whizzing by.

"You can't come to visit after all," Keith wrote me in an email in early September. His place in Pennsylvania was going to be my first stop. A couple of decades had gone by between our contra dancing together outside of Boston in the early 1990s, and his unexpected email one year, "Is this actually you?"

Since then, we have exchanged short notes back and forth each year to catch up with each other's news. I was disappointed in the cancelled visit, but I knew there would be many moments where my plans would need to be redirected. I told myself to let go of any specific agenda and move on to Roanoke as my first stop.

"I'll reimburse you for your bus ticket," he had written.

Even though I hadn't bought a ticket yet, he insisted on sending me a donation to help with the journey and wouldn't let me persuade him otherwise. I sent him my mother's mailing address in South Carolina, where I am headed next, so there should be an envelope waiting for me when I arrive.

Generosity comes in all forms, and I have already experienced quite a bit of it over the last couple of weeks. Folks have picked me up and dropped me off, fed me, introduced me to all kinds of interesting people, invited me to events. But a cash donation is way up there.

"I don't know what to say," was my response to his message. "I haven't seen you in years. This is an amazing gift."

He replied, "I get it from my father, but he would find charitable causes like a 'School for Myopic Native American Orphans'. I prefer to donate to individuals rather than big charities. I love the idea of your year-long adventure, and how special you are to have a courageous spirit. I would never do what you are doing, but I'll be able to live it vicariously through reading your new travel blog. Send me the link when you have a chance."

I believe in gestures of kindness. Like the time I was traveling to Maine on the highway one Christmas Eve: the toll booth operator told me the car in front of me had already paid my toll. *Really?* At another toll booth farther along the turnpike, I did the same for a car coming up behind mine. It felt good to do, and I wondered how many people would continue the action.

At some point, Keith's gift will allow me to experience an extraordinary place and thoughts of him making it possible will travel with me. And, in some random location, around some random person, during some random experience, I hope I can offer my own version to keep the gift moving on.

At my mother's house in Greenville, South Carolina, I endured six hours of technology panic trying to upload the new operating system on my new iPad mini while working over the phone with two Apple problem-solving gurus in Colorado.

Chapter 3

Can't Get There From Here

Greenville, South Carolina • September 2014

Over the phone in August, while I planned an itinerary for my first month of travel, my mother complained, "When we lived in Florida, you never came to visit us. Fourteen years we lived there."

It *is* true. I never visited her and her second husband while they lived in Florida. Over the phone, she aimed for my guilt. "You'll be going right through Greenville. The Greyhound station is just up the street."

"Sure, I'll stop in for a few days as I pass through," I told her before I left Vermont. My visit would be my path of least resistance—my fulfilled obligation—my wall of avoidance, since I've never told her about my long standing choice of limiting any family interactions to three hours maximum to avoid old behavioral patterns creeping in, mine *and* theirs.

I also wanted to challenge my current beliefs about our relationship with a reality check, maybe a softening into a new perspective or yet another approach for a healthier dynamic. Over the years, I've tried some things, but nothing ever changed.

I remember standing on the front stoop of our first house in Massachusetts at the age of four. Thinking that my decision to leave the family was some sort of child's game, my father had just spent the whole afternoon helping me pack. "You can take only what has been a gift to you. We'll lend you a paper bag, but you'll have to return it." Everything seemed workable at the onset of that afternoon.

I was dead serious about leaving, but the reality of darkness descending on my small body, without any flashlight in hand, paraded me back into the house with the resignation of having to suck it up for another fourteen years. I like to think I was that articulate in my thoughts at the age of four, but really, I just felt hopeless—these parental people didn't seem to be in support of my best

23

interests. In all fairness, I learned about resilience at that young age. I turned inward, learned to love myself, and found ways to circumvent feelings of emotional abandonment while being assumed inept by my parents.

A lot of years have gone by, and my mother and I have silently agreed to hypocrisy—we continually disappoint each other. Some of the daughter infractions include never getting married and giving her grandchildren, spending thirty years in a man's trade as a cabinetmaker, and avoiding visits. Maybe she's still upset at having to get back that Barbie doll from the neighborhood girl across the street in our suburban development and paying for all the sewing lessons she sent me to that didn't stick for me. Had there been a finishing school for young ladies nearby at the time, I suspect she would have sent me there as well.

I fear my year-long journey is doomed to become another embarrassment for her. If it had been a fancy cruise or a chain of hotel stays on European beaches, she could brag to her friends, *Look what my daughter is doing.*

But Greyhound buses, packs on my back, couchsurfing in strangers' homes, hostel bunk rooms, and backpacking in the wilderness just don't compute for her.

Good boundaries, I remind myself as I arrive at their home. *Here we go.*

Their condo is exactly how I imagined it to be—straight out of an interior design magazine, right down to vases that match the light sconces on the walls: fluted glass of a yellowish tint. Her second husband gets up out of his leather lounger in front of the television with a quick greeting before sitting back down to watch the news. Since they married after I was an adult, I've never thought of him as a stepfather. My mother leads me down the hallway to the spare bedroom, where I drop my packs, and shows me the bathroom to use across the hallway. They have their own connected to the main bedroom suite.

"Single women are raped and murdered every year on hiking trails, and accosted while taking buses," she projects from the living room as I come out of the bathroom. I knew this was coming.

Biting my lower lip keeps me from saying what I'd like to say, but I know I need to respond with something. Even though I doubt she will understand me better than other times. "Do we have to go through this again?" I say as I walk back through the hallway to sit down at the dining room table, then pause before I continue. *Stay calm*, I remind myself. "I'm 57, have survived fine so far, and will continue to do so. I'm not reckless, or an idiot."

"Things happen. Why do you have to take these risks? When are you going to grow up?" she continues her lecture as she brings up on her Smartphone articles written about bad things happening to women while traveling. She's probably bookmarked them in alphabetical order. Her husband busies himself with watching the local news on the television in the living room and I consider joining him. I can hear the volume increase on the TV as the commentator reviews a local Greenville High School sports event, drowning out the tension.

"Do you have any tea? I could use a cup." I notice an envelope addressed to me from Keith sitting on the counter—his donation to my trip finances—and pick it up, looking for any distraction.

She gets up to show me the choices from a drawer full of tea boxes and puts a pot of water on the stove to boil. I can see her still talking, but my thoughts override whatever she is still ranting about. Pressing in on both of my temples are the angel/devil volleys of reason and guilt.

She's just human, the angel offers. *She doesn't know how to trust you, or have empathy for you, or support you. I know she never has, but how about some compassion here?*

My temples start to throb more quickly, and I think, *Compassion goes both ways, angel.*

The devil twists my head in the other direction. *Just walk away. When other people treat you like that, you turn toward other paths. So, she's your mother. That shouldn't matter.*

I want the devil's easy way out, but know that families are not so simple. I refocus on my mother's words, still on the subject of rape, as I gather my next thoughts and purposely keep my voice low, "I could be raped and murdered in my own home. Should I never be there either? Do NOT, under any circumstances, call the state police in whatever state you think I'm in at the time. You will embarrass us both."

"You'll need to call me every day then," she pleads while pouring hot water into a flowery porcelain teacup. I get up to stuff my Red Rose black tea bag into the hot water to seep, and sit back down at the table with the cup.

"No, I won't be doing that. You can check in on my blog once in awhile and see where I have just been. Then you'll know I'm still alive."

Every time I've gone into the wilderness for a few days of hiking and camping, I've had to slowly talk her fears down, line by line, over the phone: weather, animals, injury, humans. I have no idea, still, why she thinks I can't make good decisions or take care of myself. Purposely, I stuff down any surfacing thoughts about my missing food on McAfee's Knob.

Walk away, devil? I wish.

Trying to accept that nothing will change for us, and also not allowing myself into voicelessness, I remind myself she probably did the best she could with what she had learned about mothering using the skill sets she had to work with at the time, but it doesn't help much. I'm just no longer willing to cater to her personal fears.

Her eyes betray any composure she tries to hold onto—her tears start to well up and I can already hear it coming, like so many times before—how her children continue to forsake her.

I push the chair away from the table, wanting to avoid the old pattern, and pick up my tea cup to take with me. "It's been a long travel day, I'm going to bed early. See you in the morning."

THE IOS NIGHTMARE . . . OR

How many computers does it take to download and install the new operating system?

The answer is three.

I'll back up (no pun intended): my mother and her husband had already installed the new iOS operating system onto their respective iPads under the tutelage of their local Apple guru. While I am visiting, the guru offers an hour long class on the new features of the system, so I tag along to learn some things, and he shows me the update bar on my iPad mini under "settings." The woman sitting next to me leans over and informs me that the installation on her iPad mini took twelve hours using wifi, so I decide to start the update before I go to bed and let it install overnight while I sleep.

Mid-sleep, I get up to use the bathroom and take a peek: black screen with white apple icon. In the morning when I get up: black screen with white apple icon. After a walk to Staples for pen refills: black screen and white apple icon. After my mother and I return from an 11:30 a.m. movie matinee: black screen and white apple icon. At 2:30 in the afternoon, I add up the hours—seventeen—and I panic. My whole travel life is in this iPad and I need to get on a bus the next day. My mother speed-dials the guru, but no answer.

Holding back tears, I remember the Apple Care contract that Nan insisted I have while traveling, find the 800 phone number, and dial. Before I left Vermont, she treated me to a new iPad mini, with bluetooth keyboard, for access to online research, email connections, banking, and writing. I added that to my point-and-shoot digital camera and old flip phone to round out my technology needs.

I get connected to Michael in Colorado and he assures me that he is one of the top problem-solving geniuses there. "I am here for another six hours and I am all yours." he tells me. Unsuspecting, I tell him I'm also free.

Wifi takes longer, so we set up a screen share between his computer and the main PC computer in my mother's office to more quickly download the operating system through iTunes. Michael's red arrow flits around the screen, and I follow it with my mouse arrow and click where he tells me to click, places deep within the bowels of the computer system, places I never knew existed. He assures me all is going well.

Three hours later, the main computer still won't recognize my iPad mini. We've installed and updated iTunes, added software to help the computer read my device, and disabled firewalls. Nothing. Nothing. And nothing. We decide on a fifteen-minute break—bathrooms and food.

Having told me he is in one of many personalized cubicles, I imagine him somewhere in the middle of a vast landscape of tiny squares. Continually calm, Michael reminds me of Roger Moore in *The Saint,* that old 1960s TV show. Out of nowhere, a ringed halo would appear over Moore's character's head. I have no idea what Michael looks like, but I picture that generic male headshape one sees on internet sites when "no actual photo has been uploaded," and a halo appears over it. *Three hours? Still calm?*

My theory: He didn't go to the bathroom. Over each cubicle hangs a punching bag. Each Apple Care technician gets personalized boxing gloves. The technicians are advised to tell the frazzled customer that a bathroom break is needed, the boxing gloves are put on and the punching bag is pummeled until the tech's frustration level is back to "calm and optimistic." Only then can the technician call back the customer.

I do, however, head to the bathroom. On my way out of the bathroom,

I look into the mirror, which turns black, and my head morphs into the white apple icon, then morphs into a closed fist with the middle finger sticking up, reminding me of a friend's idea that there should be a vehicle dashboard light that comes on to tell you not to bother with repairs since you are just plain "fucked." I try to scream. You know, like the kind of nightmare when you are running down an alley in thick fog, some creepy monster with blood dripping from fangs chasing you, and you try to scream? Nothing comes out, you try to scream louder, and you finally make a sound and wake up? Except this time, I keep tapping on the bell icon with hope that the volume will increase, and instead, the icon keeps having that line through it. Mute. Mute. Mute. I see the middle finger still in the mirror as I head back into the other room just as the phone rings. Fifteen minutes are up, it's Michael.

There is a laptop in the office as well, so we give up on the main computer and change over to it, starting from scratch with screen sharing, iTunes, and firewalls, except now he calls in the troops: James. Michael tells me that by now, others would be crying, laughing, or screaming at him. A fragile line, my tears leak out now, and Michael feels bad. He has been saying, "I want to be the one to fix this" again and again.

Somewhere between the fifth and sixth hours, Michael and James break the spell and we are able to download and install the new operating system, and go through the settings to make sure everything is working okay.

"Click on 'erase all content and settings'," he says and I freeze in fear. *What? Erase what will be irretrievable?*

"Hold my hand," Michael tells me, "and James will hold your other one." I breathe deeply, take their virtual hands, and tap on the bar, a free fall backwards out of the plane, praying like hell that the parachute will indeed open. It works, and I let go of their hands.

Michael has to leave now, six hours gone, and James guides me through enabling the firewalls again. In relief, I offer to buy them virtual beers as I see them both, in my mind, wearing Stetson hats as they ride into the Colorado sunset on white stallions.

And me? I'll take a double shot of the virtual, intravenous, rot-gut whiskey, please!

My cat Persistence meditates on pond life outside my home in Vermont, where frogs and snakes and birds grab her attention.

MEDITATIONS ON A CAT

In the dream, my cat Persistence and I play with each other around the trunk of the pine tree near my perennial gardens. Each summer morning, for eleven years, she and I started our day in the garden, me with a cup of tea, her snooping for newts. She was included as part of the house rental package.

As I frantically packed before I left Vermont, my cat made her own peace with the upheaval. "Mama's going on a big mouse-hunting trip for a year," I whispered to her, hoping she would understand the telepathic imagery. "I'm not abandoning you, sweetie. I want you to be here when I return."

Right before I left, I heard the crunching in the upstairs hallway. Usually she just played with the mice. I thought the eating display sentiment might have been, "Don't go, I promise I'll eat the mice like you've wanted me to all these years." I wonder, however, if the sentiment *really* was, "Look, I can catch and eat mice, in the house or not, and therefore I'll be just fine, no matter what."

Before getting up out of bed now that I am awake, I re-read the recent email from my renters again. Enough time had passed for her to acclimate to them when I decided it would be okay for them to let her out, had confidence she would come to the back door for easy food and shelter. But she hasn't.

How could I have left her like I did? Was I being selfish?

I know she'll be able to eat out there in the wild, but there are things that go bump in the night for small felines: fisher cats, owls, weasels.

Since the time is late enough, I grab my phone from the side table and call two local Vermont friends who she knows well, and they offer to stop by the house to see if she'll come out of the woods when they call her. I feel like a failure as a cat-mother. *Is this a lesson in allowing those we love to go and live their own lives?*

I pull the cotton sheet back up over my chest and shoulders as I wonder if the dream images of playing around the tree are telepathically from her to let me know she is fine. For my own peace, I imagine she has gone on her own long mouse-hunting journey, and after my return, we'll compare mouse-hunting notes.

From down the hall, I hear the TV go on—some kind of muffled morning talk show. The smell of coffee wafts into my bedroom through the crack under the door and I roll over into a fetal position and stare at the lamp on the side table. I don't recognize it, which makes sense since my mother redecorates every few years, whether needed or not, to stay up to date with the latest trends. The lampshade fabric is the exact same as the curtains and comforter and waste basket—tiny orange flowers on a yellow background.

Mothers, I would suppose since I have not had children, make choices for all kinds of reasons, and I imagine that sometimes the results don't turn out how they were initially expected or hoped for. I understand this, and in the case of my cat, I once again rehash my reasons for going off for a year and leaving her behind. I knew she had feral needs, knew there was the possibility of her choosing to stay out and living the life she wanted. The risk was always there—something could happen anytime, even if I had stayed home.

It's ultimately what I want for her—to live a good life, *true*, right up to the end, whenever that would be. I would never want to interfere with anyone's life choices, even my cat's, just to support a personal agenda of mine. Maybe this is where my mother and I differ.

I can understand the imperfection of mothering, intellectually, but I still feel frustrated, discouraged, resigned. If I don't push back, I fear the return to my child's way of dealing with my mother's judgements: voicelessness. Most of the time, it just doesn't feel like I can get *there*: more patience—from *here*: my pushing back. It's just easier to avoid visits.

I begin to sweat under the sheet and pull it off me again. Might as well get up and into the day. My bus leaves this afternoon and I need to pack.

Short-Term Goddess

Greenville, South Carolina, to Gainesville, Georgia

Her reddish-brown hair curls up around her face and cascades down over her shoulders and back. Pushing her woven shoulder bag around to her side while she steps along the aisle, she gazes past where I sit. Her shoulders slump, and I can tell that every pair of seats has someone in it.

I move my bags off the cushion next to me and onto the dingy floor as I catch her eye. She sighs, smiles, stuffs her bag into the overhead bin, sits down, and leans over, "You are a goddess."

I tell her I am always up for "short-term goddess" status, as I imagine myself upon a glittery throne, seekers about my feet, the aroma of burning frankincense overshadowing the musty AC encircling me.

My fantasy shifts back to reality as the bus driver turns on the microphone: "No smoking, no alcohol, no loud phone calls, music, or video games. Keep the restroom clean. Any infractions will result in the bus pulling over to the side of the road and removal of the rule breaker. No second chances." The driver belts himself in, starts up the bus, and my throne has been reduced to a window seat.

My seat mate and I spend the next few hours volleying travel stories. No longer tied to my career labels, I have become a "traveler" who is interested in other travelers' adventures. When someone used to ask me what it is that I did, I would respond with "custom cabinetmaker, teacher of woodworking classes, musician." Now, I offer "traveler and blogger."

With these older labels falling away, I thought I might seem "less than" for it. But I don't. Even though it has been just a few weeks since I left Vermont, I actually feel "more than"—more than *just* what I have been doing for work all these years—more than other people expected me to be—more than I've expected myself to be. Forcing myself to be more outgoing in order not to feel alone, I've opened myself up to all kinds of sharings and experiences with people I never would have initiated interactions with previously.

On her phone, my new travel pal scrolls through photos of Brazil, her husband's home country, where they visited grandmothers and cousins recently.

"Guests eat first, no matter how little there is to eat," she explains as she turns the phone my way so I can see the group of smiling relatives. "It's expected that we leave a little bit for those who eat next, but not too little or we insult them."

I imagine a small village, a tiny kitchen filled with the cooking matriarchs I saw in the photos. I picture them stewing their own special recipe of *Feijoada*, with black beans, sausage and pork, onion, garlic, and bay leaves permeating the steamy air.

Maybe the photos were taken in one of Brazil's larger cities. She doesn't say. I don't ask. I just let my imagination go where it wants: how does one figure out the exact amount of food to leave so they don't insult their hosts? I might need to know this someday.

Outside, the sun has started to set and the remaining light grows more dim. The bus pulls into a route stop parking lot where a few passengers depart and collect their luggage. Seats free up and my friend moves across the aisle to curl up on both seats now that it is getting dark. But before she settles in, she leans back across the aisle and asks my age.

"Fifty-seven," I reply.

"No way," she says in surprise, "But—you are so beautiful."

I wonder if there will ever be a time in our culture where age and beauty have nothing to do with each other. My time as a "goddess" stalls, since clearly I am too old.

As the bus accelerates back onto the nearby highway, she pulls her coat over her legs and drapes a straw hat over her face. I roll up my jacket as a pillow, push in my earplugs, and faded goddess-glitter falls off my eyelashes to land onto my scrunched up jacket. Inside, as I drift off to sleep, my inner goddess lives on.

I wait with the James Brown bronze statue in Augusta, Georgia until my brother picks me up for a visit with him and his family for a few days, while remembering all my favorite songs Brown performed while I grew up in the 1960s and 70s.

Chapter 4
Bloody Grit

Evans, Georgia • September 2014

Echoing out of my Rock 'n' Roll memories, I can hear song lyrics about "destinations not too far," and "finding out who you are on the way" flowing down the main drag of Augusta. Yes, the words from "Living in America" land flat at the feet of James Brown's statue.

Forbidden grit. It's not quite the kind of grit that the wind blows into the eye, and the only way to release it is to flood it out with tears. It's not quite the kind of pebble grit that pushes its way in between a foot and a sandal, wearing away at flesh until there is no choice but to stop and manually remove it. It's not quite the kind of grit that lands on a tooth from unrinsed seafood-in-shell, positioning itself just right for the bite, then grinds enamel.

It is the grit that embeds itself into wounds, glueing itself to the raw and tender places. Slowly eroding whatever is around it and reopening traumas as soon as they start to heal. It's the grit of history—the deep, bloody grit dripping from hearts with painful stories to tell, and no amount of flushing can ever wash it away.

The Savannah River separates Georgia from South Carolina. I stand with my brother, just a year younger than I, along the River Walk near the rapids that separate Augusta from its northern-half namesake across the state line. Farther behind us, his wife and daughter linger, looking at a group of ducks floating along the river's edge. I don't know if my visit here is out of duty or a longing to heal what has long separated us as siblings. After years of silence between us, I had needed to track him down during our father's last years of life.

"You have to fly up to see Dad. This may be your last chance," I told him over the phone that year. When he came, our long-standing silence stuffed itself into every remembered crevice to protect us from any emotional holes.

Over the last five years since our father passed away, we've made awkward attempts to connect, to converse, to recover.

"If you come through Georgia, we'd love to have ya, sis," he had offered a few months ago. I hadn't seen his wife since 1996, and had never met his two kids, now teenagers.

We've danced a strange dance as siblings over the course of time. The camaraderie of our youth split apart as we walked our separate paths that opened up in front of us as adults. The family blood now holds us in this place, and I can only lean in so far before I feel the discomfort in my eye, under my foot, and in my mouth—rubbing, gnawing around the swollen edges of each and every childhood memory.

Even with his thinning, graying hair dyed blonde, his facial features morph into our father's features. It's the nose and eyes specifically, even though he has our mother's thin body frame. He lights a cigarette, like our father always did to distract himself from tension, and puffs out the smoke over the river rapids, billows that resemble the difference between us that has always been there. He lives in some cloudy dimension; I walk heavy on the ground.

I try to look into his eyes, but he won't allow it—it's a destination that's too far, too old, too raw. He takes another drag on his cigarette and flicks the ashes onto the ground, then looks behind to see what his wife and daughter are up to.

I watch the ripples at the river's edge along the walkway, and feel another rush of memories flow, a slideshow carousel in my mind of him and me, an unspoken "us against them" while growing up in silence and having each other's backs by keeping secrets from our parents. Like the time he took a hammer to the player piano keys in the basement when young, or as teenagers fooling around in the kitchen, he and a friend broke the glass in the storm door three times before my father got home from work one day. My brother knew where the cash was kept in my father's sock drawer, and the two of them rode their bikes, faster than I have ever seen, all the way to the nearby glass repair store.

"There you are," says his daughter as she jogs up to us, knocking the slideshow screen over. Her olive skin glistens around her denim shorts and halter top since the Georgia weather is hot. Her dark brown hair, her mother's lineage rather than my brother's, is thick and long. She sidles up next to me. "You know, I follow you on Facebook," she says.

"Really," I say, trying not to show her I've caught her bluff. I've never been on Facebook. *So, who has she been following?* Perhaps this is an attempt at Southern politeness.

"Yes, ma'am," she replies as my brother's wife finally reaches us as well, sharing how the last time they were at the rapids, she and my brother were doing a photo shoot on one of the rocks near the shoreline. A flashback from their wedding day surfaces in my memory—she was wearing a long curly wig of black hair, and quite the bosom-revealing strapless wedding dress. Supposedly she was a model when they met in Spain when he was there on a job assignment, and I wonder how she's acclimated to being a Georgia housewife and mother instead.

We keep walking, along the flow, under feathery, gray Spanish moss dripping from trees over our heads and I duck to avoid getting ensnared in some low hanging moss. We have nothing to really talk about, which in all fairness, we never have. We just walk. I stop to remove a pebble from my sandal that has been riding my heel for a while now.

For my brother's Spanish wife, blood is blood, and it doesn't seem to matter how much grit has been worn down from ages and ages of Euro-abrasion into smooth, soft, clean blood droplets. A state of grace—I honor her for it. It's not easy to do living in America since families break apart for all kinds of reasons. Mother and daughter start to lag behind us again, maybe to give my brother and I familial space, but what does it really matter?

"Have you talked to Mom?" I turn to ask him, and notice he's physically bulked out a bit over the years. We both were always thin—the maternal side of our lineage, but he shot up in height during high school and I did not. I have more of the paternal side, which has always been my concern as I age: the image of the Polish peasant woman, what I have described as a four-by-four-by-four cube, wearing a full apron, a head wrapped in a scarf tied under the chin, with two arms and two legs poking out. My father's sisters were all full-figured, to put it nicely. As soon as I gain a few pounds, I reduce my food portion sizes and cut back on sweets as I can.

Having just visited our mother in South Carolina, I know the answer already.

"No." He pauses for another cigarette hit, agitated. "She pissed me off and she needs to apologize to my wife. I've had it with her husband. They are not allowed to visit anymore." I don't know his side of the episode, and he offers no other details. Even during those ten years of no contact with me, he refused to tell me the reasons for his disconnection. I still have no idea what incident triggered his avoidance, and don't feel it matters now.

"She's the one who feels betrayed, and is waiting on you," I respond. "Maybe the two of you can meet in the middle. Just the two of you. Vomit what needs to be vomited on the table and make some peace. No spouses. You've always been closer to her, and now she's annoying me by being hyper-focused on me."

I want to step out of the middle of it all, but again, feel like voicelessness is not the answer. Maybe it's my selfishness that I want him to distract her over the next year, so I don't have to deal with her fears.

"I'll think about it," he mumbles.

We pass by the Boll Weevil Cafe and Sweetery and my niece and I wander in to look at the huge slices of cake. I'm relieved for the change of focus, and consider options through the glass display case, choosing the *7th Heaven* with layers of dark chocolate, creamy buttercream icing, and a layer of white chocolate cheesecake topped with chocolate ganache. She picks out the *Tropical Dream*—sweet coconut and pineapple cake layers, with coconut cream-cheese icing. I hand over a twenty-dollar bill for both and wait for my change as she reaches up to grab a few plastic forks, and we shuffle back outside.

"Anyone wanna bite?" she asks her mother and father. My brother just lights yet another cigarette and I step away from the smoke wafting over at me. Our father gave me a try on a cigarette sometime in my early years and I thought I would cough to death. Never again picked one up, even with high-school peer pressure. His wife shakes her head no about the cake. Just as well, more for us. Maybe my niece takes after *my* blood, sweetened over the years by sugar highs that mask wounds. I try to wrap humility in some compassion since I know no one has history that is completely grit-free. Ganache lingers on my tongue and coats my teeth as we find our way over to the bridge crossing from one state to another. The bridge won't save us, there is no bridge that can re-open our hearts, he and I. Graciously, we play out our niceties and our hypocrisies, and drive back to the house.

My brother's wife, missing Spain, seeks nostalgia for the depth of familial celebrations, no matter how hypocritical. Sweet, leathery saffron permeates the shellfish simmering in broth on the stove, yellowing the rice she spoons into the dinner pan harbored in this Augusta suburb. I sniff at the steam rising and watch the crab and shrimp slightly bounce around in the boil. "Smells great," I say to her. "Thank you for your efforts on my behalf."

"Family is the most important thing," she slurs from her Spanish tongue, adept at pulling grit out of the way. I just swallow any words in response to her statement.

My brother, outside, finishes his beer and another cigarette, then comes in. "We should take a family photo," he says, not knowing how to fill in the gaps. I cringe.

Our mother has this loyalty to imagined tradition as well—the *let's all put on a happy face for the photograph* thing—toothy smiles betrayed by saddened eyes. Ignoring him, the kids hunker down at the table, hungry, tethered to their phones and social media. His son, tall and lanky like my brother was at his age, also bears the olive skin of mixed ethnicities. Just out of high school and working a low paying job, he still lives at home. Since he's hardly spoken to me at all, I just let him be. It somehow feels more honest that the other interactions I have been having.

A woman of pride, his wife labors alongside the ghosts of her culinary matriarchs. "My mother made *paella* this way," she announces proudly, "and my grandmother." I sense her offerings during my visit are out of duty, not out of the desire to smooth woundedness into healing for my brother and I. She can live with abrasion in a way I cannot.

Seafood, shelled, drapes over the rice on my plate. Without any more words wanting to be spoken, we all chew to the tense clicking of forks, not unlike the shared childhood meals for my brother and me as we watched sit coms on the small television my mother put next to the dining room table for distraction.

In the morning, my brother drops me and my bags onto the Augusta sidewalk next to James Brown's statue. In James' hand leans one of those old-style microphones on a stand. His cast bronze coat flows to the ground, and I can hear his voice screaming "I feel good!"

I have no idea when I'll see my brother again, and relieved to be moving on, scar tissue starts to re-form already.

Not My First Rodeo

With six hours to go until my bus to Atlanta arrives, I fold up my jacket as seat padding for the coated wire chair and settle in. Four weeks into my journey, I've grown familiar with these layovers and I extend my legs to rest them on my piled up packs on the floor. Nervously aware I am the only white person in the room, and the only woman, I accept there is no way to blend in, and try, at least, to look comfortable.

As I shift yet again in the seat, an older Black gentleman in a worn brimmed hat, brown sweater, blue jeans, and cowboy boots heads for a seat along my row. While he places his two small, stuffed white plastic bags on the seat between us, he turns and looks over at me, smiles, and says hello.

"Where ya heading?" I ask him, relieved for the connection. He drapes an arm over the seat back between us and his loose sweater sleeve seems to drip off of his shoulder.

He explains his itinerary, "I'm heading north to Chicago, then two locations in New York. I have eight children, lots of grandkids, and a couple of great-grandchildren to visit."

"Great grandchildren?" I inquire, since he doesn't look a day over seventy.

"I married my first wife when I was fifteen," he shares nostalgically. His dark eyes light up with the memory. He must have been a good-looking man in his younger years, and quite the catch at fifteen.

He's had many jobs over the years, he tells me, but mostly he has spent his younger years working in rodeos. As we lean in even closer to hear each other over peoples' phone conversations, I learn about his daughter who is a brain surgeon, and the houses he built for each of his children and their families. We are in our own world.

The earlier bus to Atlanta, his bus, comes. He hands me his business card for a bar he owns outside of that city and I watch him leave.

But he comes back in to tell me that there is room on the bus, that the Augusta station will close up before my later bus comes, and that I will be sitting outside for a number of hours in the dark. I had been assured that the bus terminal was not in the "seedy" part of the city, but one never knows. I picture myself outside on the curb all alone.

"I didn't catch your name?" he asks.

"Gail."

"You could lay over in Atlanta and be more comfortable than here." He looks right into me, a look that makes me take him seriously. I check the possibility with the driver and get on the bus.

We sit together and continue our conversation, working our way through family, life, work, health, love. Almost whispering, he says, "I couldn't see them, but I could feel them looking at us in the terminal and thinking, *What in the world do those two have to talk about?*"

The interior lights are off as people try to sleep. I can just see his smile peeking out from his dark skin by the street lights shining through the windows as the bus moves down the streets of Atlanta.

Now, here's the interesting part, the late-at-night surreal part, the food-for-thought part. His smile morphs into the darkness as he whispers, "When I saw you sitting in the terminal, I knew we had met before, maybe a thousand years ago, not sure."

My skin tingles as I feel a familiarity with him as well. Being from the South, he associates it with God. I don't believe in God, but I do feel that there is an energetic connection between all of us, so I wonder, *another lifetime, another plane of existence?*

"Yep," he says, "I could tell this is not your first rodeo, and I know that we will meet again sometime."

Shivers run up my back as the bus pulls into the Atlanta terminal.

Down on the platform, we say goodbye again, and I awkwardly give him a quick hug and wish him luck as he heads north. He asks me to call and let him know when I arrive safely to my destination in Louisiana. I pull out the card to make sure I have the right number to call. There are three names on the business card, and he points to the number for "Albert" as he races off to make his next connection.

I lay over for hours in Atlanta, starting to process all that Albert and I had talked about. The next evening after my final arrival, I pick up the business card to call the number next to his name. But the voice mailbox is full and won't accept any more messages. *Maybe he'll just know that I'm okay?*

Or maybe, somewhere along my travels, I'll chance upon the business card stuffed in a pocket in one of my packs and try to call again.

Because, you know, after all, this is definitely NOT my first rodeo.

When perusing handcrafts in a small gallery in downtown Lafayette, Louisiana, I try on an art frottoir (rub-board used for percussion in zydeco bands)—sort of Madonna meets Swamp! Lafayette has been on my zydeco dancing bucket list for over twenty years.

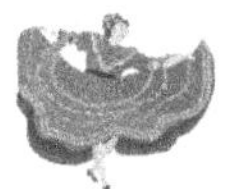

Chapter 5
Bon Temps Rouler

Lafayette, Louisiana • October 2014

Sweat immediately seeps along my temples, down the spine of my back, and across my chest as I descend the stairs of the air-conditioned bus onto the sidewalk at the Lafayette Greyhound terminal. I check my scribbled notes for the walk to my couchsurfing location with a University of Louisiana professor who accepted my recent request to stay, near the weekend dance festival site. While wiping the dripping salt away from my eyes, I find my bottle of water in one of my bags and guzzle it down, then start walking. Worn paint feathers off the small houses on either side of the road, and I can feel the penetrating gaze of random folks sitting on their front porches. Not sure if this is a safe neighborhood, I hustle through the beating sun, woozy from the dense humidity, and feel like just another traveler passing through, even though I expect to see a few familiar faces from up north while at the weekend festivities.

Freed from the protective embraces of friends along the eastern states and the obligations of family visits, I'm looking forward to seeing how I respond to different cultures and perspectives as I continue my travels. There isn't anyone now to try to please, so I wonder how to present myself to the world without wearing some kind of facade. It's strange to both yearn to be known, completely and deeply like I've always wanted, and for this peace I'm feeling now from anonymity. I have hope, not for reinvention per se, but for transparency. Back at home, people seem to expect me to be one-dimensional: strong, practical, steady, available at any moment, but I am so much more than all that. I know I have to be willing to let people *see* my other dimensions and complexities.

As I turn down my host's street, scanning the houses for numbers, my spirit softens, and I wonder, *If I am true to myself, how will the world around me perceive me?* Darn my mother's voice lingering in my psyche, always concerned with what everyone else might think.

Two days before the dance festival is due to start, my friend Carol flies in to join me for the weekend event. With perhaps a slow transition into my anonymity, I welcome the connection with an old friend as we find our way around historic downtown Lafayette. Searching out painted murals celebrating the land and culture of Acadiana, we come across illustrated cypress trees periscoping out of swamps, animated alligators with jaws wide open, and fiddlers bowing their strings. A craggy five-hundred-year-old live oak rests its heavy limbs on the lawn outside the Cathedral of Saint John the Evangelist. In the Sans Souci Gallery, we try on modern art *froittoirs*—glorified rub boards that Zydeco bands use for percussion by rubbing a spoon up and down the washboard grooves—and giggle at one that looks like a Madonna show costume: Viking meets glitz.

Bead necklaces from past Mardi Gras drape from skeletal tree branches over our heads and wrap around fence boards in front of columned white houses. Walking along side streets, we listen to locals speaking Acadien French, and we try to recognize words for translation without much success. In the evenings leading up to the festival, we visit local dance halls that we can walk to since neither of us have a rental car—like the Blue Moon Saloon, with its walls lined with old license plates and street signs. Mostly, we're excited to finally make it here to Zydeco dance where it all began.

At Festivals Acadiens et Creoles later in the week, the organizer, for good luck, lifts the stringed sections of the *boudin*—the local spicy sausage—and snips the sections apart. Others slice the links into rounds and place them on small paper plates to hand out to those waiting in line to receive the ritual offering. Having avoided pork since the late 1970s, I aim for the music stages and dance tent situated at different corners of Girard Park. Just let the music begin.

Old name bands are gone, but their children and grandchildren carry on the traditions of old-style Cajun and Creole music, as well as bringing in their own modern Zydeco styles. Once I rendezvous with Carol, we dance to old favorites such as Beausoleil, Geno Delafose and French Rockin' Boogie, Corey Ledet, Steve Riley and the Mamou Playboys, and CJ Chenier performing with Rockin' Dopsie, Jr.

We run into a few dancers we know from the Northeast, but mostly we dance with locals who know how to party, celebration cemented into their

DNA. I suppose, when history is in the blood and bones, thinking stops and utter abandon oozes out with the sweat. The locals are uninhibited and leggy, and nothing is held back as the pounding rhythms of the music find flight across the dance floor, the sidewalk, the grass, and the dirt. Dust covers our clothes and dance shoes as we shuffle around tree roots and stones, happy for the dust rather than wet mud.

For those who have learned to dance in a workshop or perhaps by watching others, there is a stiffness honed from counting out the steps, searching for the right place to break the tension in the knees. I've been told, in the past, that I dance like I'm from Louisiana. In other dance forms I've done, I've been told to calm down. I don't want the calm, I want the full immersion, and find others dancing the Zydeco trance, stepping and twisting and bouncing to the accordion and fiddle and frottoir.

BEFRIEND A LOCAL CAJUN

Now that the festival is over and Carol has flown home, I decide to stay on in Lafayette for a few more days. I thank my host and book a bunk bed in a six-bed hostel room at the Blue Moon Saloon and Guesthouse on East Convent Street near the downtown grid. For years, I've heard visitors from the Northeast tell me the Moon is the iconic place to stay if ever in Lafayette. Other festival lingerers from afar occupy the other bunk beds in the "Band Room," one of the two hostel rooms at the Moon. A young woman working at the registration desk near the front porch entrance places sheets and a towel on my lower bed near the back window and air conditioner, and hands me the keys to the entrance door and the room.

Free admission to their stage dances and music jams offsets my daily bunk price to less than half, and upon registration, I'm given a red ticket for one free drink at the stage bar.

"You came to stay at the Moon," says Doug, a local Cajun dancer I met at the festival, and who works part time at the hostel. "No more couchsurfing?" We sidestep around each other in the communal kitchen, and from the "shared food" shelf, I help myself to an instant soup packet and pour it into a ceramic bowl, then turn the stove burner on for heating water in a kettle.

"Yeah, I thought I would stay on for a bit before I head to New Orleans for a wedding later this week."

Coffee drips into the coffeemaker pot on the counter where Doug is waiting. "Great. We can dance some more. I work the stage area to help set up and then after the show to clean up, but in between . . . I'm allowed to dance. I'll look for you. We love it when y'all come around festival time." Doug pours his hot, black coffee into a mug taken from one of the cabinets and heads out to the stage area to help musicians unload their gear while I sit down at the large communal table to spoon some bland version of chicken noodle soup into my mouth.

According to Doug, I have "personality" while I dance, so that's why he sought me out often during the festival. I've been setting aside my introverted self in favor of practicing the new extroverted version, so I sought him out as well. Doug also offers himself out as dance instructor and tour guide to travelers.

"Boy, I'd love to see alligators in their habitat," I comment the next morning while cooking up some oatmeal for breakfast, another offering from the free food shelf.

"I can take you sometime while you're here," he tells me. "My favorite place is Lake Martin over in Breaux Bridge. We'll see some there. It's a good time of year for them to be out sunning."

Since I don't have transportation, and can't afford to hire him as a guide, I'm thrilled by his offer to show me around the area for free, taking me under his wing as "Cajun Ambassador."

A few days later, as we drive the rutted dirt road around Lake Martin, we scan the road's edge where it meets the water and look for alligators, snakes, egrets, owls. Cypress trees rise out of the swamp, bell bottom roots holding firm in the mud. It is chillier than it's been, so we hope that the gators will be out of the water to soak up the heat of the setting sun. We "get down," as Doug puts it, out of the truck, to walk a boardwalk over the swamp and through part of the Nature Conservancy's Cypress Island Preserve. Feathery Spanish moss hangs from the cypress branches over the wooden walkway while white egrets wade in the murky water and roseate spoonbills watch us from tree branches high up.

"Keep an eye out for snakes," Doug reminds me as we head back to the truck to keep driving. He spots a small gator sunning itself on a downed tree not far off from the road edge and slows down. "See it?" Doug points over to the left in a shallow pool. "It's about two feet long." Hidden within the grasses,

I barely see the gator and open the truck window to try for a photo anyway, but the shadows blend into the gator's body silhouette under the water's surface. Farther down the road, Doug spots another one, just the head out of the water. I see two bumps and a dark hump. Doug tells me that the gator is about eight feet long. He can tell by the size of the head and the distance between the eyes, a skill he picked up as a kid.

Pink starts to fill the underbellies of the low clouds, so we head more quickly to The Point to look across the body of Lake Martin for a glimpse of the sun through the moss-bearded trees. As we walk up the path, we spot another gator out in the water. It turns to swim toward us, and I scoot over to the other side of the path. Nearby frogs *ribet*, and Doug thinks the gator is interested in them, not in us.

"But they can jump out of the water about six feet, so we want to stay clear of the edge," he tells me. "And snakes can hide in there too." He chuckles as he picks up a long stick to use as a weapon if need be. I move closer to Doug while the cypresses glow pink from the sunset and another gator's eyes balance on the water's surface as we pass by, its long back laying just beneath among the weeds. We hustle back along the path to the boat launch parking area where a swamp tour boat is unloading passengers.

Another day, over shrimp Po'Boy sandwiches at Old Tyme Grocery, Doug tells me stories about his childhood on the Atchafalaya Basin and about the swamp people who live deep, deep into the backwaters. His father knew them—they were his folk—while moving the family houseboat around the marshes. "People who would shoot you if they did not already know you. Even though I grew up there," Doug explains." Since my father passed away, there is no safety even for me going back in there now. They don't want anyone to know what they are doing out there. They'll feed you to the gators, never to be seen again."

Having grown up trapping alligator with his father and uncle while living poor on the Basin, walking the bayou inlets barefoot with a piece of rope as a belt to hold up his pants as a kid, he embodies humility and a kind heart. He is a simple man and I like his lack of pretense. He shares stories about the swamp legends that were told to kids, not unlike the bogeyman stories I heard as a child—stories to inspire obedience. Like the legend of the *Parlangua*, half human and half alligator, that comes out in the full moon where one swamp inlet meets another. And the *Rougarou*, the bayou version of the werewolf—half man and half wolf or dog. These superstitions still keep the swamp children in check.

He tells me about the time his father took the family out to the larger nearby cypress trees and with rope, tied each of them to the backside of a tree to endure the high winds and rains of an upcoming hurricane. I try to imagine what it must have felt like to be tied to a tree, not knowing if I would be uprooted with the tree and drown or get grabbed by a gator. It's what the bayou folks did though, and later on, refusing to head inland for safety, his father stayed to wait out yet another hurricane, but did not survive.

BICYCLING THROUGH THE BAYOU

With a small mirror taped to his glasses, a fellow hostel guest sorts through a box of instant grits from the shared food shelf. Doug and I, along with a San Antonio friend of his also staying in my bunk room, have just returned from an early Wednesday night dinner across town at Rachael's Cafe, followed by dancing at Randol's restaurant near there, where one can dance to live music for free every weekday evening.

In the microwave, we heat up the bread pudding we ordered as take-out from Rachael's, the perfect end-of-night snack. I've eaten bread pudding before, but not as good as this. As I savor each bite, trying to determine what's in the sauce, our bicyclist boils up some water and adds in the instant grits.

"Where did you start the bike trip and where are you headed to?" Doug asks him.

"I'm taking a three-year sabbatical to bike around the globe," he tells us. Having started in San Diego after leaving his park ranger job, he's made it as far as Lafayette, and plans to ride through the bayou over to New Orleans.

He laughs nervously as Doug tells him the rules of the road through that area: no bikes or pedestrians allowed on the highway, which is a narrow strip of connected bridges that goes on for miles and miles. And then there are the snakes and alligators.

The bike guy gets excited about the alligators since he imagines himself hunting one to eat. Doug reminds him that hunting season for alligator is over for now, so any gator eating would need to come from roadkill or self-defense. I imagine our young hero in hand-to-scale combat with an eight-foot gator while trying to wrestle the thing to death just for some meat.

"It's a bit chillier this week, so the gators may not be out so much," Doug tells him. Our adventurer jokes about smothering himself with chicken fat and standing on the bayou, beckoning the unsuspecting alligator for an altercation. I just hope he takes enough of those instant grits packets with him. I think he'll be okay, since he told us he met a lady coming through Austin, and now there is a love interest who cares if he is eaten or not. I like our hero, though, since he is *following his bliss*, as he says.

As am I, each of us in our individual ways. I wish him well and head into the bunk room to sleep, my tummy filled with bread pudding. Late-night Cajun jam music permeates through the uninsulated Moon's wall between the stage and the bunk room I'm staying in, the rhythmic ting of a triangle in the background a fitting bayou lullaby easing me to sleep.

After crashing the wedding of a friend's daughter in New Orleans, Louisiana, I grab an umbrella for the ritual Second Line parade down the neighborhood streets to the reception.

Chapter 6

Louisiana's Crescent City

New Orleans, Louisiana • October 2014

"I'm a friend of the bride's mother," I say at the gate, then pass through to find Kari. Wooden chairs radiate in rows out from a pond where lavender lilies nuzzle into the variegated red and green pads that skim the pond's surface. I drop my bag on the chair closest to the water and cross the lawn toward a refreshment table.

"Gail!" I hear from behind me.

Turning, I see Kari heading in my direction.

"You made it," she says while hugging me.

"I did. A couchsurfing friend from Georgia lined me up with an acquaintance of hers here in the city. I'm sleeping on the living room floor for the weekend."

"I told everyone I was bringing a guest, but left the mystery hang," she whispers. "I know they've been wondering who it could be." She giggles and waves to someone across the lawn.

The man behind the table hands me a lemonade, and I leave Kari to greet other friends who have arrived. Kari's daughter and her girlfriend married legally back in Vermont over the summer since Louisiana doesn't recognize same-sex marriages. This is just a local commitment ceremony for those who couldn't get to Vermont.

A red rose adorns the right ear of the accordion player who is sitting down next to the wooden fence, while dreadlocked friends, in flamboyant garb, congregate near the lemonade table. October sunshine filters through ornamental trees and oozes golden honey-light onto the two brides during the short ceremony. Then the happy couple takes to the street while umbrellas are handed out for those of us unfamiliar with a *Second Line* parade. Accordion and fiddle riffs march us down the street toward the French Quarter for the reception.

"We don't do *this* in Vermont," Kari says as she sashays to the marching tune, yellow orange swirls bouncing on her umbrella. The yellow fringe along mine boogies to the beat as well as I zig and zag giddily, and the umbrella's row of dark blue fleur-de-lis herald the rich French history of party rituals here in the Crescent City. A sea of umbrellas floats over the paraders like the carved animal seats going up and down to calliope music on a merry-go-round. I pump mine back and forth into the air as I weave through and around everyone doing the same, laughing with glee that parades like this can take over a street, forcing cars to pull over to the side to wait it out.

Neighborhood residents rush out of their houses with trumpets and trombones, adding their brassy blares to the march. Some fold themselves into the parade line while other onlookers rush to the sidewalks to hoot and holler us on. Once at the reception, we eat and dance late into the night under the full moon.

BLUE: A TEARDROP IN THE DUST

Blue sky fills with white puffy clouds, a steamboat motors up the Mississippi River, a soft breeze blows wisps of my hair around my face, and shade cools me from the hot southern sun. Silent moments creep in, and I breathe them in deep, exhale a peace not remembered in my body for too many years. A freighter chugs upriver and I close my eyes, remembering the stories of Huck Finn's adventures on a river raft, his desire for freedom and experiences—his own version of being a traveler, of living *true*.

Smoke stacks rise and shipping yard piers jut onto the lumbering river. In this silence, this peace, is my desire for the simplicity of rafts, and the freedom of not having to be anything to anyone. Disappearing into this city full of strangers, my body surrenders a bit more of the tension I have been carrying and I release a breath, allowing the road to feel more solid beneath my feet as I make my way across the city to Lafayette Park.

Blue is the color in the sky, in the voice, and ringing from guitars. Blue drips a fine sky-dust onto my skin, and seeps from my heart. A young couple stand in front of me, whisper love onto each other's necks, and I scan the innocent love of my past: hope, faith, resilience, lust, duty, disappointment, resentment. Years of failed attempts at relationships have turned me towards skepticism, and although the wedding was filled with a naive hope of long lasting bliss, I know that life will challenge them.

Will they make it? Do any of us make it? What sacrifice is needed to keep the union alive? Am I willing to go there again, give up anything or everything for the sake of it—be willing to let it syphon off who I have worked so hard to become? Yet underneath it all, there remains the yearning for what might be—a possibility of sustainable togetherness.

Blue vibrates along St. Charles Street where Vasti Jackson whines life's regrets out of his guitar strings, and Valerie June twangs her southern drawl over the rumblings of her banjo strums. My wedding crash has coincided with another NOLA blues fest where I find myself deeply connected to the music of humanity's heartaches. My tear drops into the blue dust.

DRIVING WITH DANIEL

Even when both of us were back in Lafayette at the festival, I had started to receive email suggestions from Daniel. While Cajun two-stepping around the dance tent floor, I had mentioned my upcoming trip to his city. I made a list, but didn't have a vehicle, so Daniel offered me a circuit of his favorite city attractions.

Tourists wait in line to order beignets at Café du Monde and climb into horse-drawn carriages to explore the district. They hop on and off buses and buy tickets for voodoo tours. They flood onto riverboats headed up the Mississippi and ship home boxes of pralines.

Sated from my take-out beignets, I peruse the plein-air market in Jackson Square across from Café du Monde and wander around the French Quarter to be entertained by street performers. Modern high-rises dwarf the iron-railed porches on Creole townhouses that loom over the jazz clubs lining Bourbon Street. Scents of vomit and urine waft from the early morning's sidewalk wash down as I stop to listen to a full-figured Black woman belting out her lament over the oompahs of a large white tuba engulfing her busking cohort. At the next corner, a magician dazzles those crowding the sidewalk's edge. I maze through the gawkers to find my way back to Café du Monde to meet up with Daniel.

"Nawlians don't leave this city," Daniel tells me when I get settled in the passenger seat. "We have too much memory here."

Southern architecture flavors the city boroughs—the bungalows of Mid-City and Lakeview, the Creole cottages of Marigny, the gallery houses of Carrollton and Uptown. Daniel shares tidbits of history as we wind our way through narrow streets, proud to show off his favorite spots.

We pass by the 1906 wooden carousel in City Park that he frequented as a youth, then stop for lunch near Lake Pontchartrain—half salt, half fresh water resting beneath the twenty-four-mile causeway holding title to the longest bridge over water in the world: 9,000 concrete pilings.

Family burial vaults sprout through grass and weeds and vases of dried flowers and beads dig in their heels on altars, relentlessly guarding the doors against ghosts wishing to party once more along Bourbon Street. Cities of the Dead: Greenwood, Lake Lawn, Metairie. We get out to walk the alleys, look up at stone cherubs, and find the vault for Daniel's family.

"Inside the tomb are long chambers, one above the other, separated by shelves," he explains. "When a casket goes in, it rests on the top shelf, and the vault is re-sealed with simple brick and mortar. Heat and humidity act like a slow form of cremation." I've seen a few burial vaults in the Northeast, but mostly, folks get buried below the ground's surface.

"I would think only so many deceased family members would fit." I say.

"After a year and a day, another may be buried there. Whatever's left of the first one is moved to the bottom level, and the casket bits are removed. In some tombs, that shelf has a gap toward the rear, and the remnants just get pushed back, where they fall through the gap to the vault below."

With more and more people being cremated, the vaults will be able to hold more bodies. I think about having my ashes strewn from the top of a mountain someday as we walk down another narrow alley to the car and continue the tour.

Daniel pulls into the Rock 'n' Bowl bowling alley and dance venue. "I have something to show you," he says, and I shuffle alongside him up the ramp. The wooden floor spans between the bandstand and bar and the bowling lanes line up to the left.

"You won't be here this weekend for the Zydeco dance," he says. "Here, give me your hand." He pulls me into an embrace, his right hand firm along the middle of my back. He sets a beat through our bodies, sits down into the Zydeco step, and twirls me around. We dance to our individual memories of last week's festival favorites.

"Now you can say that you have danced at the famed Rock 'n' Bowl," he says with a grin.

Daniel suggests the ferry ride across the Mississippi to Algiers and back so I can view the city skyline from the other side. He drops me off at the pier where I purchase my round-trip boat ticket for the next crossing.

OUT OF THE GARDEN

At the last minute, I get a couchsurfing acceptance from Charley, who is excited to have me stay for the duration of the week. In his thirties, he had decided to take a sabbatical from his teaching job sometime after hurricane Katrina blasted its way through the levees in 2005. Wanting to help save the history of this section of the city hit hard, he was able to purchase a devastated shotgun house for cheap and start in on renovations.

The now-gutted shotgun house nests in a row of other broken houses. Open studded walls re-frame the long architectural style that evolved to allow breezes to flow through each room from the front of the house to the back. Legends also claim that bullets went in the front door and left through the back door, hence "shotgun."

"I'm hoping you can help me with my kitchen design ideas," Charley remarks as he shows me the open room with the spare bed. My design expertise is something I can easily offer as a thank-you for his hospitality. I look through the open framing into the corner of the house meant to be the kitchen eventually. It's a small space but options for a cabinetry layout surface in my thoughts already.

"Oh, yeah . . . I don't have running water yet. Not sure I mentioned that in the email. We just pee in between the houses since no one is living next door right now."

I peek out the back door to see the three-foot-wide stretch along the length of the houses, and cringe. *I'm a backpacker*, I remind myself. *I can handle this*. I hesitate for a moment, then turn back to look at Charley and nod okay.

"We usually head over the Y to use their showers and bathrooms for the rest," he continues. He sits down on a pile of lumber stacked across the open hallway to relace one of his sneakers.

Knowing I can use a coffee shop bathroom for freshening up, I smile awkwardly, then change the subject. "There is a bus stop about two blocks up according to my Google map. Do you have a neighborhood bus schedule? I can walk the couple of blocks and catch the city bus downtown."

Charley plops down his sneakered foot, looks me squarely on, and shakes his head *no*. "Not a good idea. Not safe in this neighborhood."

Large southern cockroaches scurry past me on the floor. I quickly pick up my packs to hang on nails protruding from the studs in my open room. Charley doesn't even blink, he is so used to the roaches. Steadying my growing anxiety, I slowly ask my next question: "There's another bus stop in the other direction . . . how about that one?"

Maybe this is why, when Daniel dropped me off here at my couchsurfing stay, he looked worried when I brushed off his concern with my naive confidence: I had already researched the city bus route map and knew my transportation options for this area.

"Nope," Charley offers as he heads for the front room, also gutted, to give me time to settle in.

Nope? . . . Nope, he said? No way to come and go from here? Daniel had already driven off, but maybe if I called him . . . But, then what? Daniel never offered to take me in, so I can't ask him to. I don't know him well enough to even think about asking.

I have nowhere to go for tonight, I need to stay. Resigned, at least for right now, I head outside to the grass to pee while it is still light, scanning the adjacent houses for anyone lurking in the shadows. Adrenaline causes me to pee as quickly as I can and get back inside.

Charley, his roommate, and a French couchsurfer also staying, get ready to head out to a pickup kickball game for the evening. "Hey, want to come along?" Charley calls from the front room.

"Absolutely. Be right there." There's not a chance I'm staying in this house alone knowing about the neighborhood. I grab a jacket and anything valuable I don't want to leave behind and join the others in Charley's car.

As the streetlights brighten against the darkening sky and a ball is kicked around the field, I watch the game from the sidelines and consider what more I want to see and do here in the city. I can't believe my naiveté has trapped me, a single and vulnerable female traveler, in a crime district. My mother's concerns race through my head while I push up against my comfort zone, and I stuff them back down where I think they belong, and instead, think about Charley's enthusiasm to buy and fix up a piece of history, his courage to land himself into the dark of this district, and his desire to join into a community surviving the best it can after the hurricane's devastation. Other onlookers cheer on the teams, and I watch Charley run the ball around the field and pass it on to his housemate. The moon is now waning overhead, and I zip up my jacket and reposition myself on the wooden bench along the field's edge for the duration of the game.

DIXIELAND GHOSTS

The buzz of Dixieland music settles on the hairs of my arms, its history lingering along Frenchman Street and Bourbon Street, regardless of the vomit and urine lingering under the cast iron fleur-de-lis overhead. Bar employees have been hosing down the sidewalk from last night's partying, but the rank smell of bodily fluids still gags me.

A taxi drove me to Preservation Hall's wooden seats, worn from decades of the Dixie party, still holding the ghosts of sax and trumpet wails, piano players' keyed licks, and drummers' rhythms pulsing out the city's heartbeat. Starting as an art gallery hosting jazz jam sessions in the 1950s, the Hall quickly became a destination for hearing local jazz greats of the time. I squeeze into the rows of pews, these sainted hymnals of transcendence, and watch other tourists settling their tushes into the scalloped benches in anticipation of live jazz preserved against the momentum of modern rock, hip-hop, and blues. Old New Orleans jazz standards shake the room, and we all stand to sway and clap to the gospel of interwoven cultures beating out a singular, primal ecstasy by the Preservation Hall All Stars, some of whom hail from the lineage of the early musicians jamming in the gallery.

Once back outside, clarinet laughter still circling my head, I slowly wander back toward the river. Hawkers in front of voodoo shops offer discounts on haunted house tours and buskers pass their pails and hats around for spare change.

"Gail!" I hear from across the square, and I turn to see Charley pedaling over in his pedi-cab to offer me a free ride around the French Quarter during my last night here in NOLA. The open cart beckons me to take in the dazzle of evening lights and jazz jousting along the sidewalks. Curling into the cart, I watch Charley's meaty thighs pedal our combined weight through the district streets while tourists scurry to and from the myriad of venues and clubs in the district, not unlike the roaches scurrying the length of Charley's shotgun house.

Without being able to walk through Charley's neighborhood to grab a bus, I've decided there is no reason to remain here in the city. The morning will allow me time to offer up some kitchen design ideas before I ask Charley for a ride to the Greyhound station.

But for now, I remind myself to ask more questions ahead of time.

Sight-seeing around Lafayette, Louisiana, I find my way to the Cathedral of St. John the Evangelist and its almost five-century-old oak tree with a circumference of around twenty-eight feet.

Chapter 7
Louisiana After-Party

Lafayette, Louisiana • October 2014

Back at the Blue Moon, I am once again called "Miss Gail" by the young women who staff the guesthouse. While bunking in the bandroom, the world feels right again.

Duckweed and hyacinth cover the murky swamp water as Champagne's tour boat, a flat-bottomed crawfish skiff, glides into a Lake Martin inlet in search of alligators sunning on downed tree trunks.

Kate, another Moon bunkmate joining Doug and me, asks lots of questions and our boat captain answers, ending each reply with the word *cher*, although it sounds to me like "sha." It's Cajun French and Kate leans towards Doug to ask what it means.

"Little one," he whispers to her over the quiet hum of the boat's motor as we inch along.

"It must be an age thing since *I* don't get the *cher* treatment when I ask questions," I remark to Doug. Kate is only in her twenties, so it makes sense.

The boat winds its way through a thicket of cypress trees, and we duck away from low-hanging moss, scanning the trees for dangling poisonous snakes, like water moccasins and copperheads. Stark white egrets nest high up in the cypress branches, easy to see. The captain watches for any of the other 205 wading birds nesting here so he can point them out.

We chug past old houseboats, not unlike the kind that Doug grew up on as a young child before his father built a small house on an inlet land point in the Atchafalaya Basin. The swamps are deeply emotional for him. Through his stories, I feel privy to a way of life no longer lived. Times change and the old ways, whoever's old ways they are, start to get lost forever unless these stories get retold once in a while.

"Le Grand Derangement" is deeply rooted in the DNA of Acadiana. French immigrants to Nova Scotia refused to pledge allegiance to the British crown and church, causing their expulsion from French Canada in 1755, some returning to France where they were no longer welcome. Survivors of sea and land travel during a second "derangement" a few years later made a sheltered home in the bayous, etc Harsh landscapes, weather patterns, alligators, and snakes gave them privacy and protection. To flourish, they ate what could be hunted, fished, picked, or raised, like pigs. Tougher times forced their culinary creativity to use every part of the animal they could . . . hence boudin began its place in their diet.

I can see the root in Doug's eyes whenever he recalls childhood memories. Life was not easy.

"We are Cajun strong and proud," he says, nodding to no one in particular. I place my hand on his shoulder, my new friend, and give it a gentle rub.

As the boat navigates around a grouping of cypress "knees," like breathing tubes gathering more oxygen for the trees and perhaps stability in the muddy swamp bottom, a gator sunning on a downed tree trunk comes into view. The captain slows even more to a glide so we can snap photos of the gator, jaws wide open with a toothy smile of sharp incisors. Kate scoots along the side bench to get a better view. Tree reflections ease across the shallows, and in the shadows, turtles splash into the water next to the boat as an egret swoops low across the water's surface to find dinner.

BLACK POT FESTIVAL AND THE KILLER BOUDIN

Aromas tickle the nostrils of festival attendees as they congregate around the food booths competing in the cook-off for gravies and gumbos, cracklins and jambalaya, desserts—all cooked in black cast-iron pots. I'm learning that here in Louisiana, anything is fair game to be made into a festival.

Doug and I mosey up to a booth with chicken gumbo roux being stirred, steam gently rising into the air. The chef chops onions vigorously and scrapes them off the cutting board to add to the gumbo base. The pot will continue to simmer until judging time later on during the weekend. This is just Friday night. Small paper cups filled with the first round of the stew are lined up in front of the pot, and Doug picks one up to try.

"Want one, cher?" he asks me. After my comment on Lake Martin, he's been using this term of endearment more often, and I feel younger and younger because of it.

"Any sausage in the gumbo?" I ask the stirrer.

"Of course, we put sausage in everything," he responds.

"Nothing for me, thanks," I say to Doug. "I haven't eaten pork since 1975."

Down the path from our gumbo pot, other competition chefs spice up their secret recipes for rice-filled jambalayas, fry up their versions of cracklins—fat-covered pork skins— and other Cajun favorites. Pork, pork, and more pork that I do not eat.

There is no dividing line in the Cajun culture between food and music, so Doug and I make our way over to the crowded dance floor, where other local dance friends occupy personal space as well as they can. Hard-drinking campers and attendees push their way onto the floor, beer bottles and cups in hand, to flail around to the live music firing up the dance energy. Doug twirls me under his arm, straight into a wobbly flailer, whose elbow whacks me in the back. His hoppy beer sprays over my shoulder and down the front of my dress and beer foam permeates my hair. When Doug moves on to dance with other women friends, partiers ask me to dance. I less-than-patiently endure their heavy alcohol breath and lack of any recognizable steps. Annoyed, my dance bliss falls flat as I rush around the dance floor's spilled beer puddles to search for a bathroom where I can hose myself down, but only have access to port-a-johns.

Without a vehicle, I am at the mercy of Doug and his time frame, so I try to make peace with being all sticky by sitting and listening to the music only, or finding an open piece of floor away from the pavilion to dance free-form on my own. I eventually look up to see Doug coming over and force a smile—I don't want him to know I'm unhappy.

"It's getting really crowded out there," he says, panting.

"Yes. I needed some breathing room for a bit, too." I take in a few fake audible deep breaths for effect. "Thought I would get off the floor for a bit."

He stays to dance with me on the sideline as people buying more beer stagger their way past us during this opening night of the weekend festival.

"What will tomorrow be like?" I ask Doug as he adjusts his Black Pot Festival baseball cap from a previous year. Every cap for every event for every past year has cultural importance for him or so he has told me.

"Not so bad for the first few hours since most of these folks will be sleeping it off, but as they wake up and join the dance floor, it will be worse than tonight."

Well, not a chance I'm coming back anytime soon—*Too much boudin, beer, and bruising for me.*

On Saturday of the Black Pot Festival, I decide to research this sausage phenomenon in a different way at the parallel Boudin Cook Off at Lafayette's downtown Parc Sans Souci. Hopefully without any bruising involved this time. From my stay at the Moon, I hoof it downtown just in time for the initial "Blessing of the Boudin" by a local clergyman.

Boudin is just sausage, right? Well, like any culinary staple, different cultures make it their own. Historically poor, the Acadiens used what they had around: pigs, rice, veggies, herbs, and spices. It was a way to use up less-desirable parts of the animal. With a variety of permutations with the ingredients, family traditions flourished in competition.

Start with pork, pork fat, pork blood, pork organs, pork feet, pork snouts, pork . . . well, maybe not snouts. Grainy rice. Add in some of the "holy trinity" of celery, onion, and bell pepper. Stir in some cayenne, paprika, garlic, or parsley. Then poach or smoke the hell out of those links.

Folks buy tickets allowing a set number of boudin samples from any of the booths set up around the park. The festival goers carry trays with groupings of small paper cups filled with a selection of recipe favorites, determined to cast their vote for the People's Choice award. Teams of judges also taste and vote. I, of course, have no desire to either squeeze the slimy contents out of the casing onto a cracker . . . or eat all with casing, the two preferred methods of ingesting boudin. Sitting on a bench in the middle of the park, I have a good observer location from which to spy on all these boudin-eaters as they wolf down sample after sample of what looks like bland slime. I can almost feel my arteries clogging just watching the spectacle. For the non-pork eater—me—the food and drink offerings are limited: boudin, beer, over-sweetened lemonade, and praline candy. Maybe the pralines clear the palette for more boudin—sweet and savory balancing on the discriminating tongue. Beer washes it all down, unless you are an up-and-coming boudin-eating youngster. Then, sugar and fat work just fine together with the over-sweetened lemonade. To feel part of the festivities here, I buy myself a lemonade and a praline, both sickly and sticky sweet.

As I wander past the booths, I wonder if any sellers offer the "cajun works": boudin filled with not only pork, but bits of crawfish, shrimp, and alligator. What about boudin po'boy sandwiches? Boudin étouffée? Boudin beignets?

Anyone peddling a variation on those options?

How about an eating contest with "killer boudin" soaked in Tabasco's Scorpion hot sauce, Tobasco's hottest, made nearby on Avery Island?

Now, that I would want to watch!

Six Degrees West

Greyhound Bus
Lafayette, Louisiana, to Austin, Texas

By 3:45 in the morning, the snorts and grunts bouncing around the bunk room push me out into the Moon's shared lounge with my belongings, ready for travel. Coffee brewing in the kitchen jars my nostrils this early in the day, but Doug is obviously up already after only a couple of hours of sleep.

The Moon's open-air stage had been unusually chilly last night and Doug and I had been the only ones dancing, bundled up in coats and hats. Due to the poor turnout, the band packed up early, which was fine by me, since my bus is due to depart at five this morning. Even so, I would imagine he would have liked to sleep in instead of driving me to the station.

Personally, I would have regretted making the offer, but cheerily he says, coffee in hand, "Ready to go, cher?"

Once on the bus, I wave through the window at my new friend while he waits next to the terminal building until the bus pulls away, and I can no longer see him, another stranger having worked his way into my heart. The Louisiana bayou diminishes behind me, and my new friend weaves his way into my nostalgia.

Nearing Lake Charles on highway I-10, the new day stretches into focus through the milky bus window. The pink clouds dissolve onto the horizon, and the blossoming blue sky waxes above that thin line to the east. Since my return to Lafayette from New Orleans, restlessness, like a pot of gumbo bubbling around its edge, pulled at my attention. Rippling throughout my visit was the concern that poor timing might result in lost opportunity.

While still in NOLA, I sent couchsurfing requests via email to hosts in Austin, but no one replied. My research turned up a youth hostel, but they had no beds available over the first few days I'll be in the city.

Too early or too late?

Having resisted being on Facebook, my limited networking options forced me to ask for help again, undermining my confidence. Frustration led me to again contact my couchsurfing friend in Georgia, well-traveled and connected, who scoured her contacts within Texas. She found me a stay for a couple of days with some old family friends of her mother's. They'll be meeting me at the bus station.

There is something to this *six degrees of separation* thing and I'm grateful to have a safe place to be for a couple of days while I keep researching other housing options. Next time, I'll start earlier with the requests, so I can send out a second batch if need be—or create more backup plans.

Oil wells, dipping their heads towards the ground like grazing ponies, pull crude liquid up from the depths along the highway's edge as Texas welcomes me into its flat expanses, and if anything, I'd rather be too early than too late.

All about trust, isn't it?

Of course I have to travel to Austin, Texas to honkytonk two-step once done with my zydeco dancing. I got here just in time to dance in the famed Broken Spoke during its fiftieth anniversary celebration.

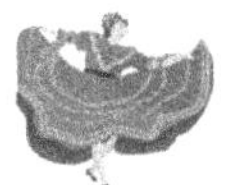

Chapter 8:
Austin Honkytonkin'

Austin, Texas • November 2014

A wooden cane clicks on the asphalt coming up the sidewalk in my direction, supporting the gray-haired Mexican man hobbling his way over to where I am sitting. Texas' capitol building looms on the other side of the avenue, overlooking all the busy traffic flowing past the bus stop.

"May I sit?" he inquires, and I twist to face him and nod, then move some of my packs off the bench and onto the sidewalk. I'm waiting for the #7 that will take me to the youth hostel, closer to the dance halls, now that there is a bed available. After eyeing my stack of packs, his dark eyes penetrate into mine. "Are you traveling with your husband?"

During a recent phone conversation, Bruce shared his frustrations of having to tell his story over and over while traveling. Having started to understand his annoyance, I think about how to tell my story differently this time. I keep it short and light. "No husband. I travel alone."

He ponders my response, then offers, "At least you have God."

So much for keeping it light. I pause to consider a reply that's respectful, and note a group of suited men crossing the street to walk up the quadrangle to the capitol.

"I have my own kind of spirituality," I say, trying to stay detached.

I can't tell if he genuinely is concerned for my personal well-being or if he feels all women need protection from a man . . . any man . . . any man-figure. Brought up in the Catholic faith, I no longer believe the doctrines, but, instead, have explored over the years a more "energetically shared-consciousness" answer to the mystery that I feel we all wonder about. I choose not to engage him in any kind of debate on the subtleties of different religious/spiritual philosophies.

"Thank you for your concern," is all I offer and leave it at that.

67

But he can't leave it there. He unfolds the story that brought him back to church: about his wife, the love of his life, dying, and the years of depression, of reaching out to prayer, of hearing Mary's voice telling him to go back to church, of the peace he found there.

And I think, *To each his own in the process of healing.* Who am I to judge where another person finds peace?

As a homeless woman wearing Winnie the Pooh pajama pants pushes an overloaded shopping cart along the sidewalk in front of us, he turns to face me for the story finale, "I would have been like you if Mary hadn't spoken to me."

Wait a minute . . . like me? Like what? Without a husband . . . or God . . . I'm wandering about in chaos . . . lost? My new travel tee-shirt slogan idea: "Really, I do not need saving."

THE BROKEN SPOKE

Amanda Cevallos and the High Hands play the opening show in the Broken Spoke's front restaurant. The Spoke is one of the oldest honkytonk dance halls in Austin. Diners pour glasses of beer from pitchers and chew burgers as I pass through to the back and main dance hall.

Not having known about this week's fiftieth anniversary festivities before I scheduled the Greyhound ticket, I shake my head at my concern about arriving too early or too late. I've landed here right on time.

Two tiers of tables and chairs flank both sides of the dance floor leading up to the stage at the far end of the hall. At a free table, I drop my bag and coat and change my shoes just as a special eight-minute video documentary rolls on the hall's history.

While well-known performers, such as Jerry Jeff Walker, Kris Kristofferson, and Willie Nelson, performed here, Austin grew and changed. Different kinds of music have taken the lead, so places like the Spoke have been important to keep honkytonk music and dance alive.

Jerry Jeff Walker, in person, joins Alvin Crow and others as the movie screen lifts and the band steps up onto the stage to start the first set. Alvin sets his fiddle on his shoulder and saws an intro for the first tune.

Lingering at the edge of the crowded dance floor, trying not to seem desperate, I peruse the scene to see who I'd like to dance with. As fiddles and slide guitars toss out melodies, men donning cowboy hats, boots, and large belt buckles strut by, twisting and turning their partners as they go.

But it's a less flamboyant invitation that pulls me onto the floor, and before I know it, I'm two-stepping through the crowd with a partner who never once looks at me, or says one word to me. After our turn, a new dance begins and a hand offers to take mine.

Like Cinderella, midnight-stricken, with city buses that stop running by eleven-thirty, I keep an eye on the time. Either I have to leave the ball early, or find a ride back to the hostel, so I start to work the crowd. I explain my situation to one man I've danced with several times, now that I'm feeling some familiarity.

"If I can catch a ride with someone, I get to stay and dance some more." Maybe I do need a bit of saving once in a while.

Whatever goes down will be okay, I remind myself. *I need to trust that the right thing will happen.* He personally makes the offer and I'm back on the floor, honkytonkin' in style.

The recommendation from my ride back to the hostel last night had been to go to a different dance hall tonight where more locals might be convening. I check the bus routes, but nothing services that section of the city, so I bus back to the Spoke.

As dancers arrive, gather up in groups, and carry plates of bar-b-que and bottles of beer up to the tables, the band checks their microphones, and I work the crowd right away for a ride. I pick a man who responded to me favorably the night before and seems to know a lot of people. After another couple of dances with him, I ask him if he knows anyone heading in the direction of Riverside and Lakeshore east of Interstate 35.

"Done," he says, and in good faith not to forget, he hands me his car key and I slip it into my skirt pocket. One nice thing about my travel: I have no time agenda, I am in the universal flow of serendipity. As the night goes on and guest performers join the house band on stage, the crowd starts to thin out. Once regular friends and dance partners leave for the evening, the remaining men start to ask me to dance. Don't get me wrong, I am grateful for the handful of men I've been dancing with, but I'm a sucker for those iconic Texas cowboys.

There's the leggy one with a brimmed black hat and cast belt buckle with a horse head who dances a bouncy two-step just the way I like it. Then I'm asked by a short Hispanic man with a clear lead and some fun swing moves. They're followed by an older man who nudges me into the center where we hardly move at all while other dancers circle the room around us. Oh well, at least I'm dancing.

The remaining dancers pack up to leave and my ride is ready to go. As we drive, I ask him what he does for work. My payment for the ride is to be an audience to his life story, since I'm learning that nothing is without *some* form of payment—even a free couchsurfing stay has the expectation of a small token gift to the host as a thank you. Many stories seem too interesting to be true, so either they have been honed as fiction over the years or they really are true. It doesn't matter to me; a good story is a good story.

"I was trained in classical music as a pianist and conductor, but couldn't make any money," he tells me. "So I became a lawyer and commodity broker in New York. Sure, there was stress and a fast pace, but I made millions. I never looked back."

"I have training in music too. Do you still play or anything?"

"No. I made some bad economic choices and I lost everything. We were living the high life when it all went down." His voice trails off, "My wife took the kids and left."

Feeling awkward, I don't say anything.

He quickly shifts to a nervous laugh. "But there's a new business venture that will either make me back the millions or leave me totally broke."

I listen but feel sad that the damage was too great to repair the deep love he still has for his wife and kids. Even if the millions come back into the bank account, I sense he feels there is no hope for reconciliation. What I don't find out as we pull into the driveway of the hostel is why he is here in Austin.

RAINY DAY WITH A LOVELORN PROFESSOR

Ethan, a neatly dressed, forties-ish college professor, and I stare out the hostel window from our shared breakfast table in the common room. He turns and asks, "What are you planning on doing today in the rain?"

With no choice but to accept the weather, I made tentative plans to suit up in rain gear, grab an umbrella, and catch a bus downtown. "Museums that I can get to from bus routes," I say.

He considers my plan, perks up, and offers, "I have a car . . . can I join you?"

Our first stop is the Mexic-Arte Museum where we find ourselves among the exhibition of pine coffins in folk art effigy. Smiling, masked papier-mache faces look up at us amidst orange paper flowers. As we check out the wooden rosaries draping over the open coffin edges, he tells me that his temporary teaching position came to an end, that he needs another job, but also a change of scenery.

While perusing the black and white photos of Mexican women and colorful illustrated cartoons that line the walls, Ethan tells me about his road trip beginning in Illinois where his last post was. After Austin, he plans on driving into Colorado and Arizona to apply for teaching positions available at universities.

"My road trip is about a change of scenery, too," I add and we decide to move on to the museum at the University of Texas for an exhibit about the making of *Gone with the Wind*. I reminisce about Rhett Butler's famous words to Scarlet in the movie about "not giving a damn." While inspecting the aged casting photos of Clark Gable hanging on a nearby wall, Ethan tells me that his travel, also, in part, is to create distance from the dysfunction of his previous on-again off-again love relationship. Surrounded by the images of Clark Gable and Vivien Leigh, I imagine Ethan as Rhett, and his girlfriend as Scarlett, not ever getting the love right.

We move over to the costumes of blue and red velvet draping off of mannequins, the exact costumes worn by Vivian Leigh and Olivia de Havilland. "She's not good for me," he says. "If I stay in Illinois, I'll be sucked back in . . . just because it's easy." Not wanting to dredge up my own most recent relationship woes, that I, too, needed space from, I just let him vent, nodding my head.

I wonder why people open up to strangers. Maybe the safety comes from knowing paths will most likely not cross again. Intimate details bond those sharing road moments, and those moments see us through until the next bonding happens with someone else farther along the journey. We leave the memory of southern plantation angst and drama for the sculptures at the Elizabet Ney Museum.

"I do love her," he continues as we study busts of Sam Houston and Stephen F. Austin. "But I just can't subject myself to her manipulations anymore." I listen and nod, since I no longer feel I have viable advice for anyone else. And he's got the transportation for today, so I'm along for the ride no matter what.

"How is it that we can live, love, and learn, and at that critical moment of using all this new wisdom, we blow it?" he muses, then walks across the room to view another sculpture.

So true, I think, and feel grateful for my chosen transience.

We end at the Hope Outdoor Graffiti Gallery where we climb over the old cement blocks to peruse the flamboyant pinks, greens, and purples of the geometric designs from local graffiti artists. They come to paint anywhere a small blank space lurks between psychedelic flowers and the latest buzz phrase.

As a writer, Ethan hopes to make sense of his relationship issues and publish a different take on mainstream advice. "Ah, such a universal theme and the subject of every therapy session and self-help book on relationships," I remind him. "Good luck with the plan, though."

He just smiles at me. I can't tell if the smile shows confidence or trepidation.

ZEN STILLNESS

The sun's warmth dries the lingering chilly dampness from last night's rain and the sky feels brighter in its blue because of it. Just up the road from my rental car pick up is the Zilker Botanical Garden with an affordable entrance fee. I tune out the highway noise and the festival waftings from the Fun, Fun, Fun Fest nearby as I wander through the cactus and succulent garden near the parking lot. Saw palmetto leaf fans block out the garden's fence near the road, allowing me to enter into a state of solitude before anyone else wanders in. Barrel cactus and prickly pear line the bark mulch pathway through the garden and out the other side toward other botanical areas.

Cravings for stillness compel me to balance out the movement of travel, the movement of dance, the movement of conversation, and regenerate. Pruned bonsai trees accent the passageways of the Japanese garden, and I pause to sit on a stone bench half hidden amongst bamboo. Flowing water streams out from a wooden pipe, dripping over hanging ivy as it cascades into a rock-framed pond across the path from my bench. Orange and white koi fish gather along the pool's edge, slipping around the stone pavers traversing the shallow water. Dragonflies hover and land on the leaves of the nearby bamboo surrounding my bench. Hanging in an overhead branch, wind chimes ting a rhythmic release of any residual tension held in my body, and I resonate with the duet improvised between chime and water.

As I study the koi flippering and flitting under the water's surface, the scent of a nearby rose bush infuses into the atmosphere, motivating me toward the remnants of dying flowers clinging to bushes in the Mabel Davis rose garden.

I think of fall's "brown" back in Vermont, the season resting from too much summer burst, preparing for another type of stillness blanketed in snow. While nature finds a balance from its seasons' movement, I stroll the gardens and unwind from my own recent bursts.

GINNY'S LITTLE LONGHORN SALOON

Texas state flags cover the walls and ceiling around the tiny band stage near the entrance. A drummer has tucked himself into the corner and a stand-up bass player hovers on the edge of the stage flooring. Rosie Flores, sea green fingernails painted to match her sea green electric guitar, adjusts her black rimmed cowboy hat with her silver-ringed fingers. She leans into the microphone and twangs her honkytonk tune to the bounce of the driving bass notes.

Sitting near the even tinier dance area, I wait for other dancers to show up. As I sway in time to the rhythms, couples arrive and take to the floor, leaving several of us lone females out of luck for partners.

Screams drift onto the dance floor, through the tunes, from the back of the Saloon, and I abandon the dance floor disappointment to explore the excitement at the back. A large cage over a bingo grid offers a cash prize to the lucky estimator of the exact location of the chicken's dropped poop. Yes, here at Ginny's is her famous Chicken Shit Bingo game. Those with grid tickets *egg* on the poor chicken to nudge it toward their ticketed grid square since a couple hundred dollars is on the line for the cash pot. The chicken's clawed feet wobble from square to square on the grid, and turning from one nudger to another, she clucks as she steps, full of feed in her gut. Finally, she stops and lays one on square number ten, and the lucky winner explodes with glee.

During the band's break and a re-set up of the bingo cage, I pose for a photo with Rosie outside the Saloon. She pulls me in close with those sea-green fingernails across my back and smacks a quick kiss on my left cheek in a passing moment of fan adoration—a fitting last day here in the city trying its best to keep everything *weird*.

From Austin, I bus to San Antonio, Texas to see the Alamo and the other missions comprising San Antonio Missions National Historical Park. I stand in front of one of the many ornate doors into Mission Concepcion.

Chapter 9
Deep In the Heart

San Antonio, Texas • November 2014

According to RB, a documentary filmmaker, poet, and my current couchsurfing host, one can learn about the entire history of San Antonio in less than thirty minutes, but not chronologically.

Air chilled from centuries of change descends on San Antonio tonight, so we grab some bean-bag chairs and a wool blanket and settle ourselves at the Main Plaza smack in front of the San Fernando Cathedral. We are here to watch the video art installation by Xavier de Richmont known as "San Antonio/The Saga." Without narration, the surround sound music pushes the colorful projected visuals across the church's facade. In the first scene, lightning cracks and driving rains pour over petroglyph images wrapping themselves around the cathedral's architecture. Native flute melodies transition red bison crawling across desert plains while missionaries descend from the cathedral spires to glove the church in painted frescoes. Helmeted conquistadors gallop onto the "screen," flags flapping, and pull roaring cannons across to conquer civilizations that had lived off the land for thousands of years.

Fringed leather, raccoon caps, and rifles defend the rights of Texas Longhorn cattle ranchers and the New Mexicans, as a lone fiddle introduces a circle of stars around Abe Lincoln's face and some chained slaves. Oil wells drill along a jazz clarinet tune, and train steam laces over iron tracks as San Antonio rises like a phoenix from the river valley. Spot-lighted skyscrapers erupt across the church face to showcase historical businesses: Cavendar's Boot City, Scheuer Butter-Krust Bread, and Rosie's Lounge and Beer.

The presentation ends with projected fireworks and flowers twirling themselves into a collage of the diverse cultural flags of present-day San Antonio. We pull the blanket tighter around us, giddy at the spectacle, and stay to watch the cathedral light up for the second showing.

TO DIE FOR

Just below the surface of my skin, an epidermal layer hangs onto the memory of my past work obligations. Now without a vehicle and beholden to city buses, their routes and schedules, the epidermal tightness releases ever so slowly, scar tissue softening into an accepted flow of time and space. What would previously have been a fifteen-minute drive can take me an hour of bus transfers, walking, and waiting on street corners. But no longer crammed into a tight moment, time settles out, and the only accountable hour is the one when the bus stops running. Not unlike what I seek in my mountain backpacking treks—time fades into only what is at stake in the present—survival, movement, and the inhalation of sensory bliss.

Through the city bus windows, billboards, banner ads, and posters inundate me with vowels and consonants whirling around, and my head spins. Maybe it is Vermont that has sheltered me from billboard overwhelm, or perhaps it is my desire for simplification—the study of choosing just the right word for what I am trying to communicate. I close my eyes and feel as if I am standing in the eye of a letter hurricane. The alphabet seems to settle into the puddles dotted along the sidewalks that line the streets. I imagine children stomping through, splashing out gobbledygook phrases.

Three city bus transfers gradually maneuver me downtown to the first of five missions: the Alamo. The other four comprise the San Antonio Missions National Historical Park.

There is no rush. The Alamo has withstood history and will be there whether I arrive in fifteen minutes or sixty. Tucked among downtown city buildings, amidst tourist trinket stores, the Alamo seems diminutive in comparison to all the stories woven over time about it. I thought it would be more "fort"-like. From what I've read, the iconic Alamo roof hump wasn't even part of the original mission architecture, but that hump seems to have become a San Antonio symbol, not unlike the historical lore of the battle fought there for Texas' independence from Mexico.

New controversy around the 1836 battle opens a window into what is unflattering about the history of the United States. Like most school kids, I bought into the hype, remembering the Alamo defenders as heroes against a tyrannical Mexican government. But there is new knowledge. Those battling Texas landowners wanted to keep their slaves and Mexico wanted no part of that. Through the arched wooden doors, bullet holes crumble as I stick my finger into the stone walls that had barricaded defenders against the Mexican force led by General Santa Anna. The same walls pushing back against Spain's attempts to extend its power north out of Mexico in the mid-1700s. The same walls reminding every visitor that, at times, people were willing to fight what they felt was injustice. But, in light of the controversy, whose injustice?

Lists of those who sacrificed themselves for a higher pursuit embed themselves here *in memoriam*. Not only Texans, but defenders from as far away as England, Ireland, Wales, Germany, and Denmark—even someone from Vermont, a place not known for its part in pre–Civil War slavery. Those fighters, willing to die for what they thought was a *greater good,* fought against all odds for Texas' independence. They had no hope to win.

I do understand, though. I've fought losing battles over the years, holding fast to outdated beliefs. I've barricaded myself behind walls for the sake of my principles, or so I thought. Only later did I recognize that I had limited perspective. And there weren't any guns involved.

RB, a kindred realist, and I, agreed this morning that there is little that we would be willing to die for. Do we lack the passion, the cultural roots, or the desire for martyrdom? Regardless of cause? Yet, throughout history, people have fought for, defended against, and made their "last stand" for all kinds of reasons.

As I gaze into glass display cases filled with historical weaponry, I realize I've had my own versions of weapons—stubbornness, discipline, small ways to feel in control against what I felt to be injustices of culture and family. I *was* willing to die on some level rather than succumb to what my world around me demanded: a dutiful woman posing no threat to the status quo. *My* rebellion has been a quiet one—I've stood up for what I've believed about myself over the years.

But . . . have I also bought into my own limited narratives? Have I rewritten my own history in order to survive my childhood challenges intact?

Continuing to Mission San Jose, Mission Concepcion, Mission San Juan, and Mission Espada, I learn more about the mission's role in erasing indigenous cultures under the guise of protection. The "First Texas People," as RB calls them—the Coahuiltecan hunter/gatherers—sought refuge in these area missions to save themselves from attacks by aggressive Comanche and Apache natives from the north and displacement from Spaniards from the south.

"In order to survive, they gave up their beliefs," RB told me this morning over breakfast. "Well, mostly they succumbed to the dress code, rules, and religious rituals demanded by the monks. Many natives eventually died from smallpox and measles, the very diseases they were hoping to avoid. They might as well have been slaves."

I felt the weight of sadness in my gut for this too-common story of attempts at cultural homogenization. I saw it in RB's eyes as well. He had studied the history while making a documentary film about the Coahuiltecan.

Before I left RB's house for the day, he offered me his version of the rest of the mission history not included in the recent video presentation on the Plaza: any indigenous cultures surviving ongoing epidemics, warfare, migration, dispersion by Spaniards to work at distant plantations and mines, high infant mortality, intercultural marriages, and general demoralization were diluted in history. Their last stand of cultural survival faded away.

With its two-story arched window corridors overlooking manicured gardens, San Jose y San Miguel de Aguayo is home to the famed Rose Window. Flowing limestone swirls of plaster roses and curling vines frame the nearly seven-foot-high window of memory and love and tragedy.

According to one legend, Pedro Huizar came to New Spain to make his fortune before sending for his dear Rosa, who was said to have perished while sailing from Spain to join her beloved in the new territory. On the last day of Pedro's carving, her spirit supposedly appeared to him next to the window.

Through a curlicued iron grate covering the glass, a shadowy shape resides—maybe my own reflection, or is it Rosa's spirit? If I look closely enough, I can almost see her, roses adorning her hair and dress, and wonder, if there is an afterlife, were Rosa and Pedro reunited along a path of real roses? Clearly, it was the kind of love to die for. Maybe someday I'll feel that kind of love.

On Sunday morning, though neither of us is religious, I invite RB to accompany me to the noon Mariachi Mass at the historic chapel tucked into Mission Concepcion's eroding stone towers, mortar slowly crumbling.

"Come on," I say, "It'll be fun." RB's father was a Baptist minister, and according to RB, anything fun was sin. RB is reluctant but agrees to join me. We arrive at the mission, follow a group of churchgoers into the chapel, and pick a worn bench not too close to the front, but in good view of the mariachi band. Incense smoke burns my eyes and makes it hard to breathe in the tiny chapel. RB leans over in my direction, his lanky body folding over itself to meet my right ear.

"I've experienced enough," he whispers. "Can we go?"

"We haven't heard the band yet," I whisper back.

"Okay," he sheepishly says, "we'll stay a bit longer."

The priest, purple robe swishing, saunters over the mosaic stone floor with his procession. While the incense ball swings up the aisle, the mariachi band plays a hymn, the singer belting out lyrics in Spanish. I turn musty pages to the hymn number listed on a sign at the front of the chapel and follow along the feathery page to see where in the music they are. Two women play violins, scratching bows across strings, while the men fill out the harmony on trumpet, guitar, and bass guitar.

A small Mexican girl steps into the aisle, flouncy white skirt with blue border bouncing as she twirls to the music, her long dark hair coiling around her neck while her parents kneel, eyes closed, and pray.

"It's okay to dance in church?" RB asks me in awe. The man sitting next to him puts down a kneeler on top of RB's shoe, then kneels onto it. RB rolls his eyes while he quietly tries to free his foot without making a scene. Finally, he taps the man on the arm and points to the trapped shoe. The poor man, embarrassed, frees RB's shoe, and the three of us hang our heads low to hold back laughter.

While parishioners read Bible passages from the hand-carved pulpit at the front, RB asks me if the priests usually drink real wine. I tell him that I don't remember from my Catholic childhood if it is real wine or not. He wonders too, in the Mexican version of Mass, whether the wafers are actually tortillas. I tell him, "No, Catholicism is traditionally rigid."

The Mass comes to an end and the mariachi band finishes their last hymn. RB and I rise from the pew, stroll back outside to breathe deeply the fresh San Antonio air, and head on into the Texas day.

FIRST ANNUAL HILL COUNTRY FAIR, SAN MARCOS

Thigh High Gardens is the dream manifest of a 27-year-old woman who studied permaculture. While working on the farm, she had a freak farm accident, then at the hospital, to everyone's shock, died mysteriously. Friends have gathered this weekend to hold her dream in the golden cup of reverent memorial, and in her tribute, invite others to join in this celebration of farm life, local music, and organic food.

Standing in light drizzle on a chilly, gray November day, about seventy-five people have gathered at this fundraising event, the median age about thirty-two. RB and I are among the older minority of those here to partake in the experience, but my hope for a better world is rekindled because of the dedication of these kinds of young people. They are a newer wave of "back to the land" life seekers. Due to the intimacy of the small festival group, stories flow easily, offering farm education in order to change the old attitudes of Texas culture.

Charred dark pink, turning slowly as it roasts over glowing coals, the spotted pig's bulging black eyes rhythmically stare at me as they carousel down, around the rotation's backside, and up and over the arc's crest again and again. Lucky for me, vegetarian chili and chicken tacos are for sale for those of us who don't eat pork. A local beer tent hunkers under a row of trees along the grassy path between the two stages set up for alternating performances.

Local artists such as Grace Park and Merlin Scott intimately sing over the backdrop of their guitars to a handful of listeners sitting on makeshift wood benches that encircle the Persimmon Stage. Following them, the Old Time Gospel McMercy Family Band spreads out along the Main Stage, snare drum and cymbal keeping time, while the layered vocal harmonies pierce their way through the mist toward those huddling near an open fire pit. I stand behind the pit, my umbrella shielding me from the dripping sky, fleece hat pulled low over my brow and ears, and compliment Merlin on his acoustic set. RB chats with folks along the other side of the flames.

Sunday morning, gospel abounds on the Persimmon Stage while campers help themselves to breakfast burritos, filled with another harvest of farm-fresh ingredients. In between sets, musicians like Merlin Scott sit in the makeshift bleachers behind the fire circle to serenade the morning still coated in mist. Over his soft background strumming, he and I speak of Big Bend National Park, where I plan to go in two days to hike in the Chisos Mountains and walk in the desert. He has been there before and makes some suggestions.

Back down by the fire, RB asks if I am still feeling afraid of the mountain lions living in the national park. Overhearing RB, Merlin, now standing near the food table, picks up a smooth red stone from the ground.

"Take this with you," he says. "They know you are coming. Buy some tobacco and stop along the road to make an offering." He drops the stone onto my palm. I close my fist around it, assuming the stone is supposed to connect me with the land somehow, or maybe the mountain lions.

I turn to RB. "No, I am not afraid."

Usually meant to protect horsemen from trail dust, a full length black, canvas *duster* coat drapes around the tall frame of another Texan as he turns away from the fire and looks straight at me. I wonder if his coat is a fashion statement or if he works with cattle for a living.

"How *can* you be afraid? You've already taken the first step," he says, and my gaze lingers long in his mysterious, gray eyes before I look up at the sky and let the mist kiss my cheeks. He turns back to the fire to warm his hands, and I feel both seen and anonymous standing around the fire pit for warmth with him, RB, and Merlin. I seem to exist in a transient state of witness—watching, listening, feeling, as I hover like a hummingbird feeding on the nectar of a flower.

But I have no stake here, as it is now traveling *on the road,* and I slip through the sagas and dramas of those steeped in rooted lives. I deposit the red stone into my pocket for safety and think about the wind blowing again soon, my wings taking me farther west out of San Antonio and into other dramas and sagas, none of which will root me either. None of which I would be willing to literally die for. But, in this moment of serendipitous Texan hand-holding, those of us still circled around the crackling fire celebrate humanity, mystery, death, music, and locally grown food changing Texas one veggie at a time.

From San Antonio, I rent a car and drive the ten hours to Big Bend National Park near the border with Mexico for a four-day backpacking trek in the Chisos Mountains, and another six days exploring and camping in the valley desert. Days are hot, and the nights are chilly enough to wear fleece and down.

Chapter 10
Big Bend Prophecy

Big Bend National Park, Texas • November 2014

As I grab the info sheet on mountain lion behavior off the counter to read later, the visitor center glass door swings wide open.

"About a mile up the road," a man puffs the words out. "A mother and two cubs . . ." He takes a deep breath. ". . . crossing the road." His arm extends straight toward the main road into the expanse of Big Bend National Park, then he scampers over to the counter next to me, and interrupts my conversation with Ranger Jim, who was just telling me about how rare it is to see mountain lions in the park. Two days ago in San Marcos, I felt no fear, but now . . .

Jim had just smiled when he was telling me, "This is a big park and most of the lions have been killed off. We know of only about twenty-five still roaming the area. If you see one, it will be a big deal. Let us know."

Hardly see any? The info sheet crinkles in my grasp as I make plans to read it as soon as I get back to my rental car.

Jim makes note of the sighting with the lion observer, then guides me through my camping itinerary for my next ten days in the park. A ten-dollar backcountry pass covers designated sites scattered along dirt roads, specific sites dotted along the hiking trails in the Chisos Mountains, and free-form camping by zone. This is my first time in a desert environment, so I don't want to miss anything; I choose a bit of everything. We carefully create a schedule of camping based on the fact that my rental car doesn't have the clearance for some of the backcountry roads and I head off toward the Chisos Mountains for four days of backpacking before the Thanksgiving weekend crowds pour into the park.

THE SOUTH RIM

Chisos has been translated as "ghost" or "phantom," but the Apache word *Chishe* means "people of the forest," which seems the more likely translation of the name. At least, I want it to be since I consider myself a person of the forest, too. There is something about a tree's strength and resiliency, life-force sap juices permeating the meat of its girth, pushing out spring growth toward the heat of the sun—transformational adaptability in response to whatever cyclical elements offer opportunities for growth. I can totally relate.

"Pack all your water in," Jim had reminded me. "You can fill at the Chisos Basin Lodge where you will park. No other water is guaranteed along the trail up there."

Since I only have a couple of hours of daylight still available today, I'm anxious to get to my first site along the trail, the very first one on the trail map, and set up before it gets dark. With all my water bottles filled and stuffed into every spare nook on my pack, sloshing mixes to the rhythm of my steps. My lower back, already tightening from the water load, protests by the time I gladly reach my site within a grove of tall piñon pines for the night.

The morning light filters through the Texas madrones' glossy green leaves, illuminating clumps of red berries and the twisting branches of the manzanita shrub along the rocky trail. After my early hiking start, water shows up everywhere in Boot Canyon en route to the rim. My back curses Jim with each labored step since I usually carry a water filter with me, but did not this time due to the "lack of water en route." My mood lifts by late afternoon once I reach the short path through the inland grasses heading away from the rim cliffs to my reserved site. With camp set up and food stored in the provided metal animal-proof box, I settle myself onto the cliff outlook to watch the sun set over the vast wilderness opening south toward Mexico. Shadows slowly darken the sage covering the lower hills within my view until the hills themselves seem to fall asleep.

Morning oatmeal warms my shivering body at the overlook while the night shadows below my panorama creep toward the eastern light. Horizontal clouds, seemingly laced with gold leaf, glow as the morning rays squeeze through the lacy fluff until the gold bleeds into the hues of the rising sun now illuminating the ledges on the rim. From the rim, the hills look like a huge hand has reached down to the desert valley floor, all fingers together, and pinched up a piece of earth. From those peaks, folds cascade down back to the plains where, way off in the distance, the Rio Grande glistens as it snakes through the valley.

The mid-morning quiet lulls me into a state of "white noise" and even my wandering thoughts blend into a low hum underlining what my senses absorb—the musty sage lifting onto the flitting breeze from the rim's bushes, and each new sound floating above the silence abruptly plucking me out of myself: the wind, a fly, a bird, the human voices of day hikers in the distance. Three white-tailed deer graze in the grasses near my site as I weave through them back to my stored food to get packing for the day's needs. My plan is to head out along the Rim Trail to look for other overlooks for exploring, sitting, writing, and contemplating.

Walking the rim toward the southwest, I run into Tim and Eric, Houston residents who I passed yesterday on the trail before they headed for their own scheduled campsite.

Tim asks if I'm also planning to visit the Grand Canyon on my trip and I say, "I hope so."

"I suggest the North Rim—more spectacular. After I visited there, I read a book of case stories called *Death in Grand Canyon*. Before coming here, I read the sequel *Death in Big Bend.*"

I ask him what the main cause of death has been in Big Bend.

"Males, eighteen to thirty years old, thinking they are invincible and being ill prepared."

"Well, I'm happy to hear that it's not females in their fifties hiking alone." I ask him about the Grand Canyon and he says "murders," usually by someone who knows the person. I ask Tim how well he knows Eric.

"Really well," he says with a laugh.

"Did you see the fresh mountain lion scat over there?" Eric adds.

"*Fresh*? No, I didn't," I respond. "I haven't seen any lions."

"Ah, well, they're watching you though." Tim reports as if he's spent time studying lion habits. I imagine a lone mountain lion laying down in the grasses across from my tent watching my behaviors through binoculars.

Since I'm camped only about a half mile from the scat, I wish Tim and Eric a good rest of the afternoon and hoof it back to my tent site to re-read the lion behavior tip sheet, just in case: "stay calm, upright, and hold your ground, or slowly back away. DO NOT run, crouch or bend over, you will seem like prey to them . . . throw rocks if need be."

At the overlook on the rim, I place a few sage leaves I brought with me onto the ledge next to the small red rock given to me in San Marcos by Merlin, and take out a match. In my ceremonial offering, sage smoke encircles the red rock and lifts up into the breeze as I send a telepathic message to all lions—*Eat lots of small animals so you aren't hungry for humans.*

In the middle of the night, clomping surrounds my tent and awakens me. Adrenaline races through every inch of my groggy body. *Hooves*, I try to convince myself, *not pads. Must be deer, not lions.* The hooves continue past and I drift reluctantly back to sleep for my last night on the rim.

DESERT MEANDERING

Distances mean nothing. The flat desert rolls out to meet the hills and buttes far along the horizon, and one just walks toward the destination seen from afar. Few actual trails exist in the park outside of the Chisos.

Sand parts from under my boots along a wash as I follow what seems to be a path not heavily traveled. I follow cairns where the trail loses clarity and look for boot prints or any other sign of past human traffic through the small side canyons. The sun's heat lowers itself through the quietude surrounding me and my breathing syncs to the sand's swish under each of my steps. Back home, during my summer backpacking treks, it usually takes about three days of silence to release built up tensions in my body, emotions, and thoughts, until I begin to feel the connectivity to what is wild around me.

My honed senses start to absorb the wildness of the desert sights and sounds: a black, shiny raven whooshes overhead, then lands on the high branch of a thorny tree, black beetles scurry into a sandy hole, and two tarantulas scuttle across the path toward sun-drenched cholla cactus. I give them plenty of room and time; I am another creature of the desert, in no hurry. Once the sun's trajectory lowers in the still-bright sky, I retrace my steps along my own past footprints, and rock cairns, back to my rental car to head toward tonight's camp spot.

Once there, having backpacked only about a half-mile into this scheduled zone, the minimum legal distance from the road, I set up my tent behind a large rock so no one can see me as they drive by. Wilderness is not about miles, but instead, a state of mind.

As the sun winds down and desert brush sets out long-fingered shadows onto the still-warm sand next to my site, white cottontail rabbits pop out from their hovels, bounce around the shadowy brush as a large jack rabbit scoots past me, but is too quick for a photo.

"It's the animals," I whisper out loud to myself. The deer allowing me close. The rabbits. A coyote crossing the road earlier, turning to look right into me through my windshield. The roadrunners. The mountain lions that see me without me seeing them. The tarantulas and the beetles and the raven. *They* know I am here.

I think about Merlin's prophecy: "Stop along the road and make an offering: *They* know you are coming." The crescent moon appears over the darkening hills across the sandy desert and the first star appears high in the big Texas sky as I zip up the tent for the night.

Santa Elena Canyon on the Texas/ Mexico border in Big Bend National Park not far from my camping spot at the end of the Terlingua Abajo Road.

SENSATIONALIST GRIT

Fifteen-hundred-foot vertical cliffs squeeze the Rio Grande River that cuts the Santa Elena Canyon through the Mesa de Anguila, on the Texas border, and Mexico's Sierra Ponce in the Chihuahuan Desert. The short nature trail at the end of the Ross-Maxwell Scenic Drive funnels the hiker over a shallow crossing of the Terlingua Creek feeding into the river's flow at the start. Once on the other side, and up a steep bank, the dirt path follows the contours of the canyon until concrete steps lead to an overlook, allowing one to view the green waters lapping up against the lower limestone layers beneath the iron-rich red rock of the upper canyon. Sunlight sluices through the canyon to spotlight the Mexican canyon wall and canyon wrens fill the narrows with song.

Uninspired by the idea of hiking into another camping zone, I pop into the nearest ranger station once done with the nature hike. "I made it down the four-wheel-drive dirt road to Santa Elena Canyon no problem with my rental car," I tell the ranger. "I'd like to trade in my scheduled zone camping for a drive-in site tonight. Anything available near here?"

He brings up the park camping schedule on his computer. "The only one available near here is at the end of the Terlingua Abajo Road. Site #2."

I agree to the change and he gives me my new permit.

Once on the road, I slowly negotiate the initial bumps and gullies leading to the three sites. Incrementally, the road narrows, erodes from being washed out, and I begin to wonder if this was a good idea. Without any safe way to turn around, I am committed to going forward, which has become a theme for my travels. I slowly straddle even deeper ruts and stones that have lifted up in the piles of dried mud along the middle of the road. My steering wheel grip tightens as I swerve, give the car more gas, and try not to bounce over rocks that might puncture the oil pan or a tire. Without having been able to afford to buy the extra insurance for the rental, I mumble some version of a prayer to get me to the site without trashing the car. Then, I come to a sudden halt.

"No, *please* no."

The road's vertical split contains a mound several feet higher on the right than on the left. If I straddle it, the car will flip over onto its side. With the car in park, I get out and slosh through the sand to assess the severity.

I study the lower section width, glance back at the car, back at the road, back at the car, and the thought of backing out for several miles feels equally as daunting as continuing on. I feel stuck between the proverbial rock and hard place and wish someone would come along and tell me what to do. My tears are certainly not helping me make a decision.

Considering the road again and wondering if the smaller wheel base of the car will fit through the lower cut, I gather up my courage in a leap of faith, pull the outside mirrors into the sides of the car, get back in the driver's seat, say another prayer to the road gods, and brace myself for scraping sounds, but I can only hear the swish of sand coming to rest in the wake of my tire tracks. In spite of my heart racing as I crawl my way through, I eventually turn the wheel again at the gully's end and slowly climb my way back up onto the rutted road. Never did I hear the screech of a scratch against car metal. Softening my white-knuckled grasp from the steering wheel, I drive on at a snail's pace, even though the road is now flatter.

Once at the site, adrenaline still racing through my body, I gather my gear from the trunk and set up my tent in the shade of some manzanita bushes.

Two pick-up truck campers pull in to the TA-3 site and a jeep and its inhabitants drive out from TA-1 at the end of the loop, leaving a tent behind.

"Hi," one of my new neighbors says from over the bushes. "Would you mind if our dogs are off leash?"

"No, not at all," I respond. "I'm Gail."

"Gus. And over there is my friend Curt. We're starting with Bloody Marys soon if you'd like to join us. We had a rough day."

"Me too. Thanks. I'll just finish setting up and head over." Vodka is just the thing I need to take my mind off the drive back out in the morning.

"You said you guys had a hard day. What happened?" I ask Gus as I arrive for cocktail hour.

Having gotten into the park after closing last night without being able to get a camping permit and pulling into a campsite with the intention of paying their entrance and backcountry fees this morning, my neighbors thought they had picked a site with road maintenance materials and an empty RV. But the people camping there, and their RV, left in the morning, and drove straight to the ranger station to complain. It didn't take long for a ranger to visit Gus and Curt and ask if they were carrying any weapons.

Curt tells me he started to take his small pocket knife out of his pocket to show the ranger, but then they were accused of possibly smuggling drugs across the border. He recounts, "The ranger yelled at me to keep my hands away from my pockets. He made it really clear that his waist belt contained all that was needed to keep us in check."

"It's just a darn camping violation," Gus adds. "They tacked on a $50 fine to our backcountry camping permits and entrance fees." Gus plans to file a complaint in writing and may not come back to this park again. "There are plenty of beautiful places to visit where we won't be treated like criminals," he says.

"It was *only* a camping violation," Curt reiterates as he points to the permit hanging on the TA-3 campsite sign near where we are sitting. I didn't bother hanging mine out on my TA-2 sign, but maybe I should take my tiny pocket-knife out of my pocket and put it elsewhere.

Gus reminisces about an old experience he had with a different friend from years ago. They came to Big Bend to play, to drive down all kinds of eroded roads. High-wheeling without the high wheels, they were able to fix two of the three flat tires on their rental car, then drive out on the rim of the third. By the time they made it out to a paved road, the rim was square rather than round, and they had punctured the oil pan, therefore destroying the engine. The nearest town for towing was Fort Stockton, about eighty miles away.

Gus chuckles as he remembers his friend calling Avis to say, "We don't know what happened, man. The car just sort of broke!" It feels good to laugh with them. The vodka is working.

I share my white-knuckling experience, then ask, "What time are you guys leaving in the morning? I'd like to drive out when you do, just in case I need some help."

When Gus offers to drive my rental car back out the dirt road to the pavement, I cringe at the thought.

"I did get in . . . I should be okay. But, just in case . . .," I say.

The night descends onto us with the sunset shifting variegated reds over Santa Elena Canyon's walls in our view, and as we continue to sit and talk, the sky darkens with a plethora of stars twinkling their way onto the night's canvas.

BOQUILLAS CANYON

A small roadrunner scampers along the edge of the parking lot and up onto the desert hillside next to several hand-painted hiking sticks leaning against an oak tree. Glass-bead-covered rocks and earrings span out over a cloth on the ground. No one is in sight. As the path catches up to the treasures, a glass jar announces the need for sales: children in Boquillas, Mexico, just across the shallow of the Rio Grande nearby, need schooling. Around the bend and from across the river, Spanish crooning echoes into the canyon. Another jar sits at the trail's edge: "Donations for the Singing Mexican Jesus."

While I stop to read the note, Jesus stops singing to yell across the water to me, "Want me to sing something special for you?"

I tell him I am not carrying any money, but if I was, I would definitely donate to his singing. His tune bounces around the canyon rock walls again as I look back to watch two Mexican men wading a low spot in the river, their arms filled with more trinkets for sale.

The late day hues drip down the canyoned facades, salmon colored, and steeped shadows rise to meet them. I finish my hike and head toward my last scheduled camp spot in the park. As I prepare to drive back across the Texas girth to San Antonio in the morning, golden sun broad-brushes the sky until yellow-tipped peaks disappear into the starlight emerging from the night's deepening darkness. Heat dissipates from the degree-dropping dusty desert cold, and I wrap my solitude into the lingering warmth waiting inside my sleeping bag.

Like Some Secret Tryst

Greyhound Bus
San Antonio, Texas, to Tempe, Arizona

There is a whole lot of nothing to see out of the bus window. Flat ranch lands, a few cows, and the occasional oil well dipping its head up and down to a tiring rhythm. Even the shadows seem more flat than usual—wilting, timid.

Due to a lengthy delay in the departure from San Antonio, many of us might miss our connections in Big Spring. Having bitten my fingernails down over the miles so far, I start to pick at the nails with jagged edges. Dreams I had last summer when preparing to leave Vermont haunt me.

I recollect waking up from those nightmares trying to remember the details. In one dream, I stepped off a late bus into the middle of a Texas plains crossroads. Cowboys, having gotten drunk in some nearby saloon, drove recklessly down a dirt road next to where I was standing. Their dusty pickup trucks roared by and guns were blazing. There wasn't anything else in sight and nowhere to go in the gloomy darkness.

This is just the kind of dream my friend Bruce likes to analyze for buried symbolism. Crossroads: choices, directions. Guns: danger. Cowboys: wildness. Drunkenness: irrationality. Darkness: the mystery of the unknown. *It's just a dream*, I would remind myself when I awoke all flustered.

As I check my phone's clock to see if the driver is making up lost time, it's beginning to feel like those dreams might be coming true. With my temple pressed against the glass, I nervously vacillate while the views whiz by, the arc of the sun fleeing fast below the horizon. The rising sliver of moon unhinges from the light of the day and locks my fears in the emotional ebb and flow of what lies deep in my psyche.

What's the worst thing that could happen if the lost time isn't made up? There has to be a town of some kind, or a terminal building I could overnight in, maybe a hotel room available. I'm carrying a credit card, for goodness sake, and I can use it if I need to. My agitated nervous system doesn't fully trust my logic.

Let it go, I forcibly think and close my eyes from what cannot be seen out the window anymore. My head droops away from the glass, waiting for sleep to take over, and no dreams invade my short respite as we finally motor into Big Spring.

Two other Greyhound buses wait at a crossroads intersection—starlight bounces off the buses' chrome and eerie glows emanate from inside the parked carriers. In this dark and barren Texas landscape, no other light seeps across the desert. Without any competition from city lights or much of a moon, bright shining stars fill up the night sky.

As those of us changing buses get off and collect baggage, the three vehicles assimilate passengers into their empty seats. No one has to stand alone in the dense dusk along some small-town Texas road. No one has to duck from drunken cowboy gunshots. The buses set off across Texas in different directions as if leaving some secret tryst. No time had been made up along the miles, and I'll eventually arrive in Arizona, but I'll preserve how three buses stealthily met in the night, all of them late in their schedule, for the sake of our safety and connections.

From Phoenix, Arizona, I rent a car for a long weekend jaunt to Saguaro National Park in Tucson. These saguaro cacti dot the landscape, and I have fun getting up close and personal with them but without getting poked by their spiny thorns.

Chapter 11
Dust Settling

Dragging my sleeping bag across the dark hallway and onto the bathroom floor, I lean against the wall as I kneel down onto the bag in front of the toilet. Trying to focus on bursts of shallow breath in rhythm with anything other than my gut, I pull some of the bag over my shoulders to stay warm. The yellow glow of a nightlight cuts across the porcelain sink looming above me and onto the toilet seat eerily staring back at me.

In between waves of upchucking because of some Texas Greyhound Bus germ, I wonder what long-held, deep-rooted thing my body might also want to get rid of in this process. I've spent many years of my adulthood scrubbing out the rotten parts of childhood conditioning—like the voices of my parents. The judgements aren't loud anymore, but still surface when my boundaries are down. This is part of what I hope to make peace with while traveling. I stare at the shadows slicing across the toilet tank jammed between the wall and the sink vanity. Gurgles in my gut start to erupt again, but quickly settle down, so I re-wrap my sleeping bag around my shoulders, shimmy my crossed legs closer to the toilet, and lean in, just in case.

I want my time in Arizona to be about life's dust settling—to be silent enough to hear the questions I want answers for—to understand why this road trip is so important. I know I'm not alone in this kind of life quest. My new tribe is out there—traveling into unknowns while sleeping on couches, bartering labor for housing and meals, sharing resources, and going out of their way with generosity in order to pay something forward. Opening our hearts usually guarantees we receive more than we give, and because of this, it seems that our lives change dramatically for the better. But it's still a challenge for me to free-fall into another's arms, or maybe it's to free-fall into the arms of what hasn't yet become clear. To trust that some event or chance meeting with another person will shift something important for me . . . in me.

Gut contractions convulse but nothing heaves up, so I close the toilet seat lid, lean my forehead down onto it, then turn my head to rest my cheek on its clammy ceramic surface. My head throbs a dull ache to my heartbeat's pulse. Over my controlled shallow breaths, I consider Brian's suggestion to say *yes* during my visit to Roanoke. *Yes* is happening more often than not these days. This gives me hope and I wonder why my early life lessons were all about fear—of the world, of people, of feelings, of experiences. Why did I build protective walls as if kindness was going to harm me? Why did I think I wasn't good enough for the world around me to treat me with kindness? I know I still seek protection by keeping myself to the sidelines for a quick escape instead of allowing myself the needed vulnerability to really connect with what and who is around me. I linger on this realization as I lean back and away from the toilet, let another wave of nausea settle down. Let all the questions settle down. Once my gut feels more stable, I drag my bag back across the hall into the spare bedroom. And I whisper to myself as I drift off:

Just listen . . . and trust.

It feels longer than just one night since Terry, my acro-yoga couchsurfing friend, scooped me up at the Phoenix bus terminal and we pulled into her driveway in a tired mobile home park on the Scottsdale/Tempe city line. Terry made the work barter offer before I even left Vermont. Helping with some landlord renovations in exchange for room and board a few months into the trip allows me to regroup financially and take a break from relocating every week.

I convince her to buy a few cheap tools to have on hand, but I know my work quality will be challenged—I can't do good work with limited tools. Perhaps this is a metaphor for everything in life. I tile mosaics around the edge of her laundry room floor with a variety of broken shards from old tiles she has boxed up, a mish-mash of colors and patterns. Using odds and ends from a pile of materials in her shed, I construct a partition door between one of her trailers and an added apartment. My desire for perfection rests precariously in the space between the ego-driven need for a pat on the back and my own internal voice passing judgement about shoddy work.

"I've done what I can . . . it's functional for sure. What do you think?" I hold my breath while waiting for her approval.

"I think it will work great. I'm just happy to use up some of this scrap. It is a mobile home park rental after all."

Relieved, I breathe again, and try to honor my struggle between vision and manifestation. Even with this reality check, I try to listen to the nudgings of my gut, still queasy after the night in the bathroom. Wondering what is most important now—perfection *or* my connections with others— I listen to what surfaces about the ongoing imperfections of truly being human in this world. As Terry and I notch up the beauty and function of her properties, even with less than perfect work, we find deeper connection by dancing tango and swing, taking hikes, and sharing what nurtures us—opening our hearts to each other.

I'll be putting *that* in my travel tool box.

TUCSON MINI-VACATION WITH CACTI

"Would you like to upgrade to the convertible?" The young woman behind the Enterprise counter asks.

"No," I respond. "Nor the extra insurance or prepaid gas." For ten dollars per day and a gas tank top off, the Weekend Special guarantees me three hundred miles and freedom of movement from noon on Friday until noon on Monday.

Initially perky, she lets her toothy smile slip into a frown, and hands me the keys and paperwork to the shiny red car awaiting me in the car lot. Once in it, I negotiate my way out of the Phoenix Airport car rental garage and head south on Interstate 10 toward my long weekend mini-vacation to hang with armed cacti at Saguaro National Park in Tucson.

Along the Cactus Forest Road loop in the eastern Rincon Mountain District section of the National Park, saguaro cacti freeze in still-life, arms poised, postured for swooping, swaying, swinging. Each with its own individual personality, these columnar cacti can grow anywhere from zero to twenty-five arms and stretch their thorny skin to store as much as a thousand gallons of water that can sustain the plant for a whole year. Gila woodpeckers peck holes into their bodies for food, then leave the holes as new homes for elf owls, wrens, and flycatchers. Spiny knobs protrude from headless girthy trunks, all at least seventy years old, some between one and two hundred years—aging sentinel statues staged in the desert, sculptural and otherworldly. *Do they come alive after dark perhaps?* Cactus party—or desert waltz?

From the Javelina picnic area at the Tanque Verde Trailhead, my plan is to meander for awhile and then turn around, without any specific agenda, just to let myself be in the moment in this desert environment. I zip off the lower sections of my convertible pants and stuff my day's needs into my day pack while my sun hat shades out the baking rays soaking into my bare skin. I follow the path out of the parking area to the desert trailhead. About a half mile up the trail, I skirt around spiny prickly pear cacti with paddle thorns waiting to sting some unsuspecting hiker. Other spiky plants lay wait as well and I twist carefully as I step to avoid any collisions.

OUCH! A bunch of small slivers stick out of my left calf. Lower down my leg, a small puncture from a cactus spine puckers in, trapped, and pools of blood press a nerve running down to my ankle. As the pressure builds up, I try not to panic, but adrenaline races through the rest of my body not already pulsing in pain. Without being able to stand effectively, I collapse onto the rocky path to assess the damage to my leg. Knowing that no ranger will advise me and no clinic will cut me open to look for a mystery barb, I picture Bruce that night at Lake Gunn in New Zealand dragging the tent, talking about singing blues and paying dues, and consider what options and resource I have right now. I rifle through my pack, extract my first aid kit, and paw through my pouch of homeopathic remedies. After I place one pellet, specifically for "punctures/blood" under my tongue, I attempt to pull out slivers with the wimpy, inefficient tweezers from my pocketknife, with limited success. When I start to limp my way back down to the car, without sure-footed stepping with both feet, I slip, and gravel rips open my palms and knees, blood oozing from the raw skin. Fluid my leg couldn't seem to release through the puncture accumulates even more along my calf now throbbing in agony. Rolling over to a sitting position, I push myself up and continue hobbling down the trail to the car to access other first aid options.

To get my mind off the pain, I consider that perhaps this comedy of errors has saved me from scaring a mountain lioness and her cubs minding their own business within the boulders by me not being able to stand up straight and stand my ground. Remembering the mountain lion behavior tip sheet I read, oh, maybe twenty times while in Big Bend, there sure wasn't a chance that I would try to run away, therefore causing the lion to consider me prey.

Or maybe this incident caused me to skirt around a confrontation with a pack of angry javelinas, since, by sign name, this is *their* picnic area and they might be feeling a bit territorial. According to a warning sign near where I parked, a swarm of aggressive Africanized bees could have been nesting farther along the trail, ready to engulf me with deadly stings. The puncture, pooling blood, and pain seem pale in comparison to other less than desirable options.

From the backseat of the rental car, I raise my leg up onto the console between the front seats and wait to see if any other symptoms appear now that the homeopathic remedy seems to be kicking in. *Nope.* Just a really sore leg and another darned lesson in letting go of my agenda. And from now on, no matter how hot it is, I'll wear long pants.

Another weekend car rental brings me to Sedona, Arizona to explore the vortex energy sites. In order to stay with my couchsurfing host, I have to agree to climb up through rock crevices to the top of Bell Rock, and become a member of his Top of Bell Rock Club. Here I am at the top.

Chapter 12

Sedona Vortexes: Gender Balance in Four Acts

Sedona, Arizona • December 2014

TOP OF BELL ROCK CLUB: MEMBER #649

I press my fingertips against the red rock as the soundless whimper in my gut is ripped up through my throat and mixes with my salty tears. Pushing my boot hard against the rock face, I scoot my butt a few inches down the opening. Peter tells me to reach up and grab the overhanging edge and slide my foot down and over to a small ledge, then swing my body back around into the crevasse again. The whimper turns into a wail that silently screams through my skull as I look down to see the ledge. The muted scream turns into a meltdown, and I press my face into the red of the rock and weep.

"You can do this," Peter says to me from below.

I have come to Sedona to hike, to look at the beauty of the red rock, and like many others, to experience the sacred energies of the vortex sites—crosspoints between whirling energy fields in the earth's grid system or intersecting spiritual ley lines.

Through the couchsurfing network online, I find Peter, who runs the Top of Bell Rock Club and hosts anyone who will hike up to the top of Bell Rock and become a member. He needs to bring 1,111 people up the 547-foot elevation gain of Bell Rock by the time an interdimensional portal will open. Peter, a retired lawyer having represented UFO groups against various governmental agencies between 1977 and 2000 under the Freedom of Information Act, knows the exact route up an unmarked path to the flat plateau. Alien theories make no difference to me, I just want to feel the vortex energy.

I had assumed we would slowly wind our way up a trodden trail with the occasional boulder climb, not unlike those on trails in the White Mountains of New Hampshire where I have hiked for many years. After all, I'm a member of the Appalachian Mountain Club 4,000-footer group. I've hiked all of those high peaks, pulled myself up and over huge boulders, slumped my butt down over slick rocks, usually with a full pack on my back. That is my terrain. I do not, however, rock climb, with or without ropes, pulleys, helmets, chalk, or carabiners.

"Move your foot over to the right and put your weight on that small rock lip, Gail," says Peter, "and grab that rock over your head with your right hand. Now reach with your other hand and pull yourself over onto the ledge."

What? I look over to see the ledge, but what I see is the length of the crevasse below me, the same crevasse that I have been inching up, and my heart pounds as if it will push through my chest and plummet all the way back down to the valley floor. My mouth, all gummy from breathing in so deeply, glues my lips together so tightly I'm not sure I can take air in through my mouth anymore. My nose, stuffed from tears and mucus, seems to turn into a solid mass that becomes one with the red rock all around me.

"You're almost there, Gail," I hear from Peter.

I've asked him to stand just below me so I can't see the full scope of the crevasse opening. I pull up and swing my foot tentatively over to the too-small ledge and bring my full weight to a standing position while my fingers dig into a hand hold in solid rock near me. I take a deep breath and remember that the "road" was never meant to be a place to hide, but instead, a change from the life I had created, and to gently and hopefully allow access to opportunities for growth to appear. But all I feel is stuck and frozen on this tiny ledge.

Tears don't roll down my cheeks, they spray salt droplets onto my glasses, rush over my cheekbones like a waterfall cascade. I don't know what feels worse—the fear of falling and dying or this display of vulnerability.

I gasp through the mucus and place my foot over onto another rock ledge and follow Peter's directions, the same directions he's given to 648 other people before me. People carrying a cello. People pregnant. People older than I and people under the age of six.

I can do this, I whisper through my gritted teeth as I pull myself onto the flat area that is our destination, put down my pack, and collapse onto my shaky knees.

To my surprise, every person ascending to this plateau is expected to write about hopes, dreams, or feelings in a notebook contained in a small, metal-latched prayer box stuffed between some rocks. The blank notebook rests on my knee, waits patiently for my overwhelm to subside so I can hear my thoughts again.

With a dull pencil, I scrape some hesitant words about emotional pus and cobwebs—voices still criticizing me from my childhood—across the page, wishing to leave their residue up here. Then I put the book back into the box.

My heart begins to race again as we start the descent. Peter smiles while I attempt to work through my personal challenges, but is right there below me, ready to reach up to guide my boot into the right hole. But the tears and terror rip through me once again, melt me down, paralyze me.

"Just push your left foot against that rock and shimmy inch by inch down the crevasse. I'm right here," Peter says again and again as I move an inch, stop to regroup, then move another inch.

"You're doing it, Gail, good job!" I hear Peter say as he adjusts the bandana wrapping his bald head.

Once down to more level boulders, I look back up to the crevasse that we just came down in disbelief that I actually climbed up it, or down it, at all. Supposedly, this rock embodies a masculine energy having to do with "conquering."

I can't remember when I first felt my body freeze in terror looking down from some high place. Maybe I followed my brother up a tree and couldn't get down when a young child. Maybe I fell and got hurt, then blocked it out, but my body held on tight to the experiential memory. Over the years, I tried to overcome what I felt held me back. In my later twenties, while assisting a clockmaking friend working on a clock tower in a small town outside of Boston, I put on the safety belt and ascended four stories of staging along the outside wall, heading to paint the clock face numerals. I climbed, hooked my safety belt strap to the metal staging, and didn't look down. My gelatinous legs eventually would stop shaking and my heart rate would eventually slow down enough for me to unhook and move up another level. Did I triumph? Sure, I did not die. Did I conquer my fear of heights? *Hell no.*

At the bottom, with legs still shaky, I feel I have endured some vortex initiation ritual, intact—*barely*.

CATHEDRAL ROCK AND FEMININE EMPATHY

Morning frost sparkles on the path as the sun travels up from behind the spired rock formation and slowly sucks the moisture from glittering leaves and grasses. I hike up and over boulders, slopes, and ledges to a small crevasse, nothing at all like Bell Rock, which easily funnels me to where a juniper tree twists its branches in a self-hug. I've read that juniper trees in Sedona uniquely twist in accordance with the whirling of the vortexes, but I had also read the disclaimer that the twisting of most any tree species is a function of prevailing wind, and nowhere have the botanical sciences found the twisting of tree bark to correlate with hypothesized energy fields. I wonder, since it is protected amidst the rock spires, just how much wind this juniper has had to deal with.

Wispy cirrus clouds feather the blue sky above the eroded sandstone that towers over me like Stonehenge rocks. The midday sun sends tendrils of piercing rays through every crack and opening and coats me in warm light. With meditative closed eyes, my crossed legs invite the earth's chi to mingle with my own by a simple technique of facing my palms toward each other, holding an intention for the chi to unblock where energy might be stuck, and moving my hands toward and away from each other, back and forth, causing a build up of chi.

Years ago, a bulletin board flier at my local food coop caught my eye and I signed up for an introductory Zhineng Gi Gong workshop, *zhineng* referring to wisdom and ability. This Gi Gong variation explores a self-healing wellness process based on modern science in connection with consciousness unity of all things in nature. Between 1988 and 2001, Dr. He Ming Pang ran a medicine-less hospital in China, where people learned to mobilize chi through a combination of intentions and movements, where terminal illness lessened and went into remission, and other "miracles" of healing happened. Eventually the Chinese government shut it down.

I learned the elements needed for the practice and joined a weekly study group, where we explored the subtleties of the physical movement form, not unlike a Tai Chi form, and experimented with the mysteries of intentional healing by aiming our combined chi to some issue one of us was having that day. The first time I felt energy "gates" open on my body, I sensed there was so much out there I did not yet understand. I continue my practice wherever I go.

Tingling circles my crown chakra on top of my head as I feel pops and shooting pulses dart through my legs, more so than usual, until total relaxation sets in and I feel ready to move again. The sun's shifting light spreads through the spires to illuminate the intensity of the red rock all around me, and I gather myself up to head back to my weekend rental car.

On my way down, a strained whimper emerges from the other side of a large rock, and as I come around it, I look up to see a young woman crouched and frozen, halfway down a crevasse.

"Everything is fine," her male companion, clearly annoyed, tells me from a lower ledge, and I flash back to Bell Rock and remember my own terror. Ignoring him, I climb up towards her anyway and extend my leg across the narrow crevasse and motion for her to step behind my leg and place her foot onto a rock lip.

"You will not fall past me," I tell her and smile. She searches my eyes for trust and then slowly lowers her foot near my leg. Once she puts her weight there, I show her the next stop for her other foot. And again, she steps, sighs, then thanks me.

I continue descending a series of rock steps and hear another woman defiantly tell her husband that she cannot continue up. He scoots their two young boys up onto another boulder and orders her to come along. I step aside from the path and catch her eye.

"Is it really difficult?" she asks, ready to flee back down to safety.

"You can do this," I offer. "The crevasse is the only tricky part and then it flattens out and is a breeze after that. Go up ahead of your husband, so he is behind you, and on the way down, have him go just ahead of you."

A few years into apprenticing to become a custom cabinetmaker, I attended a New England conference for women in the trades. During lunch one day, the woman sitting at the table next to me told me about her gender equity advocacy and lobbying. Always admiring those who wield a picket sign, since it is not in my nature to do so, I told her how much I appreciated her efforts. What she said to me then changed me forever: "I can't do what I do without women like you working on construction sites, being in the trenches in traditionally male-dominated environments. Showing them women can do the work."

I had been hired by a small two-owner cabinetry business, and felt validated and respected by the two men who were my employers and mentors, who then eventually became my colleagues and friends. But being on the job sites, installing kitchens, showed me the discomfort the other men had for women being in their territory. With fists clenched, I embodied the angry feminist attitudes left over from the 1960s and '70s.

". . . showing them women can do the work . . ." loosened the grasp of my fists. The men were a product of cultural history and patterns, too. What if I just needed to do the best I could, show up with humility? My work would stand for itself, and maybe their attitudes, and mine, might slowly change because of my perspective shift.

I turn to see how the woman is doing heading uphill, find her up on the flat ledge and see her arms wave at me from her perch.

There is no *conquering* here in this place, it doesn't work. Instead, it's a gentle approach with listening, empathy, and understanding. *Isn't this the balance needed for both the male and female parts within us? Conquering with softened fists?*

BOYNTON CANYON AND THE KACHINA WOMAN: MASCULINE AND FEMININE MAKE PEACE

In legend, humans abused their gifts of free will and a questioning mind with violence and manipulation and were sent to live in Middle Earth without abundance. Kachina watched over the humans, and once the Earth was rebuilt and the humans were behaving, they were allowed to resurface. If the humans ever lost their way again, Kachina would crumble and fall, and humans would be sent to an even darker place, never to see the Earth's surface again. I glance up at the Kachina Woman rock formation as I pass in order to assess any erosion on the brink of crumbling, but sense no foreboding.

As a Native American flute song soars above me and the Kachina rock, the flute player catches my eye and tells me about the weekend sound healing gifts he and his friend offer to those who come to visit the Kachina Woman. I jump on the offer for any healing at any time, so I agree to their gift.

His female friend picks up two didgeridoos and hands him one while they explain how the instrument's low frequencies offer deep relaxation, allowing emotions to surface that are soothing and healing. Historically used in ceremonial rituals by the Aboriginal peoples of northern Australia, the primal, percussive tones overlay a growling drone note believed to rouse the spirit and promote the unblocking of energy in the body.

Lying flat on my back on the sandstone, I close my eyes, connect into my Gi Gong intention for consciousness connection and chi unblocking, then absorb the droning vibrational buzz tingling my skin. Low-frequency barks and moans surround me as the two move slowly around my form, fluttering and rippling electrical impulses from their circular breathing technique. The pulsing blends into an improvised vocalization to interweave masculine and feminine energies—both supposedly associated with this vortex site. Besides the residual tingling, I listen to my body for any signs of energetic change, but feel no dramatic shifts, just a small pop here and there. At least I feel emotionally relaxed and ready to hike back out.

THE CONQUERING OF AWE AT AIRPORT MESA

As I walk several miles of mesa circumference along the airport fencing, I try to feel energy forces either pulling or pushing on me. Once again, nothing much. But I do wonder what the indigenous tribes felt about white men putting an airport on a sacred spiritual vortex site?

It has been said that Sedona's beauty, for many people, can only compare to a powerful spiritual experience—either a person has to recalibrate a sense of awe or the brain interprets the experience as something supernatural. For me, beauty is always a spiritual experience, filled with sensual input that traverses that tight rope of center and balance. When I'm totally aware, my resulting awe is always a meditation on light and shadow, inner and outer, bringing together both the feminine and masculine.

Any vortex—whatever "whirls"—eventually comes to rest—in matter, energy, or thought. And from the swirl of chaos, like thoughts pushing at each other in my brain, the residue settles. And from that settled place of alchemy, I somehow expand.

How can this not be sacred?

Pilgrim Feet

Pre-sunset cloud cover lifts as neoprene-clad surfers wait patiently for the next swell to bulge up from the incoming waves. Like meditating buddhas, they sit on their boards and watch the horizon—sacred Zen moments.

Most likely without even thinking about it, they seem to understand this Buddhist teaching: *everything is always changing.* They wait for just the right wave.

Foam curls onto the beach's soft sand, then quickly races back into the ocean's vastness. As I gaze out over the water, mist glistens on my cheeks. My bare pilgrim feet, sea foam frothing around my toes, come to rest at the edge of a whole country land-massed behind me. My nose inhales salt as seagulls search the sand for anything worthwhile to scavenge and tiny shore birds scamper along the wet sand like wind-up toys.

Terry and I say goodbye at the beach while the tide pounds onto the shore. Her scheduled yoga workshop in San Diego allowed me a ride to the California coast and a break from Greyhound's frustrating bus schedule. We have no idea when we'll cross paths again, if ever—we're just grateful for our time of connection. As Terry crosses the beach to the parking lot and the sun lowers in the sky, I look back to the east and consider how far I've come.

I've made it across the whole country, listening to the prophecies of those like Albert and Merlin, surviving the grit of family interactions, joyously dancing in Louisiana and Texas, and looking straight into the deep, black eyes of ravens. Turning back to the west, I picture a raven, holding firm on a surfboard on the curl of a wave crest, then replace it with a buddha statue on the board, and then me balancing on the board.

I come back to the idea of balance—on the board, on the wave, on the road, along a linear trajectory from birth to death. Without trust—the wave cresting and offering its unique ride toward what is important to learn—one could get stuck inside a crashing wave from too much "juice." The surfers know; they practice mindfulness. But me, I'm just finding my pace, my place, the Middle Path here on the road, learning to temper my new-found fearlessness with my human vulnerability. I'm renewing my faith in myself, opening my heart, and allowing myself the innocence of the Buddhist concept of beginner's mind anew.

The January chill of the Pacific Ocean washes over my feet again as a rush of warm excitement travels through my body all the way up to my smile anticipating the next wave of adventures here in the West. Like the surfers still out on the water, I meditate on the setting sun finishing its day far out along the horizon and settle into my own private nirvana.

At Joshua Tree National Park in California, I drive to the geological sites to check out the Joshua trees and the park's wonderland of rocks. On a misty day, I walk through Hidden Valley.

Chapter 13

Joshua Tree National Park

Joshua Tree, California • January 2015

Where the Colorado Desert meets the Mojave Desert, cholla cacti glisten, golden in the sunlight. Ocotillo spurt scarlet flowers atop their spindly stalks and Joshua trees sculpt themselves into mannequins scattered across the the arid landscape. Winters freeze. Springs bring rain. Trees flower. Only then is the Joshua tree pollen spread by the nocturnal yucca moth flitting within the moon-shadows.

But for now, these spiky-leafed groves crawl up through the sand and smear across each side of the boulevard winding through the national park. I aim my low-clearance rental car toward the four-wheel-drive-recommended Geology Road and trails leading into the backcountry.

This *wonderland* of rocks, formed when hot magma pushed up through the planet's crust millions of years ago, towers everywhere among the groves of trees.

Remembering my white-knuckling along the Terlingua Abajo Road in Big Bend, I focus on the road rather than at the views and hope that my car won't have any under-carriage parts torn off. I steer a few more miles, past the self-registration kiosk at the weather-beaten Backcountry Board #1, to the second board to explore my backcountry entry choices. It becomes an art form when to give the car gas, when to crawl inch by inch around the road's protruding rocks.

But the trail from the second board heads into the treeless valley below the distant Malapai Hills, with their remnants of old riddled mines and tunnels. No Joshua trees or rock formations, so I U-turn back to the first board before it gets dark. I've read the night sky over the Joshua trees is filled with millions of twinkling stars, and I ask the blue sky to stay clear for an awe-inspiring experience of beholding such a star-filled celestial canvas.

111

A worn path leads me about a quarter mile into a thickly treed copse hugging the hill's contour, and I veer off towards a cluster of massive boulders. The early evening blue sky tugs at the pink-filled clouds hanging heavy above the sunset-silhouetted Joshua boughs. Once I set up my tent for the night, I watch for stars to push past the dimming gray swaths of dusk. Below a few twinklers shining through the increasing cloud cover, the looming rocks fade into the shadows. A stealthy coyote pads across the sand near my campsite and adrenaline courses through my body. The moonlit silhouette of the coyote blends into the desert flora and the lingering daylight lays down for the night.

After all the "doing" back in Arizona—all the internal musing, dancing, and exploring, I ponder the shadowy coyote. According to Native folklore, the animal is said to break illusions and reveal truths. Spotting the coyote seems to give me permission to be living *true* in this moment.

In the glow of moonlight, a raven scans me from a hanging branch. Allowing my gaze to stay affixed to the raven's black eyes, I wonder what message of metamorphosis I'm meant to hear whispering through its beak—some epiphany sliding over its black wing and landing on my palm.

The clouds dissipate just enough for star constellations to emerge and explode into the celestial canopy above. With no one watching, even the raven, my arms float out to the sides of my twisting torso to shadow-dance in the moonlight, adrenaline rising once again. Sandy granules crunch underfoot, and the coyote wails in the distance, calling me deeper into the primal. Cool air wafts around my bare arms—my only containment in this moment. Giddy and uninhibited, I continue to flail my arms and legs through the night breeze as the desert floor provides my starlit stage. And I think, *This is what total freedom feels like.*

ONE WOMAN WALKING . . .

Last night's elusive truths and I snuggle into my tent to shelter from the light rain coming down. I type words onto my iPad about my time here in the park for a travel blog post, sentiments having nothing to do with *becoming.* Now that I am out of the backcountry, the magic has dissipated.

The warmth of my down sleeping bag curls around my crossed legs as I balance my device on my knees. I've hung my headlamp from a small bungee cord strung from loops along the top of my tent, like an overhead chandelier, for a spotlight onto my work. Having a rental car for storing most of my belongings allows me ample room to spread out in my one-person tent.

Next to me is a small notebook filled with my handwritten notes from the last couple of days—historical facts about Joshua trees and Yucca moths for now. As I cross out random thoughts on the lined page after their transfer to my iPad, a splatter of moisture runs ink across the rest of the page.

Drip . . . drip . . . drip . . . *What the . . .? Oh, c'mon, my tent is leaking? I don't need this!*

I quickly push everything in that spot out of the way, unhook my headlamp from the bungee and point it along the tent seam over the zippered door. Small droplets of water slide and gather over the dripping spot, so I ruffle through my travel bag filled with clothes and other items that I use as a pillow, for something to soak up the drops now splashing into a forming puddle on the bottom of my tent.

As I triage my rainy reality, muffled voices outside drizzle glee over the rock faces of the stone monolith next to my tent like runny honey. I thought the wall of stone would be a private and sheltering backdrop for my campsite, but no, these rock climbers didn't get enough during the day or they just arrived here at Ryan Campground and could not wait for morning. Vocalizations increase in volume, from hoots to grunts, and the damn drops keep dripping in my tent. So much for a peaceful evening of writing. Rain intensifies and moisture finds its way along other seams, spitting drops onto my sleeping bag, so I ball myself up in the dry section of the bag and pull it to one end of the tent, then pull the bag up over my ears to dampen out the climbers' exclamations.

Oh . . . crap! Never mind.

I stuff what I can into the pillow bag, gather up my sleeping stuff, and run from the tent to quickly toss it all into the back seat of the rental car. There, it's at least dry, and I can more effectively diffuse the volume of annoying voices. I lay out the bag and makeshift pillow and writhe myself into some sculptural form across the seats, but the middle seatbelt digs into my hip. I twist around to find a more comfortable position and shade my eyes from the shafts of climbers' headlamp lights careening through the car windshield. Sleep eludes me as I fixate on the rhythm of the raindrops dancing on the car hood.

In the morning, exhausted, with eyes still closed, I listen for the remaining tapping of raindrops on the car. None. I stretch myself out and wrestle into my clothes. Grabbing a trash bag out of the car, I break down my wet tent, stuff it in, and toss the bag back into the trunk to deal with later. Nearby Ryan Mountain, adorning itself in the remnants of low-lying clouds, summons me out of the campground and funnels me onto its solitary trail, where I hope for a mood adjustment.

Without any other hikers along the trail, I pause at a bend to watch the gray clouds sweeping across the hills and desert floor, and gain an elevation view over the outcroppings of the wonderland of rock formations.

As I close in on the summit, footsteps behind me break the silence. A woman runs up the trail toward me, blond and gray hair braided tightly and partially stuffed up into her cap. I step aside, and nod hello, but our connective moment comes later, on her way down, as I move off the path onto a rock. She stalls to try to remember the correct etiquette of who has the right of way, but it doesn't matter now since we have both stopped.

"You have quite the glow about you," she says, still moving her feet back and forth so she doesn't lose momentum for her run.

"Thanks." I turn to move on, but something nudges me to stay and say more. "I'm partway into a year of travel around the U.S., hoping to understand more about myself. I was tired of working so much, and decided to hit the road. I'm just starting to find my pace, and some peace."

"Me, too. After ten years in the corporate world, I wasn't happy."

She digs her toe in the trail dirt, then continues, "I spent last summer in Wyoming where I fell in love with rock climbing. I'm here volunteering as a Search and Rescue EMT so I can keep practicing skills."

"You must have some resources in order to be able to do that," I say. "I have to be really creative, since I don't have much money to work with."

"Yeah . . . working through my savings, though." She inches a few feet down the trail backwards so as not to lose her rhythmic pace.

"Well, we do what we are led to do," I say, and step back onto the trail, wishing her luck on her journey.

She starts down the trail, then turns around, "Ya know, I don't think luck has anything to do with it."

Back in the parking lot, I lay out my tent next to a grouping of cholla cacti lining the parking lot edge near the road, hoping the partial sun and light breeze dry things out quickly. While I wait for drying to happen, I think about what the woman said earlier. Maybe luck has nothing to do with anything. We needed no words. I know we both felt that we have the ability to create our lives, to choose our journeys. She did. I did. I wonder if perhaps destiny prods me toward specific events, places, or people . . . like her, for example. If destiny is even something.

I pick up the tent fly off the ground and hang it over the rental car door on the sunny side of the car, then return to my thoughts.

Does my self-identified label of *alchemist* always bring about the need for some mystical explanation about why these kinds of experiences ensue? The idea of luck does seem to take away any illusion of control; I've always liked to keep life's questions in a comfortable container. Maybe it's the same for her.

And what about *chance*? The rolling of some cosmic dice?

Like this morning—I knew I needed to get an early slog up the trail— to avoid hiking crowds, I thought, but perhaps also to be in the right place at the right time. Not too early or too late. One woman walking away from what no longer served her, then colliding with another woman doing the same thing.

Of course we glowed. Our synchronicity is the reminder that we are indeed lucky. That the dice's dots are favorable. But also that we have to turn our defeats into life changes—choosing the road toward passion rather than security. Maybe this is a truth that slides down from the raven's wing.

Life is not that simple for a lot of people, though. We all have limitations and hurdles. The actual truth is: Reality doesn't always support choice. I think about women who don't have the same freedoms as I do, women with no means to leave abusive husbands, no community support, stuck in untenable situations. Even if they soul-searched their passions, dreams, and goals, they would still have to transcend their history and culture. And if they found the courage to make changes, they would still need luck to help them. Even with limited finances, I have the resources and free will to create a new life. So—am I lucky? *Darn right* . . . but I still want to believe luck doesn't have everything to do with it.

The next day, on a short walk from the parking area for Cottonwood Spring, fan-shaped leaves accordion out from the tops of California palms. Old, dead fronds droop like worn petticoats against the palm's girthy trunks.

The brim of my sun hat wards off the hot rays while allowing the cool air wafting through the fence from the oasis to protect me from the heat. Hiking past the palms farther into the canyon, more metaphysical thoughts surface about my life choices.

It took me decades to move away from the cultural and familial constraints of my first eighteen years—the "what will the neighbors think" suburban mind-set—as if what others think ever had anything to do with my own trajectory in life. My defiance started small: leaving my family's meat and potatoes diet behind for vegetarianism, causing my mother to doubt my sanity.

But the 1950s and '60s were a mixed byproduct of repression and "anything goes." Had I been a few years older, I might have embraced the '60s counterculture, but I was still too young to understand the need to question everything outwardly. My internal questioning became the ball and chain I dragged everywhere and drag even now.

My clamped fist of an anti-Barbie-doll stance—my desire to escape the expectations that culture had for women when I was growing up—left me no choice but to lean into the wind—a respite against what I viewed as mediocrity and complacency. The projected neighbors' judgments seemed to be a crime against my individuality and I pushed the doors of nonconformity wide open by my rebellions. After the diet change, I stopped shaving, let my hair be wild, dressed in flannel, overalls, work boots. I walked away from the Catholic church, and explored other spiritual philosophies. I dated artists and musicians rather than the financially secure businessmen or professionals my mother wanted for me.

However, there are times when the metaphysical crashes into the literal. Today is one of those times. A couple of miles into Lost Palms Canyon, a tail wind pulls in chilled air. Shivering, I dig my fleece hat out of my daypack and exchange my desert sun hat fastened tight under my chin for my warmer hat pulled down over my ears to drown out the wind's whistling. Still, the bright, warm sunlight continues its attempt to burrow through the icy blast.

Like the unending desert sand, those metaphysical questions about luck and destiny keep spreading into eternity. I've never been able to stop that process. Or even want to now.

Truth, generically, could only have become the exploration of "my" truth—out here I am shielded from judgement's eyes watching me like some Big Brother. Being on the road is opening me to infinite self-discovery, like the desert sand expanding ahead of me toward the ridge overlooking the canyon, where lollipop palms huddle within the split of hilly folds. There might be a trail continuing toward them, but I'd have to climb back up against the wind to get there, so I turn back toward the random prickly pear cactus and cholla.

My frozen fingers race my jacket's zipper up to my collar and tug my fleece hat as far down over my neck and cheeks as it will go and still see the trail. My boots manage only small steps in the parting soft sand swirling about me. Today, I am the literal "Wind Leaner." My thighs ache as if I've hiked much more than the mileage stated on the trail sign. As the wind finally lulls for a brief moment, I stop to look up to see how far back it is to the palms and the parking lot. As I resume my hike, the sound of the sand crunches underfoot, blending with the nearby chatter of birdsongs. Done with my nagging thoughts, I navigate back through the drooping fronds to the perfect wind-free oasis rock to lean against. Snacking on a granola bar, I wonder if I found any real answers today.

Truthfully?

I look down at what might be lingering on my palm from the Raven's message, but see nothing.

Slow Dance with Memory

Amtrak Train
San Diego to Santa Barbara, California

While boarding the crowded Amtrak Surfliner heading up the coast between San Diego and San Luis Obispo, a young woman stalls just ahead of my double seat and turns in my direction. When she sees my smile, she unhooks her bags from her shoulders, positions them on the wire bin above our row, and sits down next to me.

"I'm Vanessa," she timidly offers.

I twist my body a bit toward her. "Gail. How far are you headed?"

"L.A. I'm meeting one of my friends there for the weekend."

Since her eyes dart away from mine, I sense some nervousness, but don't want to draw attention to it.

Exposing her vulnerability, she mumbles, "This is my first time traveling away from home."

As the train car sways left and right along the tracks paralleling the sandy beach edge, I offer her encouragement with shared stories about myself, around her age, desperately seeking courage for trips like hers, and describe the trepidation I felt starting this current year long trip I am on.

Because I no longer hear the timepiece ticking in my ear—schedules that forced their pounding rhythms into my steps for decades—I free-form slow dance with my memories as she and I dialogue. We share our experiences around the concept of safety in our individual worlds—inner, outer, perceived, and real—our stake in emotional survival. It seems that neither of us felt secure as children. She can't be much older than nineteen and she's already turning away from her past so she can claim her present and therefore her future. I sense much courage in her as she faces the unknown.

"I told my family I can't have any contact right now," she states under her breath. With her head bent down, she asks, "It's the right thing to have done, isn't it?"

She lifts her head and looks over at me, a stranger, searching for approval, before shifting her gaze past me out the window, and through a line of palms quickly moving out of view. She adds, "My therapist feels I need to get away from the abuse." I wonder what she has endured as the Pacific coastline slides past the train's scratched windows like some old movie footage. I have vivid images of myself as a child, too, feeling lost and alone, trying to find ways to love myself in spite of my father's rage and judgement, my mother's constant disapproval.

Lines furrow her brow and I remember seeing similar lines along my own brow every morning in the bathroom mirror before heading out to catch the bus to school. They remained even after I went off to college.

"Sometimes we have to save ourselves first before we have enough confidence to change patterns," I say. "I hope that working with your therapist will help you find tools to keep yourself centered." Trauma runs deep. Vanessa bites her lower lip as she listens.

Now old enough to inhabit the role of *elder*, I present more layers of wisdom as a contrast to the cultural choreography that young women like Vanessa, and at one time me, have been expected to follow.

"You've clearly developed some inner resources," I add. "You can trust what you know." Her eyes meet mine once again, the tilt of her head suspending the beat of each phrase spoken between us as she considers my words.

I tell her she's already taken her *own* first step, regardless of how much fear gnaws at her. I tell her that she has declared her bottom line—defined her way—a sequence not unlike mine, still, every day. She tries to smile, her lips tense, but upturned.

"Los Angeles will be great," I add. "You'll be there to see a good friend."

When the train stops at the L.A. depot, she extends her arm towards me and her strong, lean fingers take mine for a lingering moment before she retrieves her bags from above. Through the window scratches, I watch her descend from the train and glide past the depot into her evolving life. I doubt we will cross paths again, and I wonder what she will take with her from our contact. As we all travel through our days, we seem to leave a wake behind us. I can only hope I've given her some added confidence for taking more risks like the one she takes today—just one risk at a time.

While visiting a friend in Santa Barbara, California, I leave him to work and rent a weekend car for my foray to Los Osos and Montana de Oro State Park along the coast, complete with hill hikes, bluff walks, hidden beaches, and sand dunes.

Chapter 14

California Meditations on the Sea

Santa Barbara to Los Osos and Back Again • January 2015

As the Amtrak brakes squeal to a stop, I scan the crowd for my long-time friend Ben, and spot him standing just below the sign announcing Santa Barbara. It has been years since we've seen each other in person. Over time, and despite relocations to different states, Ben and I stayed in touch. Individual challenges around health, finance, and love often pulled us off track, but knowing the other was out there to talk to made life easier.

From my window seat, I watch his eyes scanning the train for a glimpse of me. Once he notices me waving at him through the glass, he maneuvers through the crowd toward the train and I gather up my packs from the seat next to me.

While standing in the aisle waiting for the train conductor to let us disembark, I remember Ben sitting alone on the sidelines of New England contra dance halls, his tall lanky body folding into a metal chair as I overheard his awkward attempts at conversation with other dancers.

In between allemandes, do-si-dos, and partner swings, we probed life questions we were struggling with—questions about finding the balance between living out in the country and finding others for playing our individual forms of specialized music.

When we sat out dances, his long fingers would tap animated rhythms onto his thighs while he told me about being a drummer for an elite type of jazz— layering complex rhythmic patterns to improvised melodies. No wonder he didn't seem excited by traditional contra dance tunes. Interpreting avant-garde classical music nourished *me*, but finding others who felt the same was difficult. Cities held opportunities for both of us, but living in them didn't ground us the way being in nature did.

Excited, I step off the train onto the landing, dropping my bags, and wrap my arms around his thin waist for a long hug. "So good to see you in person, my friend." I lean into his shoulder, a tear or two wetting his shirt sleeve.

"Good to see you, too. I'm so happy you decided to come through Santa B. We have so much to talk about." He gives me a tight squeeze.

"Yep. I am so looking forward to catching up." I reluctantly release him and look into the eyes of my dear friend. Though we've had lots of questions to explore with each other, we'd agreed to wait until we met in person since I was going to be traveling through his area. Phone and email weren't adequate, we could wait.

This is what I appreciate about him—together, we dissect whatever life throws our way, even when the answers are elusive, and there are always more questions to keep us going.

MEDITATION ALONG THE SEA

Since Ben has some at-home work to get done, I find an Enterprise car rental weekend special I can't pass up: three days, ten dollars per day, and three hundred miles. I first chanced upon this rental deal when in Arizona, used it twice, and now look for locations that offer a coupon. Some airport locations offer it, but mostly it is the downtown agencies that sit on cars in the lot all weekend long. I search Google maps for a getaway within a hundred-and-twenty-mile radius. Montana de Oro State Park in Los Osos, north along the coast from Santa Barbara, pops out as the perfect location. I reserve a site in the state park campground and head north for a weekend coastal adventure.

Green plaited hills slump to meet the sandy beach that slips in under the breaking whitecaps. Soft, wet sand covers my bare feet as I walk into a wave and cold ocean water explodes around my ankles. Even though Vermont is a few hours away from the Atlantic Ocean, I rarely make the effort to get there. I'm giddy as the Pacific froth tickles my bare feet.

Dunes rise up from the sea in this deserted cove and I watch long-billed curlews poke their bill-tweezers into the sand for anything hiding under the grains. They race away from the breaking waves, then scurry back again for more foraging.

Is this also what humans do? I think. *Dash towards something, someone, anything? Peck? Scatter? Repeat?*

I don't know why we seem to be in such a hurry—rushing into relationships or chasing the dollar. Social acceptance, social media, social this and so-cial that. We poke at these things, and when time suggests a more relaxed pace to better assimilate an experience, we scatter and prick at something else while searching for some reward.

Tide-arranged still-lifes of leafy-headed seaweed stalks, ripped from their moorings, curl around the beach's polished rocks near where I walk. I stop to photograph the seaweed and wonder if this is what life is about—the unfolding of who we can become as time and nature rip us from our own moorings and push us to abandon the hurry, angst, and grappling. My launch back in Septem-ber was filled with trepidation, but I'm happy now that I ripped myself from my own mooring and that I am finding ways to slow down and grapple less.

Sea meditation, timed in rhythm to an aged moon's pull, ebbs and flows with my thoughts. I tuck my hair up into my hat to let the breezes swirl around my exposed neck, those same breezes swaying the purple petals of ice plants dispersed among the coastal sage scrub. My breathing slows to a sustained exhale, reminding me of the importance of releasing my own hurried desires.

Shorebirds dash and peck along the breaking waves on one of the hidden beaches at Mon-tana de Oro State Park.

One of the many tidal pools I explored while in the park

Stone cliffs break away from the mainland as if slowly crumbling back into the sea. I settle myself into a stony crook at the edge of a cliff and allow my senses to engage with the mist wafting over my face and onto my tongue. On a nearby promontory, a California condor communes with the environment from its bluff pulpit. With its wings outstretched, its feathers grasp the breeze, sunlight, salt air. Once near extinction, I've read, over four hundred now exist, some of them along this section of California coast. From the stillness of my own perch, I stretch my arms in cadence with this wild and majestic raptor. The sea breeze envelops me as the waves swell and fold in on themselves, the crescendo and decrescendo of the crashing waves below marking time against the cliff walls.

The repetition of my measured breath churns with the mysterious power of the ocean's waves slapping onto stone, each slap trying to get my attention. My inner thoughts feed on the carrion of what no longer serves me: old patterns holding me back from living fully. I know my old, deep beliefs about myself were dumped on me as a child, that my mother's fears about what the neighbors would think became my fears. I understand why I wove a web of safety around myself, tried to stay under the radar of judgment and exposure, hiding any shame around my imperfections. But does any of this serve me now?

Even with these non-rhythmic thoughts crashing into my deeply tethered beliefs, my heart swells and trips over itself on the way to rest on shore. As the condor drops off its rocky perch, its long wings power toward the south. I often imagine wings lifting me to soar along the thermals, too, for greater perspective, supported by my strong will. Maybe I do need the clamped fist once in a while . . .

The sun lowers itself in minute gradations to the sharp line of the horizon as sea foam glistens like an umbilical cord between that fiery orb and me. The surf's brawn pounds at my desire for life to be different than what has been, and the answers I seek seem to be the sun's sweet kisses along the distant horizon too far out for me to reach. All I can do now is trust the answers will someday arrive for me.

SKIN SEDUCTION

After my return to Santa Barbara for a few more days with Ben, and being mindful of his work, I continue my solo explorations along the pristine streets of the rich and famous. En route to a downtown coffee shop along Anacapa Street, I glimpse myself in the mirroring glass of ritzy storefronts. Ghostly images shadow my reflection.

Perfect southern California weather cradles the wandering homeless on the other side of the avenue. But the dispossessed seem to blemish the smooth skin of a city both tolerant *and* disapproving of those left to fend for themselves under the palms, in alleys, and on the beaches.

Turning suddenly, I come face to face with a merchant's tailored suit.

"Good afternoon, ma'am, can I offer you a free skin cream sample?"

I love free samples. "Sure," I respond, painfully aware that I am wearing clothing from my consignment closet repertoire. The most expensive item on my body cost me no more than $5, and I wonder if Santa Barbara even has used clothing stores.

"Just step this way inside and have a seat."

What? No small foil packet to drop into my bag as I hurriedly walk by? Oh yeah, I'm trying to slow down into the "moment" after my condor connection and stay open to life's answers mysteriously coming my way.

Counters of salves, creams, and gels surround the leather chair, and I feel out of place. He opens a jar and tells me about the anti-aging qualities of this pore miracle elixir, then shows me in a hand mirror the dry skin around my eyes and mouth. Maybe my time on the sand dunes with salt mist drying out my natural Vermont skin tone was a mistake.

"Ahhh," I moan as he dabs the miracle potion onto my dry skin patches. The cream makes my skin feel like satin, each pore celebrating what I think every movie starlet probably feels is a woman's basic right.

"For trying the sample today, I'll give you a sale price on one month's supply of the cream," he says, trying to reel me in. I play along for a moment more while my skin absorbs the creamy ecstasy.

"How much?" I ask as I casually tuck the fraying edge of my skirt under my leg, sure that no one in Santa Barbara ever asks about price.

"I'll sell you a one-month sample supply at discount: only three hundred and ninety-nine dollars. You'll want to continue the regimen for at least six months before you see the full benefits."

Really? I wonder what will happen to my skin if I don't eat for six months, don't leave Santa Barbara, become one of the homeless, just for the privilege of having my skin sucking in this satin magic. Let's just round up to four hundred dollars—that's my monthly transportation and food budget. Together.

I tell him I'll consider it while shopping along Anacapa Street, but I have no intention of going back for the purchase. No answers here for me today. My skin will just have to work everything out on its own.

THE BEAT GOES ON

Ben gathers nuts and fruit for breakfast in his tiny kitchen while I pour almond milk over my granola. "Ya know, I never pictured you here in southern California," I say.

"No, I didn't picture myself here, either. But I don't have much more time to try to find the music. There are only a few places that are a good bet, and this is one of them. I have to try."

I think about the condor's outstretched wings as the bird searches for what has died, and I wonder if Ben's desire to re-identify himself as a drummer will die as well, or at least disappoint him. I haven't seen his drum kit anywhere in the apartment, not even his small practice pad with a couple of drumsticks. There isn't anywhere to set anything up.

"Any leads for gigs?" I ask.

"Not many. I'm not willing to play music I don't like with a band out on the road. That's a younger man's gig. I keep looking for folks to jam with. I've checked out some leads in the papers, but nothing has felt right."

He's been here for a few years without anything working out. Sadly, he might have to let the drumming go. I don't say any of this.

"I like the weather, though, no more long Vermont winters." He shifts his chair out of the direct sun to protect his fair skin. The sunlight filters in through the kitchen window, as it has every day I've been here. Hot water for a cup of tea boils and I get up to pour some over my tea bag waiting in a mug on the kitchen counter.

"Yeah, I'm tired of the long winters, too." I move my own chair to sit in the sunshine and soak in the warmth.

"I do have my men's group," he continues. "You'd like these guys—deep thinkers. This is what's feeding me right now. We really dig deep." Male friends are a new thing for him, maybe eventually even more important than the drumming. This goal of finding friends up in the Northeast Kingdom of Vermont is what drew him to the dance halls, but bonding attempts didn't stick. He's tried working out at gyms, but no friendships were forged there, either.

He tries to smile, but his attempt is strained, and I know him well enough to know he craves a fuller lifer than this.

"What do we have to give up while we search to have it all, to feel like we really belong somewhere?" I muse, maybe to him, maybe to myself. He and I have posed this question so many times over the years, with no viable answers surfacing. He stayed in Vermont longer than he planned because of a love relationship, even without any music, but his muse kept nudging him. They broke up and he tried other places before greater Los Angeles. Music, work, friends . . . love.

Reaching across the table, I gently squeeze his wrist. Maybe he'll find some way, any way, to feel like he belongs here in California. I want this for him.

"But, *you*," he says, shifting the tension toward something positive. "You're finding a way to belong everywhere you go. That's so great."

Am I?

Once done in Santa Barbara, I bus to Ventura, California to catch a ferry to Santa Cruz Island in Channel Islands National Park for four days of camping and exploring. I walk the Navy Road to the China Pines Grove and beyond on one of my exploration days.

Chapter 15
Blocking Out the City Lights

Channel Islands National Park, Ventura, California • January 2015

Tiny fists wrap around the ferry's handrails. Transfixed, the children watch as dolphins swim alongside the boat and whale spray erupts off the port side. High decibels of giddy laughter pierce through the mist as I head to the cabin to find some quiet.

Most passengers disembark at Scorpion Harbor for the day to hike or kayak. The rest of us stay on board, motoring another twenty-two miles, hugging the shoreline toward Prisoner's Harbor farther along the eastern side of Santa Cruz Island, one of five islands comprising Channel Islands National Park.

Back in 1830, about thirty inmates were refused docking at the Santa Barbara port and left with supplies to fend for themselves at Prisoner's Harbor instead. Some accounts say that the prisoners built rafts and crossed the channel to the mainland. Some say none made it.

The national park land covers only about a third of the island acreage; the rest is protected by The Nature Conservancy. The ferry only serves this part of the island twice per week. Most of the twelve people remaining on board step down the ramp onto the dock to take the guided Nature Conservancy hike before catching the mid-afternoon boat back to Ventura Harbor. Not me. I am staying for three nights since I want more than just a couple of hours to explore whatever wildness still exists here in spite of the island's history.

Four national park–designated backcountry campsites overlook the channel from a primitive campground about three and a half miles up the Del Norte Trail. Each of my backpack pockets bulges with bottles of water to last me four days, not unlike my hike in the Big Bend Chisos Mountains. A gentle sloshing shifts from side to side as I walk the newly mown grass path funneling me over the hills toward the campsites. No other hikers follow me up the trail. Finally, I can hear my own thoughts without having to tune out others' voices.

Island scrub jays croon from trailside branches while coastal sage perfumes the island air with a twist of pungent citrus. The midday sun siphons droplets of sweat from the back of my neck. Low chaparral—manzanita, scrub oak, sage—opens to sweeping views of the channel bisecting the islands from the coast. By late afternoon, I have my pick of campsites atop the ridge. Once my tent is set up, I settle into the calm spreading over the island and scrounge through my food for some sustenance.

Santa Barbara and Ventura city lights begin to glow in dim clusters across the channel as I spoon out the last remaining tuna bits from the foil packet and munch a granola bar for dessert. With the island sounds settling down for the night, all I can hear is my own breath and the chewing of oats and chocolate chips.

Solitude covers me like an old, worn shawl protecting me from the kind of unwanted stimulation I find in cities. Even the cliffs, dunes, and beaches of Montana de Oro State Park were saturated with loud conversations. I don't know how Ben copes with Santa Barbara's crowding—having to suffer the city noises and put up with dense traffic. My nervous system wouldn't be able to take it for very long. But here, on this island, I have the solitude I need right now.

FROLIC IN THE GRASS

The ocean, like blue spilled milk, laps onto the rocky curves of the sloping hills as the morning light spreads across the trail. After the recent rains, the island has adorned itself in sprouting green. Moisture lifts into the air, mist lingers from overnight dew, and beads of water spit off of my boots' leather as I maneuver along the dragged and raked grassy path toward my goal—Chinese Harbor. Mushrooms bloom through the sod and fox scat molds in the humid air. Bombarded by my senses, I seem to blend into the green all around me.

Partway along the trail switchbacks heading down towards the harbor, the whirring hum of a motor penetrates my solitude.

Traffic? People? Here?

The mown grass paths are well maintained—whether by National Park, Nature Conservancy, or Navy, I'm not sure. Resentful of the disturbance, I leap onto a knoll to get out of the way of an oncoming tractor.

"Sorry for the intrusion," the driver calls from the rig. Cut grass falls along the path as he downshifts to slow as he passes by. I'm under no illusion that I am the lone soul on this island, yet I still feel the shock of human contact jarring my meditative stroll.

"No problem," I say as cheerfully as I can.

As soon as the tractor has moved on, I hop over the grass clumps back onto the path leading to the beach. The motor's hum fades into the hills above me as the crashing waves pull at my attention again. I return to my task of getting to the cove.

Tide-deposited *treasures* peek out from under piles of sea-battered stone or reveal themselves boldly on the sand. Purple sea urchin shells and slimy seaweed stalks disclose sea trash—tennis balls, plastic cups, a single sandal—delivered onto the land for humans to take back into possession. I like nature having a say, having the last word at times.

Small pieces of micro-trash line my pockets as I climb back up to the trail, but my efforts to *leave no trace* never seem enough against those islands of discarded objects far away and floating out of our view.

After I return to my campsite in the late afternoon, a pair of Channel Island foxes rumble-tumble through the swaying grass blades. From my perch on top of my picnic table, I watch their reddish-brown bellies flip and wrestle and their snouts poke and nuzzle. Symbolic qualities of Native American totems come to mind, such as the fox's playfulness. Due to their heightened senses and quick thinking, they are able to meld into their surroundings.

Climbing up on other tables, they search for leftover crumbs. Once the sites are scoured clean of any food residue, they cavort their way back through the grassy tufts to the Del Norte paths leading to other fox picnic sites, and I'm left with the echoes of their revelry.

The sun slowly plants itself behind the distant hills, and with wispy clouds in the sky, dusky hues paint themselves into more flamboyant spectacle than the cloudless sky of yesterday. A low-lying mist skims along the mainland shore and waits for the almost-full moon to obliterate the star-light, star-bright show overhead. With the haze blocking out much of the city-light intrusion across the channel, I am once again alone, just me, happily melding with the moon for the night.

BLOTTING OUT HISTORY

Remnants of livestock ranches from between the 1850s and 1980s—rotting wooden posts and barbed wire—frame the edges of verdant fields along the single road traversing the island's ridge line.

Wilderness is just starting to reclaim the island from its history.

Since few hikers walk the sixteen miles between Scorpion and Prisoner's harbors, I have my solitude while strolling along the Navy Road toward the China Pines and Montannon Ridge.

Abandoned orchards canopy sections of the road from the hot morning sun and I linger in their shade real estate to cool down, hydrate, and imagine the ghosts of history slipping through the field's open gates. First came sheep, then cattle. Islanders strove to be self-sufficient, but in the process, their livestock decimated the natural balance of the island. Feral pigs uprooted plants and rabbits brought for meat escaped and devoured native flora. But the annihilation of the island's wildness goes back even further to when fur traders in the early 1800s hunted the coves for sea otter, seals, and sea lions, nearly hunting them to extinction. By the 1980s, golden eagles had moved in to eat the piglets. Overhunting, egg collection, and pesticides led to the disappearance of bald eagles, and then the golden eagles went after the foxes. By 2004, the Channel Island fox was on the endangered list.

My playful afternoon encounter with these adorable creatures is a testament to the ongoing reintroduction efforts by The Nature Conservancy and National Park Service to remove invasive species. Clearly, humans have been the ongoing invasive species here, but if we were eradicated from the island, I wouldn't get to experience the foxes in their habitat.

An approaching motor disturbs my thoughts. A white pick-up truck slows, a window opens, and the tractor man of yesterday greets me with a smile and some chit-chat. I feel like he and I are the only people on this island until the ferry comes again.

"I'm after a different view of the island today," I say, my own voice sounding foreign even to my ears, but more cheerful today than yesterday. "I'm hoping to make it as far as the China Pines . . . or not. I have no agenda. I'm just out to explore." I like not having an agenda, just letting the day "be."

He leans out the window, resting his tanned arm along the door edge. "It is a beautiful day. I usually run that section of the road during my lunch hour." I wonder if my presence here interrupts his own island meditation.

"Then maybe we'll cross paths again later on," I say as he inches the truck forward along the road."

"Just might . . .," he says. Okay, he deserves to be here as much as I do.

The bucolic groves and old ranch fields transition to stark metal chainlink. Slightly rusted, a NAVY—NO TRESPASSING sign hangs askew on the fence. Even though no activity seems to exist beyond the barrier, I scurry along the road past the gates and locks anyway, almost as if I'm trespassing by my mere presence.

The twisting road leads me through the thick grove of pines, cool and sappy, and once I'm through their outstretched boughs of needles, the canopy of boughs ends, and Montannon Ridge unfurls to the west, the Pacific, and hilly Anacapa Island just ahead in my view. I can see why ranchers wanted to prevail here away from the mainland—ruggedness and peacefulness melding together. They existed here on their own terms, living true, even if not on the terms of indigenous species.

Thoughts of my foxes call me back to the road for my last afternoon viewing of their campsite visit. Their playful ease reminds me that life shouldn't always be taken too seriously. Throughout my decades of adult responsibility, I've forgotten how to have fun for the sake of having fun. Maybe, sometimes, it's enough to just frolic in the grass.

Life seems to be a juxtaposition of one thing blotting out something else—the hunters and otters, the ranchers and bald eagles, the trash and ocean. The runner through the pines. Foxes rollicking while trying to survive obliteration.

As I hoof it back along the Navy Road, I pass the tractor driver on his daily jog through the China Pines grove. I admire him for living a caretaking life on *his* terms, away from the mainland, with the jays and the foxes . . . and for putting up with the interruption by an occasional island camper like me.

Along the scenic Big Sur coastal road, I often stop to look for sea lions and other ocean creatures basking in the sun.

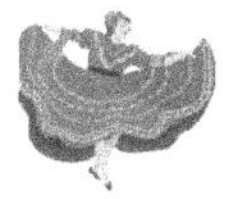

Chapter 16

Where Is Cupid When You Need Him?

Santa Cruz and Big Sur, California • February 2015

No one is really sure if I'm a traveler carrying backpacks or one of the unfortunate homeless having stepped into a coffee shop for a bit of respite. I usually just smile at anyone staring at me—let them guess. So when Jeff, my Santa Cruz couchsurfing host, texts me that he's nearing the back alley to pick me up, I grin at the man at the side table who has been watching me curiously for the last hour. I hang my packs across my shoulders and hurry down the back hallway to the alley just as my host's pick-up truck pulls up. I push through the glass door and toss my packs into the truck bed to mingle with coils of electrical wire and other tools of his trade.

I had sent a couch request to him since we both work in the trades and we both love nature. Okay, plus his profile picture was cute and he's my age. The combination stirred some romantic daydreaming, the first time since I left Vermont.

At his house, we spend the evening drinking tea and sharing stories of hiking trips. He leads the occasional Sierra Club group hike and carves out a month each summer for a longer trek in the Sierras. As he tops off my cup, I'm drawn to his strong, tanned hands, and thick brown hair like I saw in his profile photo. Since the evening is still early, we move onto backpacking gear, food, and tips until we both need some sleep.

"You'll be in the spare bedroom upstairs. There's a futon bed set up for you," he says. "I'll help you with your packs."

I pad up the stairs behind him and follow him into the spare room.

"Thanks for taking me in," I say. But, really, I want to give him a hug. He puts down my packs on the bed and gives me the rundown on the shared bathroom and towels.

"If you need anything, my bedroom is just across the hall."

Any thoughts of possible romance get buried as soon as they surface—*not appropriate*, I remind myself, *he's my host.*

Over the next three days while Jeff works, I check out downtown Santa Cruz by bus. In the evenings, we pick up where we left off—more stories about being out in the wilderness. I have yet to explore Yosemite National Park, his absolute favorite place to hike, so I listen carefully to his tales about multi-day backpacking trips along the John Muir Trail.

He describes trip details about alpine lakes and mountain wildflowers while assembling fish tacos for dinner. Sipping white wine, I flash back to feeble backpacking attempts with former boyfriends—coercions, begging. "Just try it for an overnight with me. It'll be romantic cuddling up in the tent for the night, keeping each other warm." If they tried at all, what I got instead was, "I felt a drop of rain, we have to turn back" or "Was that a mosquito I heard? We should get out of here."

But Jeff goes out on his own, like me. *Oh, dear.* As I feel myself flush, I purposely redirect my thoughts to my upcoming plans. "I'm renting a car for the long weekend to drive along the coast. Could I leave my extra bags here until I return on Monday?"

"Yes, absolutely. Where are you off to?" he asks, pouring more wine into my glass.

"Big Sur. I've seen photos and it looks amazing. Any suggestions?" A bit tipsy from the wine, I shoot him a coy glance.

"Haven't been down there for a while, but I have some nice spots I've found over the years for camping overnight. After dinner, I'll dig out my maps."

Maps? I love maps. I love that *he* has maps. Maybe he can bring them down the coast and show me in person? I bet he has better tolerance for rain and mosquitoes than all of my past citified boyfriends combined.

CUPID'S CURSE

About a quarter mile into the Los Padres National Forest, my tent overlooks the open hills that roll down to kiss the ocean where it caresses the Big Sur coastline. Sea lace wraps around rocks and dissolves back into the salt water that surrenders each night to the setting sun. Everything seems to be about love this Valentine's weekend.

The morning light spreads onto the curve of the watery horizon as I hike back down to drive the scenic coastal road before attending a tango event in

Monterey later on. I stay close to the trail, since Jeff told me poison oak covered the forest floor. Still raw from last year's relationship break-up, I trace imaginary lace around a Hallmark red heart as I recount my tear-soaked tale. Do I even have any romance left in me?

At every pull-out along the road, young lovers, with puckered lips, click giddy selfies. I don't begrudge these young paramours their affections. I would still take the lace and challenge my shaky faith. I suppose I would even go so far as to tat my own darn lacy filigree for love I could trust.

But sympatico with Frost, roads diverging in the wood, I often have taken the less-traveled one—self-love over angst and a broken core. Blades of grass sway to the remnants of last night's gusts and waves crash against the rocky cliffs below, so I urge my self-protected life's resolve to waft away on the fleeting breeze.

Trying to avoid lovers, young or old, I pad my way to a deserted point of land where cypress trees hold tight to eroding rock. Sunning sea lions flipper their way onto their sides, snuggle up against others of their kind. Watching these shiny, soft creatures summons up daydreams about snuggling out in the wilderness with Jeff, somewhere in the Yosemite backcountry. After all, this year-long journey is supposed to be my time where everything is possible.

Red fabric drapes around three-quarters of the women in the dance hall. I didn't get the memo. The bright flower print on my shirt and my black skirt seem to boycott the solid *red* of "date night" at this V-day Tango Milonga, the Argentine social event. Risky business coming alone to a Valentine's dance. As a single woman amongst couples, I might not get to dance as much as I would like, so I place a few Ghirardelli chocolates and a sliver of red velvet cake onto a paper plate, pour some white wine into a plastic cup, and find a vacant table next to the dance floor. Trying to look perky, I hold the intention for some brave leader to "take a chance on me" as old ABBA song lyrics taunt me from the back of my brain.

The first *cabeceo* happens—that glance from across the room inviting me to dance. As the soles of my heels push into the wooden floor, the staccato of Argentine heart songs, interlocked within recorded bandoneon and violin, overlay the flow of each gestured step. Infused with cake and chocolate, I dance at least two-thirds of the evening in the embrace of local *tangueros*, knowing that *all* of them will be leaving, at the end of the evening, with their own personal swish of red. I wedge open my heart and remind Cupid that it might be nice to add a "sweetie" onto the life list—a bit of clarity for the transcendental journey, framed in doily lace, never hurts.

CUPID'S RESPONSE

As I was riding the bus back to Jeff's after dropping off the rental car, I felt it again: a surprising heaviness, getting heavier as my departure to Hawaii looms. Jeff had invited me to stay with him until I leave for the airport in a few days.

Before Big Sur, I had avoided his searching glances in my direction, hoping to not read more into his intentions than were there. Now back at the house, his dreamy eyes send a rush through me from across the room. Guilt from my weekend fantasies renders me incapable of returning his gaze.

"You can't ignore there is something here," he says, nervously leaving the kitchen to join me on the living room couch.

My stomach tightens as I twist towards him. "I don't know what this means."

His breath warms near my lips, my accelerating heart desiring him to understand that nothing is frivolous, that I don't seek this out as I travel. My whole being opens up to his kiss. It has been almost a year without tenderness like this, without being touched in this innocently tentative way.

"I'll be leaving in a few days," I whisper.

"I know." His hand takes mine, and he explores the contours of my palm. "I'd like to see what this might be, but I also know you'll be moving on. I'm not sure what to do with this either."

Sensations radiate from my palm up my arm, all the way up to my heart.

Yes, I have the plane ticket and a trajectory of travel plans. But I know that I would relocate for the right man—not right away, but in time. Maybe the man for me wasn't back in Vermont, like I told Nan, but is here in California. Maybe I felt a premonition of possibility back then.

He plays with strands of my hair and I know Cupid has listened. "I could come back after Hawaii," I whisper to him. "Stay awhile to see what wants to unfold for us."

"I'd like to stay in touch," he says, as his strong arms pull me into a loving hug before he reluctantly releases me.

I choose, for now, to allow what wants to take place, and bliss permeates every part of me for a few days more. I've wanted to take more risks, be more spontaneous, be more open to life's "mysteries and miracles" like my friend Bruce talks about often. Here is another chance . . . or maybe it's luck.

While we wait for the express bus between Santa Cruz and San Jose, where I will catch my flight, Jeff kisses me goodbye against the passenger door of his pick-up and I don't really want to leave yet.

"If I have cell service, we can talk by phone," I excitedly say as the bus pulls up. "Or email. I'll find wifi."

He carries my packs to the bus and gives me a last hug goodbye. As I watch his truck pull away from the transit center and disappear down the street, I wonder if my one-way plane ticket to Hawaii is a mistake.

Insta . . .

San Jose, California, to Hawaii

Wendy's twenty-something almond-shaped eyes move between the aircraft window and her camera screen. She snaps photos of distant cloud fluffs and the plane wing near our seats. The image of Jeff kissing me goodbye replays as a loop across the screen in my mind.

"Which island are you heading to?" she asks when done. The memory of Jeff's lips fade into the atmosphere surrounding the plane.

"The Big Island to start with and I'm not sure from there. I have a one-way ticket, so I have to see how my money goes. It's my first time to Hawaii. I can't wait to check out paradise."

"One way? Cool. How long are you traveling for?"

"One year —around the U.S. mostly."

"That's awesome. Are you on Facebook?" Wendy leans onto the arm rest between us.

"Nope. But I'm blogging as I travel."

"So, you're a writer? As *I* travel, I use my GoPro for photos and post them online. Are you on Instagram?"

"No, but I've heard of it."

"Well, you need to get on board with some social media. It's important if you want to get known."

Do I want to get known? I wonder.

Wendy persists with the Instagram issue around my travel photos and I realize I've been gritting my teeth. Technology makes me uncomfortable.

Plus, how much of a writer am I really? A few poems and six months of tripping over words and images on my blog doesn't make me a writer. And I certainly don't consider myself a photographer. I'm not sure what Instagram will do for me in my future plans.

She pulls up adventure photos on her camera, talks about "tags" and "followers." Clueless, I just smile and nod.

"I've got over two thousand followers now," she brags as she scrolls through camera shots of herself hiking up a mountain, zip-lining, kayaking. "That's why GoPro gave me a free camera to use."

"Well . . . I'll consider it."

Over the remaining flight hours, once Wendy has settled down for a nap, I scan through my pics for any that I think are good enough for sharing on Instagram. If nothing else, I suppose, it could be another interesting form of creativity. I don't actually use all of my photos on my blog site and I've been reading photography tips online and trying for better composition, artistic close-ups, more interesting landscapes. Having a forum for the photos could inspire me to be more attentive when taking pictures. By the time the plane starts its descent, I'm more comfortable with the idea of the social media platform.

The plane's wheels bounce a few times, each with a thump, onto Maui, Wendy's destination and my layover. As we disembark, humid breezes waft through my already sweaty hair. Any heated memories of Jeff's kisses evaporate up into the swaying palms . . . framing the perfect snapshot, I think, for my first post on Instagram.

I fly to the Hawaiian islands with a one-way plane ticket to see how long I can afford to stay. I spend two weeks on the Big Island, starting out with a hitchhiking trek from the youth hostel to the Kapoho Tidal Pools to snorkel.

Chapter 17
Hawaiian Paradise

Island of Hawaii • February 2015

Sunshine finally infiltrates the vertical planes of tropical rain that have been battering the island all morning. With borrowed snorkeling gear from my hostel, I risk the weather and take the bus as far as I can get, then hitchhike the remaining miles to the Kapoho Tide Pools to swim with brightly colored fish. According to my hostel host, the best time to snorkel the pools is during the "slack" period, when the the direction of the tide changes before another wave swell, causing a slack period of water movement for better viewing of the marine ecosystem. I time my journey to the changing tide.

In the Hawaiian language, Kapoho means "the depression," a reference to the shape of these variably sized geothermal pools, some with a temperature as high as 90 degrees Fahrenheit. The labyrinth of pools is contained by pahoehoe lava rock causeways, similar to a barrier reef's protection from the ocean's stronger currents. Without specific water shoes for protecting my feet on this smooth, swirled, slippery basaltic lava, now wet from the slightly receding tide waters, I leave on my Teva sandals for better grip and hop from one lava causeway to another to find a pool large enough for snorkeling.

While floating on the warm, brackish water, I observe raccoon butterflyfish flit around lobe coral, black face masks prominent against their striped bodies and the iridescent rainbow colors of pale-nose parrotfish. Saddle wrasses, convict tangs, and bright-eyed damselfish converge near patches of blue rice coral growing on the basalt ridges of the pools. Paying attention to the tide coming in, I move my towel and bag to higher rocks closer to the shoreline as needed and find my way to other pools.

But once another round of downpours pummels the pools, I let go of my search for sea urchins, slog to the main road, and stick out my thumb. Without any cars driving in my direction, I walk and listen for oncoming motors. Lava grit grinds under my wet sandal straps, where blisters start to rival the quickly blooming poison oak sores spreading up my legs and the heat of sunburn emerges along my upper back. My umbrella edge drips more quickly as I stick out my cardboard sign for "Hilo" as I hear a vehicle approaching, as advised by my hostel host for easier hitching, and a sedan finally stops in sympathy for my plight back to the hostel for the night.

With the early morning rain done, the sun's heat bounces off the glassy black lava tubes as I carefully pick my way from one cairn—a pile of rocks—to another. From the Napau Crater rim in Hawaii Volcanoes National Park, I had wanted to witness the glow from the Pu'u O'o vent as it spews molten lava down the hillside and into the ocean. Stopping to pull out my umbrella, not for rain this time, but for shade from the baking heat, I guzzle a whole bottle of water. One thing I'd learned from Bruce and his many years of travel was to aways have an umbrella—for rain, sun, self-protection. It is a versatile travel item.

With each step over the lava tubes, my feet twist under the weight of my backpack. My hip aches and sweat seeps from every pore on my body.

What was I thinking, hiking for seven miles over old lava?

But in this desolate landscape, miracle life happens: delicate bamboo orchids peek out from broken lava cracks, surviving in this intense heat. The variegated purple fronds remind me that life can still thrive out of destruction.

More cairns funnel me across the open lava field and toward distant jungle and welcome shade. Once at the jungle's edge, the uneven lava trail morphs into an eight-inch-wide path through thick underbrush. My arm pushes away overhanging ferns and gnarly branches to protect my face from scrapes.

Why didn't the ranger recommend a machete while I was initialing permit line items? I mean, I had to promise to wear long pants, carry plenty of water, and be prepared for the possibility of toxic fumes blowing across the crater from the Pu'u O'o vent and its flowing hot lava. No one said anything about the thick brush.

After another two miles along the narrow path, three tiny plots of packed dirt, carved out of the brush, reveal the park camping area. To the side stands a little-used vault privy, well stocked with toilet paper. Alone here, I set up my tent near a patch of tiny purple orchids that found a less desolate environment in which to grow.

Since some daylight is still available, I maneuver my way about a half mile through tall ferns to the Napau Crater's edge. A low-lying cloud hugs the other side of the crater or maybe it's steam emanating from the vent. Hard to tell. But any actual reddish glow could only be seen in the dark, and no way will I try to come back later and get lost amid these thick tropical ferns.

Morning brings rain again, drops drumming a rhythm behind the tropical bird cacophony of high-pitched trills and warbles. Having stuffed my wet tent into a trash bag, I thrust my way back along the narrow path. As the sun appears, a side trail channels me over even more miles of slippery lava tubes toward the trailhead at the main park road.

One false step and broken lava crust will slice like glass. As soon as I think it, I go down. My arms shield the front of my face as I land, but a sharp edge slices through several epidermal layers along one of my forearms. I stare in disbelief at the oozing blood, drop my pack onto the dried lava under me, then root around for my first aid kit. Since I've used all of my bandaids on my poison oak sores and the blisters on my feet, all I can do is pull the skin together with a few remaining butterfly closures and wrap a bandana around my arm to soak up the blood.

Intense sun bounces off the lava, and with my body fighting all of its issues, I have no defense against heat exhaustion. As I start to get woozy, I slowly crawl to a nearby bush for shade and water to drink, and notice the lava tubes morphing into an asphalt road ahead on the trail. I forget that there was civilization here before a volcanic eruption flowed over houses and roads, causing the residents to flee their communities. Defeated, I want to flee out of this park as well and feel ready to move on. Once I get to the trailhead, a car eventually sees my thumb and stops to offer me a ride back to the park entrance.

Exhausted, I stumble out of my ride's vehicle and hobble across the main road. With my pack balancing on the road shoulder, upright in full view of oncoming traffic, I put out my hand to hitch a ride from the line of cars exiting the park gate.

From the bus yesterday morning en route to the park, I had seen a sign for a concessionaire-run campground a few miles south. Whatever they charge per night will be worth it for me to sleep for a few days, to rest and let my body heal a bit.

A white sedan finally pulls off the road up ahead of me, and I pick up my pack and scuff my way to the car. As we wend our way along the curving road, Laura, a retired teacher now living in the small, isolated town of Pahala south of the national park, tells me how she has come to own one of the plantation cottages connected to the historical sugar cane industry.

"What did you do for work before traveling?" she asks.

"Thirty years as a cabinetmaker."

"Really? I have a wooden rocking chair with a cracked seat. Any thoughts on how I can fix it?" Without seeing it, there are only abstract possibilities, so I offer to stop by when I have a rental car later in the week as a thank you for the ride. We pull into the campground and stop in front of the registration building. I reach for the door handle.

"Or . . .," she says, hesitantly, "you can come back to my cottage. I have a spare room."

I can hardly believe I might sleep on a soft bed rather than the ground tonight. When I trust—kindness and generosity seem to find their way to me just when I need them most.

At Laura's home, stripped out of my hiking clothes and into my sundress, I shuffle into the bathroom to clean my arm and re-dress my poison oak sores. Laura was kind enough to stop at a local store for me to buy more bandaids on our way to her cottage.

"I'll be grilling tuna for dinner later on. Please join me," she says through the closed bathroom door, and my whole body sighs with gratitude.

THE WAKE LEFT BEHIND

A hot shower washes away not only the lava grit and sweat, but the dried blood from the arm slice and some of my lingering exhaustion. The night rains have ended and early morning sun filters in through the window.

The stove kettle steams as Laura pours boiling water over loose leaves of her homegrown *mamaki* tea, its scent of butter and sweet potato wafting over the hearty breakfast already on the table. We'll be working on her rocking chair today and the fortification is welcome.

On the way back from the hardware store with supplies, Laura stops at the Punalu'u Black Sand Beach to show me where sea turtles have dug themselves into the soft sand as they prepare to lay their eggs.

From there, we visit a nearby Buddhist temple, greet the caretaking monk,

Punalu'a Beach with its black sand south of Pahala on the Big Island where I stay with my host Laura.

and push a few dollars into the donation box. In the temple, with eyes closed and incense smoke wrapping around us, I feel at peace for the first time since I arrived on this island. My legs don't itch. My arm doesn't ache. My back is not burning. Laura's breathing is like the tide, gently moving in and out.

I ponder a friend's intuitive message from before I left Vermont. "I don't know what will happen in Hawaii," she had said, "but something important will avail itself. You need to get there."

Even though the island has not been gentle with me, I think about the kindness of strangers, like Laura. There's something about falling to one's knees, not in prayer, but in resignation that all one has is humility. As I imagine gazing through the crevice between dark and light, the fragile edges of my desire for control seem to fade away. I wonder if this is the kind of awareness my friend had alluded to.

Laura and I open our eyes as a breeze blows through the screened window and a ray of golden sunlight flows across the temple floor. Neither of us say anything, but I sense Laura and I were meant to meet.

Before dinner, I teach her about two-part epoxy and clamps. Since the seat crack is free of debris, I squeeze out a line from the two epoxy tubes, and mix them thoroughly with a small plastic stick, push the goop into the crack and affix the clamps across the width of the seat. We tighten and loosen the clamps a few times to draw the epoxy down into the gap and then tighten one last time to leave on overnight. I have Laura wipe off the excess squeeze-out.

"That's it?" she asks.

"That's it," I say, hoping she will have the confidence for other repairs in the future. For over twenty years, I've taught women about tools, problem-solving, and self-reliance with this kind of instruction, and it feels good to offer this to Laura as well. As I look back at my woodworking career, my work with women has offered me the most satisfaction. This is our exchange—the wake each of us leaves behind from the synchronicities intersecting our lives. We teach each other about what we need at the time. A glued chair seat. A traveler repairing parts of herself as she explores new places and experiences. Kindness is the glue connecting those from different cultures.

In the morning, Laura drops me off to visit her friend Ginny who is the caretaker at another Buddhist temple. After years living in Honolulu, Ginny recently returned to her birthplace to work with the indigenous communities trying to survive after the plantations closed in the '90s.

Working specifically with at-risk children, she teaches meditation practices to them as soon as they can sit still for a few minutes. "I want to reach the kids early enough before they turn to drugs or crime." Her brown, half-moon eyes sparkle with hope. "If they can find a way to stay centered and focused, there might be a chance for them. The kind of chance I didn't have growing up."

We share our meditation philosophies and practices as we sit on the temple's cool stone steps. I show her a Gi Gong meditation practice I think kids can easily do—a simple movement of their palms, facing each other, moving back and forth. Excited by the simplicity of this practice, she agrees this could be a way for the kids to connect not only with their chi, but with each other and the planet.

On my final day in Pahala, Laura drives me to the bus stop to catch the early morning bus back into Hilo. Red and gold monk's robes drape over a frail man stooping along the sidewalk as his long fingers pick up shards of broken glass. Laura notices me watching him.

"Roy is homeless, and harmless. The town allows him to live behind that building over there with a couple of cats," she tells me. "I once asked him what he does all day. He told me he has a lot of praying to do."

Roy places the glass pieces into a plastic shopping bag.

"Has he done something he feels he needs to atone for?" I ask Laura.

"I think he just feels deeply for a troubled planet."

I bend down to join Roy in picking up glass and without saying anything to me, he catches my eye and smiles. Laura opens her car trunk and takes out a couple of plastic shopping bags, handing me one. There is time before the bus comes. I think back to the trash settled on Santa Cruz Island in the Channel Islands. What better way to pray for our planet than in this moment, in this way, with people who care.

Aloha

Kauai, Hawaii

A= Akahai:	Kindness, expressed with tenderness
L=Lokahi:	Unity, expressed with harmony
O=Olu'olu:	Agreeable, expressed with pleasantness
H=Ha'aha'a:	Humility, expressed with modesty
A=Ahonui:	Patience, expressed with perseverance

Tropic gusts blow loose hair strands around my face as I look up to see the almost-full Hawaiian moon and I zip up my soft-shell jacket all the way to my chin to ward off the night chill. My flight from the Big Island arrived at midnight. Unaware that the airport would close for the rest of the night, I had planned on hunkering down somewhere in the airport lobby until early morning. Instead, I haul my bags across the terminal road in the floodlight blotting out the moon's glow.

"Excuse me, ma'am," a security guard says as he crosses the road behind me. "Are you waiting for a ride?"

"Actually, no," I tell him. "I'm getting a rental car first thing in the morning and can't afford the extra night of rental. Sorry, I thought the airport would still be open. Is it a problem for me to sit here for a few hours?"

The security guard hesitates as he assesses my packs. I look him straight on and explain about my year of travel, my one-way ticket to these islands to explore the beauty here.

He agrees that it is ultimately safer for me to overnight outside the airport. He tells me it's a long walk into Lihue in the dark to look for a twenty-four hour establishment that's open so late. The officer is reasonable and I also know he will surely keep an eye on me through the security cameras, just in case.

"At some point, we'll make a run to the 7-Eleven for hot coffee. Would you like anything when we go?" he offers.

I wonder if this is the "A" or the "O" part of Aloha. I'll take either—the agreeability or the kindness. "No, but thank you," I respond, then watch him walk back toward the terminal building.

I put on my rain gear as a buffer against the wind and pull my fleece hat down over my ears. With a pillow I've made from my packs and extra clothes crammed into a light weight stuff sack, I lay myself down for a power nap along one of the benches under a protective overhang across from the terminal's main entrance. I scan the eaves for security cameras. I feel safer seeing them, just in case I need to ask for assistance.

Just as the morning light peeks through the palm trees, now calm after the night's gusts have stopped, I get up to use the nearby rest room. Then, I stuff my pillow and rain gear into my pack and stride across the parking lot to the row of rental car offices along the maintenance road.

While I sit on a bench outside the large glass window in front of the rental car office, waiting for a clerk to arrive and unlock the door, I read the sign tacked up on a nearby pole:

Don't feed the chickens.

Suspiciously, I look around, but don't see any.

I pose in front of Hanakapiai Falls on the island of Kauai, two miles along the Kalalau Trail, and up a muddy side trail during my week-long stay to explore the island.

Chapter 18
The Razor's Edge of Paradise

Kauai, Hawaii • March 2015

Low-lying clouds hover around Mount Wai'ale'ale in Kok'e State Park after the night's light rain stopped. With my eyes still closed from much-needed sleep, morning bird songs serenade me from the lush, wet foliage around my paradise campsite. Only the intermittent itch of dwindling poison oak scabs distracts me from the bird concert.

But . . . what? You have to be kidding! Right next to my tent? Bird song overshadowing by a red-headed and black-plumed cockle-doodle-doo crooner and his bevy of coo-clucking gal pals? Do they have no respect for the morning bird symphony?

"Go away! Shoo," I croak through the fabric of the tent as I try to channel the patience of Ahonui. I don't know why I thought each new morning would be different with these guys. Just as well—this morning is my last one in the park. I might as well get up and descend from the misty hills into the sunny day along the coast.

A need for wifi leads me to the Princeville Public Library en route to the Na Pali coastline, where I ask the librarian about the feral roosters and chickens everywhere.

"They're on the roads, in the parking lots, along hiking trails—they do take this free-range stuff seriously," I remark.

The librarian laughs. "There's a history of cockfighting on the island, brought over from the Philippines. During Hurricane Iniki in the early '90s, the cages were opened and the fowl went into the hills, reproduced, and now roam free. Yes, they can be a nuisance at times, but they do eat the centipedes that have always been a problem on the island. We're used to them now."

The roosters are indeed colorful. And I have to admit I haven't seen many centipedes climbing over parked cars at stores. Or circling my tent in the hills.

View of Hanalei Valley, with its taro fields and lush mountain folds, en route to the Kalalau Trail.

Or partying under palms. Folks who live here on Kauai must just be early risers. *I* certainly was up by 5:15 this morning.

SLACK KEY LULLABY

The green folds of the volcanic Hanalei Mountains flow down to the valley's semi-submerged taro fields, their presence looming over a few restaurants, art galleries, and tourist shops along Hanalei's main street.

Pairs of shoes line the porch along the outside wall of the community center. Keeping with the Hawaiian custom, I slip my sandals off, adding to the collection. After purchasing my concert ticket, I take an empty seat in the back of the room and gaze through the open window where several roosters parade across the lawn, their black tail feathers bobbing with each step.

"Always instrumental, the songs are slow and sweet, never fast," Sandy McMaster tells the audience as she quietly strums her ukulele. Her husband Doug shapes a gentle guitar melody with his pick on his guitar strings.

"The tunings are unusual for the guitar and can number up to seventy-five different versions, many original to specific family lines," she continues, explaining that she is the keeper of the stories and Doug is the keeper of the music.

The openness of the chords, reflecting the nature of the island and people, started in the 1830s when Spanish and Mexican cowboys were hired to contain the overflow of the populating cattle that had been gifted to the Hawaiian king.

Having started playing *slack key*—meaning the loosening of the strings— at the age of six on a toy mail-order Roy Rogers guitar, Doug's years of study with island masters informs each flowing guitar melody. Layered over Sandy's supporting ukulele chords, each note, punctuated by the influence of Spanish strumming techniques, blends smoothly into the next.

Each new guitar lick is like the constant breeze blowing away the island's cares. As my eyelids close to half mast, I feel like I could curl up for a much-needed nap right here on the community center floor, even with the now-familiar rooster crow echoing around the nearby taro field.

Sandy's words drift off into the palm trees as Doug's fingers slide up and down the guitar neck, leaving only the ringing tings of harmonics to settle onto the hills of Hanalei. My thoughts wander to tomorrow's hike, but each anxious concern breaks like the tide on the grainy shore of my five-dollar-per-night city beach camp spot.

THE RAZORS EDGE

Today is the perfect paradise day. The sun is bright as its rays poke through white puffy clouds. The jungle flora is thick and lush. The air warm and moist. The ocean is a deep, deep turquoise blue.

Starting early to avoid crowds, I ascend the soggy red dirt trail along the mountain's rolling edge. The sweet scents of tropical blooms cascade down the hillside to the wild and powerful, white-crested waves crashing against its rocks.

The Kalalau Trail, traversing five valleys and skirting cliffs, loosely follows a path used by ancient Hawaiians to link their coastal settlements. Even at this early hour, young hikers geared up for camping pass me in both directions. I know where they are headed or where they have just been. I know because my decision-making demons have been battling it out since I decided to come to Kauai: Could I find the courage to make it to the very end of the trail?

This is my razor's edge—a slice so sharp it cuts me no matter which side of the edge I am on.

No one seems to know for sure if the precarious "Crawler's Ledge," at mile seven, eroded over time to its current eight-inch width, or if the narrowness allowed for the protection of the inhabitants residing in the farther valleys. It doesn't matter—the image of falling to my death hundreds of feet onto the rocks below haunts my internal debate. An uphill cliff barricades the mountain's lush folds with no possible inland escape. People fall from the ledge every year . . . and *Die!*

In photos and videos I have seen online and in books, the verdant mountains spill onto a silky sand beach at the end of the eleven-mile trail. The destination is on every backpacker's bucket list. For over thirty years, I've been preparing myself for and daydreaming about exotic trails like this one. Over the years, I've asked myself if I could find enough courage to hike the more dangerous ones, like the Kalalau Trail.

Now, I'm dragging my feet in Hawaiian mud. My demons have won. Another group of intrepid youth passes me along the winding trail, and my decades-old "I can do anything" facade disintegrates under the weight of my longing to feel their kind of confidence. It buckles under the shame I carry for having decided not to hike all the way to the end. As if they might be able to sense my shame, all I can do is smile, look away, and quicken my step.

And yet, I have made peace with not climbing Mt. Everest, not jumping out of an airplane, and not being in a boat in the middle of the ocean tossing atop tsunami waves. How many people have told me they would be too afraid to get on a bus to travel alone for a year? Or how much courage it takes to build one's own home? Or even head out into the wilderness to hike and camp by myself for days? I know we can't rationally choose our personal fearlessness. The razor's slice is clean and neat, but my heart still bleeds.

At a large volcanic rock along the trail, I kick clumps of red mud off my boots, and lost in thought, I keep kicking, even without any mud left to fall off. Relieved no one else is coming along the trail, I slump onto the rock and hold back my tears.

Because this is *still* the perfect paradise day. The sun is *still* bright, and the puffy clouds *still* hang above the turquoise ocean.

Nudging myself up a side trail, I end at the Hanakapi'ai Falls. Mist sprays onto my face as I gaze up the mountain side and the water cascades down to the clear pool below. My once-again mud-caked boots slosh through more slimy muck as I hike the two miles back to the Hanakapi'ai Beach. Small, stacked, sculpted cairns, like an altar's offerings to the ocean gods from those battling their own demons before me, mock my disappointment in myself.

Once I'm ready to leave the stony beach, my bare toes search the stream pebbles for footing while my boots swing from around my neck. My hand methodically grips a suspended overhead rope as I traverse the flowing water that has been known to wash the unprotected into the ocean's deadly rocks.

Two miles later, the mountain remnants flow down to pavement and the sandy Ke'e Beach. Rust-hackled roosters declare their territorial freedom as I find a shady place to sit in my personal silence. Almost as if taunting me, they scratch into the sand nearby and brush their plumage against my bare feet as they pass me. Wild waves continue to crash up against the coastal rocks. And a brisk breeze blows through the palm fronds of my *bittersweet* paradise.

Bluebirds Might Fly

Lihue Airport Terminal
Kauai, Hawaii, to Santa Cruz, California

Constant breezes blow through the palms outside the terminal, and in the sky above, patches of blue filter through low gray clouds. Through the palm fronds overhead, a vocal rendition of "Somewhere Over the Rainbow" drifts into the waiting area.

As planes intermittently take off and land, I listen to the familiar lyrics about bluebirds flying and dreams coming true. *Might they?* I wonder.

It had taken a while for Jeff to respond to the voicemail I left about meeting up again once on the mainland. "Come back to Santa Cruz," he had finally said.

The memory of those words obliterates the continuing slack key guitar melodies pouring from the airport speakers and sends me into my own hopeful thoughts. I've made no assumptions he'd want to continue our romantic exploration, but over the phone, his enthusiasm relieved my doubts. Secretly, I've been fantasizing about the possibility of finding an apartment for a couple of months so we could date for real.

Come back to the house were his exact words. But I wonder if he means the spare room again . . . or his bed? No, it's too soon for that conjecture.

As I board the plane, a new softness dwells in me. Honed by my challenges over the last few weeks, I've humbly accepted more of my limitations and acknowledged increased honesty within myself, now that I've bled some—both inside *and* out. A thin scab covers my arm slice from the lava tube fall on the Big Island and the poison oak oozing is on its way out. Internally, I found some peace around not being able to do everything all the time, allowing myself a bit more imperfection. I wonder if Jeff will see me as changed in any way? If so, will he feel differently towards me?

With nothing below the plane but clouds and ocean, I sit in silence, staring out the window, relieved the person next to me is plugged into his device so I can ponder my questions in peace. *Do I even want a new relationship? Would I ever consider moving to California?* I shift in the seat and lean my head against the window edge, taking a deep breath, and gaze out at puffy cloud variations. Memories of Jeff's kisses swell again in my mind as the plane continues east to the mainland—the moistness of his lips on mine, his breath next to me as our sweaty bodies clung close, our whispered pillow talk as he reached to hold my hand in his.

The pros and cons battle it out in my thoughts over the remaining flight. Raw recollections of my last relationship in Vermont wend their way through my consciousness—the shutting down, the pushing away, the disappointment and tears. The clouds give way to darkness, but I continue staring out the window anyway.

Trying to shake loose from old heartbreak, I imagine listening to the ocean waves crashing against Santa Cruz's shore just five blocks away from Jeff's house. I picture him putting his arms around my waist, resting his chin on top of my head, watching the sun lower over the Pacific Ocean. I daydream about us sitting on a mountain summit near our tent, perhaps in the Sierra, or the redwoods. And then, at other times, in the evenings after he returns from work, cooking dinner together in his kitchen with a glass of wine in hand. And now that I feel less guarded and more honest with myself, I think about feeling happy. And maybe, just maybe . . . falling in love again.

I return to Santa Cruz, California after three weeks in Hawaii to check out a bit of romance started prior to my Hawaii trip. My possible paramour and I hike through Pinnacles National Park to see how we do together on a trail.

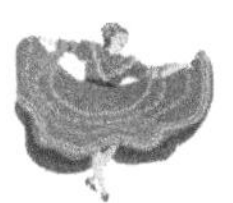

Chapter 19

California Pinnacles of the Heart

Santa Cruz, California • March 2015

Rock spires for scaling protrude from the rolling hills and flat valleys that surround Pinnacles National Park, home to talus caves, condors, chaparral vegetation, and a few hiking trails. Unfortunately, what it doesn't allow is overnight backcountry camping. Jeff and I came just for the day, so we won't be able to camp among the towering rock needles in the park.

My love of backpacking originated decades ago from that place of longing for the brush of a wind-blown mountain fern against my calf, the view of shadows gliding across valleys and lakes from the arc of the setting sun, and going to sleep under the star-lit night sky. With no one excited to join me on those adventures, I went alone.

But I've also wondered what it would feel like to wake up again in a tent snuggled in *his* arms, whoever *he* might be. To feel cocooned, our bodies as one, resonating with the primal and the dark, then the morning light. My fantasies will have to wait for another backcountry opportunity to find out how it would feel to experience this with Jeff.

Shelving my daydreams for the moment, I follow him up the trail that loops through the center of the pinnacle crags. Spring buds line the trail, tiny flowers flouncing their skirts—Shooting Stars, California Poppies, Monkey flowers.

As the trail parallels the West Fork of Chalone Creek, Jeff stoops close to the edge of a field to take photographs with his phone. There is something vulnerable and tender about his love of the tiniest wildflowers. I saw it in his eyes over our very first cup of tea, and felt relieved at having met someone who clearly understands my love of being in the wild.

Each day since my return to Santa Cruz, he's taken me to his favorite wild places in the area. Each day, we've shared our dreams and our histories. Each day, we've touched and kissed and laughed.

The view from the bottom of steps down to the Pacific Ocean's rocky edge provides a romantic moment.

I kneel down beside Jeff to see which flower he's photographing—yes, the Baby Blue Eyes. The low clusters of five-petaled blooms proudly show off their blue edges and blue-veined white centers for the photo shoot. I proudly show off my spreading grin while I watch Jeff click photo after photo.

THE HEART'S RISE AND FALL

Along the Santa Cruz coastline, the bright yellow-orange poppies sway in the gentle breeze.

I reach to touch a petal and within its velvety softness, perhaps like Alice in her Wonderland, I wish I could shrink to a size where I could curl up inside the petals and nap. The sun would warm me; the petals would shelter me from the breeze. Jeff could take a photo of me curled up in the flower.

Instead, we walk past a cluster of small swirls of poppies but stop so he can snap a few. Once at the end of the trail, we scoot down the hill below ocean cliffs to a protected sandy beach. Waves break around the protruding rocks and rush in toward the shore as surfboards ride and flip along the crests out past the shoreline. I close my eyes and listen to the waves, listen to Jeff's breathing and my own.

My heart opens as we continue our conversation from earlier in the hike. Jeff and I sit and watch the tide come into the cove as we talk—I want to know everything about him. I've been asking lots of questions, but now I sense his discomfort, so I back off.

"I need to let go of so many questions," I say, returning the conversation to my personal perspective, trying to lighten the mood. "I'm working on it. I get so excited about digging deep, that I may ask too much too soon. Sorry. And I know, for you, it's hard to open up. We each have our challenges."

Jeff holds my hand in his and rests our clasped hands on his knee. I turn to look into his eyes, but he just looks out over the salty foam reaching higher on the damp sand.

"We should climb out of here before the water gets too high," he remarks without responding to what I just said.

We pull our way up the cliff along a steep but trodden path among the towering rocks and return to where we left our bicycles at the trailhead.

Once back at his house, his silence thickens as he pours himself a glass of wine—but doesn't offer me one. I watch him saunter over to the living room couch. I watch the newspaper go up. I watch the television go on. His walls build up fast, as if his heart closed when mine opened.

I stand at the edge of the kitchen, frozen in astonishment. *What the hell happened? What did I do?*

He picks up the remote and flips the TV channel, ups the volume, then turns the newspaper's page to another section. The light from the setting sun slices in through the living room window and across the floor, as if providing Jeff and me with a dividing line. He never once looks up at me still standing on the other side of the line like a fool. Letting him lose himself in solitude, I feel I have no other choice but to retreat to the spare bedroom upstairs.

"What is it you expect?" was Laura's question to me while staying with her in Hawaii, when I talked about Jeff and my desired return to Santa Cruz.

"I simply *hope*." Just using the word itself felt open and innocent at that time; my heart felt ready.

Another friend recently said to me over the phone that hope is what tortures *her*. That too. I often wonder if those who have lost hope have a simpler, more accepting life without the aspirations. I don't even know what to hope for now as I sit in the dark on the futon.

Hours later, I pad quietly down the stairs to see how Jeff is doing, but he is wrapped in his numbness. He just stares at the television that is still on, his face swollen from alcohol and emotion. An empty whiskey bottle roosts on the end table near the couch.

Each day, Jeff gets up early and heads off to work without even a morning hello. I spend my days downtown at the library, at coffee shops, walking the sidewalks listening to street musicians. I buy cupcake after cupcake to make myself feel better. Each evening, I return to the house with anticipation and each night, I hole up in the spare bedroom and wait.

Each emotion that surfaces abrades my optimism as I mark time, criticizes every choice I've ever made, grinds down my confidence. Those feelings keep chipping away at me and I want to shove them out of my way. But I do want to hear the truth—whether I like it or not. I also know that I cannot heal anyone's wounds. To protect my heart, rationalizations comfort me as I drift off to sleep: "He's not the right one," "It wasn't meant to be," "Someone else at another time will be better for me," "I deserve more than a man who shuts me out."

Acceptance through this kind of alchemy fends off some of the despair. *Damn it, am I giving up already?* It's not that I don't want to feel all that I feel, it's more that I've grown weary of feeling *old* feelings—like the one where I'm somehow not worthy of the love.

Disheartened, I remind myself that I don't have any attachment anywhere I travel through. But, in reality, I *want* to. I push away images of all those men who have bitten into my heart and left teeth marks. All I know is that I don't want to go through heartbreak again so soon.

Yet again, I watch a single glass of wine poured in silence. I try to look through his wall, into his eyes to find connection there. I hold my salty tears in the palm of my hand and offer them to him, but there is no taking them. If taken, his stance is weakened. I have no choice now but to turn the palm to let the salt drop off and then turn myself away from this discomfort.

"I'll be leaving on Tuesday," I say, and wait for any light breaking through his facade.

Earlier today, I reluctantly secured two couchsurfing stays in San Luis Obispo, along with a one-week Workaway exchange, and bought a bus ticket online.

Several birds land on the feeder seen through the window, and Jeff just continues to gaze at them. I watch his grip tighten on the wine glass stem, aware of his pain clenching through his body. Time slows to a halt while I wait for anything at all from him.

"That would be best," he slowly responds while taking a sip of wine, then stares down into the liquid as if all the answers were beneath its surface.

"What happened?" I whisper, without stake now, and pull myself up onto the counter stool next to him.

He looks at me for the first time in four days, angst emanating from his eyes, then looks away again. "You said something that confused me."

I reach over to touch him, but he squirms away from me." Why didn't you ask for clarification?"

"I couldn't," he finally says, gulps down the rest of the wine, and storms off to do some chores, leaving me standing in the kitchen, once again alone. A male cardinal balances on the bird feeder outside the window. I wish I could just up and fly away too.

I know that this issue is his, I've done nothing wrong, and he just won't let me in. Pushing aside my disappointment, I tell myself I deserve better than this, and decide to *choose* what I haven't been able to before now . . . to love *myself* first.

Sightseeing downtown San Luis Obispo, California looking for free things to do, I find my way to pungent Bubble Gum Alley, where gum chewers have created years of gum-art on the concrete walls.

Chapter 20
Navigating the Maze

San Luis Obispo, California (SLO) • April 2015

Paths criss-cross the lush, grassy hillside of a local nature preserve. Once at an intersection, Kelly, my couchsurfing hostess, points to a path less crowded than others we can see. She takes the lead, her strong runner's leg muscles pulling her easily up the hill.

Since I arrived from Santa Cruz, she and I have been exploring not only local trails, but old love expectations no longer working for either of us. Laughter and humility unite us in kindred frustration as we dissect our old relationship patterns.

"Can *you* compromise on your integrity?" Kelly asks me as we leave the sunny, open pasture and head for shade.

"I doubt it." Carefully watching the sides of the trail for poison oak now that the oozing on the backs of my legs has totally dried up, I contemplate past relationship toxicity that could have been avoided.

"And you?" I ask.

"I've tried," she bemoans as we enter into the scrub oaks shading this section of the trail. "Guys think I'm one of those ditzy blondes, and they think they can get away with anything. I'm getting tired of it." Her long, blonde ponytail sways back and forth as she walks.

Now that I'm in my late 50s, it seems harder and harder to meet a man who has worked through his issues. Or to meet someone who has at least somewhat lowered his walls. I feel discouraged after so many experiences with those in my past who hadn't. Being in her 40s, Kelly hasn't allowed this kind of cynicism to affect her . . . yet. Based on other places she has lived, she feels that California men don't seem to have any real depth. I consider Jeff and wonder if she's right.

We agree that spring, with its new beginnings, might inspire us to search out new perspectives on love and dating. We come out of the trees onto an

167

open hillside and branch our way back down the trails to the parking lot. And as we hike, we continue to debate: *Are we willing to bargain in order to make some mediocre relationship work? For the sake of companionship, are we willing not to?*

Another day, I see two women place yoga mats they carried up the switchbacks onto the summit edge facing south. The sun is to their backs as they start to stretch while other hikers, including me, pass by to climb the remaining rocks looming above the flat ledge the women have chosen for today's yoga practice. I love the idea of doing yoga on top of a mountain but wouldn't want to carry the mat all the way up.

Like a line of camel humps, *morros*—volcanic plugs of magma that welled up long ago and solidified into softer rock—align towards the open sea in Los Osos. I wonder if the plugs, named the "Nine Sisters," feel the sisterhood of geographical root, not unlike Kelly and me, both having grown up in New England. Where the land ends at the Pacific, I can barely see the statuesque Morro

The morros leading out to the sea from San Luis Obispo.

Morro Rock in Los Osos, the end of the line of morros.

Rock from the top of this morro, Cerro San Luis. Supposedly in the outline of a Moor's turban, the Rock looms in hazy silhouette against the bright sun.

Once I've taken in the view, I descend from the upper rocks just in time to see the rolling of the yoga women's eyes. Laughter leaks out from behind their tightly held grins and I can't quite tell what image is on the flag waving from the pole carried by a man walking away from them with a clear *humph*. Temptation gets the best of me, so I stroll nearer to the women to ask about the altercation.

"He asked us to face our fannies in a *different* direction," one whispers to me as they snicker.

"His group of boys over there, facing away from us, are supposedly impressionable," the other adds. "Really, have those boys never seen women exercising?"

I glance over at the herded boys as the women pack up their mats to move to another outcropping for uninterrupted yoga. The boys don't look that impressionable to me either, and I feel certain they have most likely seen women's fannies before—clothed or not. But still, out of some kind of respect, I keep my fanny pulled in as I pass by the boys on my way down the switchbacks. Nothing is simple when it comes to boys and girls.

Having Googled "free things to do" in SLO, intrigue lures me downtown to Bubblegum Alley. Connecting Higuera and Marsh streets, the narrow walkway, whose vertical walls, as high as can be reached, emits a sticky-sweet stench, initiating a slight gag reflex.

Small pockets of intended gum-art, both disgusting and colorful, showcase dried goo affixing plastic sunflowers, business cards, bottle caps, and photo portraits. Love poems, spelled out in multi-hued gum strings, seem to drip down onto the asphalt, almost as if love itself is disintegrating. Is this what *love* has come to?

Now gagging from the assault on my sense of smell, I exit at the other end of the alley in search of better sensual delights, like something sweet to eat, then head back to Kelly's, where she is swiping at her phone while her cat Biscuit pads along the back edge of the couch behind her. Tinder is Kelly's current vehicle for meeting men. She swipes left and right, meets up with some for coffee, maybe some kissing.

My own memories of online dating make me want to chew some gum and create a skull and crossbones in Bubblegum Alley right next to some gooey love poem about being together forever.

"Anyone interesting?" I ask, falling into a nearby arm-chair, still basking in the glow from my earlier love affair with an ice-cream sandwich.

"No." She puts down the phone, allowing Biscuit to drop down into her lap. "You mentioned some guy in Santa Cruz. What's with that?"

I spill the whole story— the spark, the return to Santa Cruz after Hawaii. I plunk down the details of the wall-building and the shutdown.

Intuitively, she says, "It's not over. You'll hear from him."

"I doubt it," I reply. "He wanted me to go. I couldn't stay there any longer even if I wanted to. I hoisted my packs onto my back and hoofed it up the road to the bus station. Never looked back."

"Hmmm. We'll see." Kelly smirks, then gets up to go out for a run.

Within a week of my arrival in SLO, the text arrives from Jeff. "Where are ya? How are ya?" Kelly was right.

"I don't know what to do with this," I say to Kelly one evening after her return home from her work-day teaching at a local college.

"No one does," she says."He can't let you go, but he didn't want you to stay either. Who needs that crap?" She plops Biscuit onto her lap and rubs his belly, but Biscuit isn't interested in the love and wants an *actual* biscuit to snack on.

"I'm not having much luck either," she continues. "I'm *also* tired of men pushing me away, then showing up again when they get lonely." She tosses a cat biscuit onto the floor near the couch.

Later, as I curl onto the futon bed in the back room, I wonder if he's figured out anything yet, or might even be ready to share what happened with me. I've had to put up my own defenses and I don't want to get sucked back into his dysfunction. I tap out a return text to Jeff on my phone: "Having a great time in SLO with new girlfriends." With nothing more I'm *willing* to say, I tap "send."

Before I leave SLO for Yosemite National Park, I treat myself to one more ritualistic hand-made ice cream sandwich from Batch, a downtown ice cream shop. From the small storefront tucked on the corner of the alleyway, a nostalgic, warm, melting chocolate aroma seeps out the open door onto the sidewalk. At the counter, the young sandwich maker rolls the frozen sweet vanilla round into hazelnut crumbs and slaps one still-warm chocolate cookie and one oatmeal cookie on either side of the round. With a handful of napkins ready, cold, creamy, sensual drips run down my chin, daring me to wipe them away.

Because, if there can't be actual love, there can, at least, be ice cream.

This is my first time to Yosemite National Park, outside of Merced, California, to hike in the backcountry. My first day is a warm-up day hike to the top of Yosemite Falls, in full view of Half Dome.

Chapter 21

The Wild West of the High Sierra

Yosemite National Park, California • April 2015

Yosemite is one of the few national parks accessible by public transportation. When I arrived by bus, I was able to obtain a walk-in tenting spot at Camp 4 for six dollars per night, where rock climbers from around the world gather. During the day, they jam fingers and fists into crevices, dangle from ledges, and rappel with fury, all with impressive strength and seeming fearlessness. The climbers slowly regain grounding each evening by telling the day's stories over whiskey and beer. Some nights, exhaustion sends them to sleep early and on others, they party throughout the darkest hours. Non-climbers try to shush the loud whoops and hollers, but I just push my earplugs farther into my ears. Due to the lack of any camp rules, I've nicknamed the camp area "Yosemite's Wild West."

Once I had settled into camp after my arrival, I set out for a warm-up hike to Yosemite Falls, with close to sixty switchbacks to navigate. From the top overlook, Half Dome's silhouette loomed across the valley, larger than life, and certainly more stunning than all of the photographs I have seen over the years in coffee-table photo books. By the time I retraced my steps downhill along all those switchbacks, I had to practically crawl off the trail into camp from the pain encapsulating my right knee.

Numbing cold spreads across my iced knee cap while I elevate my leg on a dining hall chair at the food court across the road from Camp 4. While I limped my way to and into the lodge for breakfast, backpackers lined up outside the court for buses heading to trails I had planned to hike. The pre-season weather can be finicky, according to the rangers, but today the sun is illuminating the valley in warmth, making it the perfect kind of day for hiking. As the ice melts and drips along my calf, I massage my thigh just above the knee cap and reconsider what to do with my time until my knee heals enough to get onto a trail. A hiker running through the court to catch the next bus whacks me with his pack on the way by and I feel like smacking him. I thought I'd learned enough lessons about *letting go,* but here I am again. Trying to take my mind off the hiking loss, I study the valley bus map for other stops that I can limp to. Once figured out, I ditch the melting ice into the public bathroom sink, drape my daypack over my shoulder, and hobble out to the bus stop to catch the next ride. Across the valley, I've located a good spot to watch the spring sun slowly warm the earth, complete with a different view of Half Dome in the distance.

Adaptation, once again, feels like the right path, so I've created a writing retreat to entertain myself while I await better mobility and my knee to heal, however long that will take. After all, wouldn't writers pay big bucks for a writing retreat here in Yosemite National Park? There is access to inspirational scenery, cheap lodging at Camp 4, internet at one of the campground lodges, transportation around the valley, and time. Lots of time. I've decided to work on turning blog posts into poems, experimenting with rhetorical devices, and creating fictional stories from my poetry. If I can't hike, damn it, then I will write! I spend these sunny mornings outside near Mirror Lake or in the grass within view of Half Dome, and afternoons on large leather couches near blazing fireplaces in fancy lodges while daily thunder crashes up against the granite valley walls. I think about all those backpackers hunkered in their tents fearing the lightning strikes. Maybe the Universe intuitively knew about the weather forecast and wanted to save me from death by lightning strike. Each night, I seek free entertainment at ranger talks across the street at the lodge—or eavesdrop on the day's harrowing climbing stories told around hot campfires in Camp 4.

LITTLE YO BACKPACKERS CAMP

Alex takes his turn with the kindling while two others join us around the fire. He moves his snow-soaked boots nearer the heat. While starlight pokes through the blue-black of the sky, licks of fire wiggle their way around the stack of sticks crumbling in the fire ring. Even though my knee didn't feel ready for the arduous hike, I obtained a backcountry permit for five days anyway. I lower myself onto a log away from the shared campfire smoke shifting in the tenuous evening breeze.

I like being around people who are willing to take risks and push up against limitations. Each strain of a tendon or muscle willing to be the vehicle of motion, each challenge shoved aside by will, each labored breath, brings us closer to the raw edge of not only what we have already been, but what we ultimately want ourselves to be.

We move forward, knowing that we might or might not cross paths with strangers within the vast terrain of wilderness. Maybe, or maybe not, we might sit around a ring of stones, red flames flickering through gossamer smoke and reaching up through feathery pine branches to touch points of starlight.

"Backpacking alone?" Alex asks, and the flames imprinted in my vision turn to ash.

"I am," I reply. "As it seems for you as well."

Alex spreads out his wet insulated jacket near the fire next to his drying boots.

"Yeah . . . good thing, though, since it's my first-time backpacking: I wouldn't have wanted to drag someone over those seven miles off trail before I found boot prints in the snow heading in this direction." He speaks softly, yet boldly, but the rest of us know the question that rode on his shoulder the whole seven miles—*I am lost, will I die out here?*

"Bummer, man," Ed chimes in while spilling a few pills onto his hand and chugging them down with a swig of whiskey from his canteen. Ed notices that we all silently watch him swallow the pills.

" . . . car accident. I refuse to let the pain stop me from comin' up here. Most of my joints are held together with pins. As long as I keep poppin' pills, I'm mostly good."

We throw aside whatever gets in our way, whether a lack of experience, like Alex, or physical pain from injury like Ed. Maybe, as some kind of kindling, we toss onto the flames the twigs of stories, like traversing the backcountry after having lost a trail, or the sigh of muscle memory cursing the mind's will as each step up bores down with gravity, each landed boot pounding vibration up each leg and through the torso, exhausting calories and cramping calves.

In our comfort zones, we don't think we need each other. Just walk down a street in any city and try to make eye contact. Others look away, cross the street to avoid what they think we might actually want from them. But out here in the wilderness, we might need each other—for safety, food, water, or for conversation and knowledge. Age, gender, religion, or ethnic lineage don't matter.

I step off the bus from Merced to see this iconic view of Half Dome from Yosemite Valley.

"It's weird camping here, though," Ed continues. "I usually ask the ranger what they will accept for a camping destination on the permit." Ed pulls his sitting log closer to the fire ring, chuckles. "Then I tell 'em I'll camp wherever I please. Isn't that what being in the backcountry is all about?"

His mood shifts. "The hike up today was tough, though. My joints hurt more than usual. Probably due to the cold, so I'm stayin' here just the one night to rest a bit."

I know what he means. I hardly ever stay in a habituated camping area either. These are the places where animals will come to find crumbs and dangerous people might come to find victims. If I hadn't needed to ice my knee over the last ten days, I'd have continued past here and camped off trail, as Ed would have done.

"Yeah," Brian interjects in response to Ed. "I'm darned fit, hike all the time, and the hike up from the valley did me in, too. How do you do it being in pain like that?"

"Sheer will. Almost died in that car crash. Just wanna keep livin'." Ed stuffs the container of pills in his jacket pocket, then stirs the coals in the ring.

My right knee holds tight onto a dull ache and I move closer to the fire's heat to keep it warm.

"You really hike alone, Gail?" Brian asks as he puts on his fleece hat, pulls it down over his ears.

"Yep, mostly I have for the last thirty years." I let my words balance on the flickering of the flames. "It's hard to find someone to go with me within my schedule or with the same pace and perspective. I'm just resigned to go it alone. But—I've found resourcefulness and grit I never knew I had."

"Wow . . . brave," Ed says. "I've been packing out here a lot of years, in all kinds of conditions. Don't see many women out here on their own."

Bravery, grit, or whatever it is, we go into the wild places anyway. We come out with stories of vulnerability and humility and connection with what is primal, simple, stark.

Brian tosses a few more branches into the fire and we all pull our logs closer to the warmth. Each of us settles into our own thoughts.

I think about how we keep reinventing ourselves with each step we take along a trail. Our energy reverberates into the ground, stirring up the remembered energies of those who have walked here before us. We watch for danger and danger watches us—our senses sharpen to the shifting whoosh of the wind and the whine of the coyote, the snort and sniff of the black bear, and the chirps of the evening scrub jay.

We each have our reason for stopping here in Little Yo. We are the ones who hear the sirens call us into the mountains. We jam a spike into the granite's cracks and hoist ourselves up a rope along vertical rock. We paddle without control through a river's churning rapids. We go where we need to go to find who we are on this untamed planet and in this untamed life.

Lingering smoke wisps along the fire ring's edge and my thoughts finally recede. We quietly watch the constellations shift in the sky as the moon arcs above.

"Heading back to my hammock," Alex says as he gathers up his dry boots and jacket.

"G'night," the rest of us say. Brian throws dirt on the few remaining coals and we wander off to our respective tents.

I hate that half-dream state where I have to pee. The awake part of me tells me it's part of the dream and the dream part tells me to get out of the toasty sleeping bag and into the cold to pee next to the tent. I try to ignore the debate and roll onto my back from my fetal position inside my bag. To get my mind off peeing, I think about the free evening ranger talk about black bears from the other night.

During the Q&A after the talk, I raised my hand, "Okay, all the food and toiletries, anything smelly, has been put into the bear locker . . ."

Bear lockers are metal cabinets installed by the park at campsites, and sometimes in parking lots. They have a latch bears can't open.

". . . What if there is a scent on you? For instance, you shampooed your hair with a fruity shampoo that morning. What then?"

"They really aren't interested in you," the ranger had said. "They can tell the difference."

But then he told us the story of a man who oiled his bald head with perhaps not the usual oil a bald-headed man might use and went to sleep in a hammock. The man woke up in the middle of the night —to a BEAR LICKING HIS BALD HEAD!

Really? Not interested? I roll over to my other side and feel pressure pushing against my bladder. Then I sense something.

Unless one of the guys is sleepwalking and snoring, I can guarantee something is out there. A lumbering shadow, backlit by moonlight, spreads across the fabric on one side of my tent . . . I suck in my breath and hold really still . . . I lie as quiet and calm as I can in order to endure the snorting and sniffing circling around my tent.

I flash back to the "Bear's Bill of Rights" poster on the kiosk over by the composting toilet—explaining that bears are curious, they get to explore the park as they wish, to forage anytime day or night, and to live a wild, healthy, and fruitful life, hopefully unchanged by humans.

I know my tent doesn't have anything of interest, and believe me, not that I didn't trust what the ranger said, I had made sure NOT to shampoo my hair for a couple of days before heading up here. With my understanding of Native American totem animals, I try to send a message telepathically: "If you *are* a bear, I meet you in this dream place, feel the power of our connection, and honor it . . . you can move on now."

What if it's some other wild creature? My fight or flight thinking quickly kicks in: *mountain lion?* Mountain lions don't snort. What else could it be?

Exhaling a shallow breath to slow my heart from pounding, I pull my sleeping bag tighter around my body as if that would help.

Moving away from the tent is the diminishing padding of paws. The distant clicking of claws on stones. Allowing myself to take in a deeper breath, I slowly unzip my sleeping bag and wonder, *Was it real or part of my dream?*

I pull open the tent zipper, slowly peel back the fly flap, tentatively look out into the moonlight to see if anything is nearby. All is quiet.

With a sigh, I jump out and pee quicker than I ever have, peeing out all my fear, then dive back into my tent and bag.

Courage? *Maybe.* Humility? *Oh, yeah, for sure.* Continuing to find myself out in the wild?

Absolutely.

Once done with two weeks in Yosemite, I rent a car in Merced for the drive to Sequoia and Kings Canyon National Parks for some day hikes and a backpacking trek into the sequoia and redwood groves. I feel nested while sitting in front of a giant redwood in Redwood Canyon.

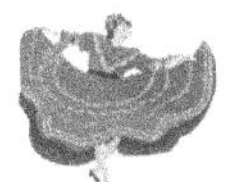

Chapter 22

Symphonic Proportions

Sequoia and Kings Canyon National Parks, California • May 2015

Sequoia and Kings Canyon national parks couldn't be more different, even though they are a continuation of the Sierra Mountain range. Yosemite's east/west road through Tuolumne Meadows allows many points of access into the backcountry, but here, one main road leads into Kings Canyon wilderness from the east, and access to the Sequoia wilderness lands are bunched into a different corner of the combined parks.

Unlike Yosemite's long wait at the valley ranger station to obtain one of a limited number of permits, I won't have to wait for a backcountry permit for backpacking—a few self-permit stations are scattered along the main roads.

While I drive my rental car toward the end of the only road into Kings Canyon, blackening anvil-shaped clouds in the otherwise clear sky chase my progress. As civilization diminishes behind me, I aim for more secluded parts of the park's wildness. My car hugs the road's sharp curves through the craggy slopes. Down below, Kings River carves a path into the canyon.

I had hoped for three nights of backpacking along the Rae Lakes loop, part of the Pacific Crest Trail between Mexico and Canada. The blue sky, benign with its current calm, tries to deceive me, but I'm not buying it. The weather report recently shifted to an 80 percent chance that thunderstorms will soon betray the current fair weather. Tomorrow afternoon forecasts storms shooting lightning and driving rain everywhere. Since lightning along open granite is dangerous, I have no choice but to change my overall plan, *again.*

At the wilderness permit kiosk near the parking lot, I fill in the backcountry camping form for only one night, since I don't trust the impending storm. Remembering what Ed had told us around the campfire at Little Yo last week about filling in the backcountry permit with a ranger-approved camping spot, then camping wherever, I peruse the trailhead kiosk map for the closest legal

181

site listed on the self-serve permit. Then I put a check mark next to the site name and stuff the form into the permit box.

About a half mile along the trail, as I search for my camping spot for the night, I choose to avoid the bouldered rocks to the left—boulders sure to have caves that might house dens for all kinds of animals likely to snort and sniff their own version of middle-of-the-night taunts around my tent.

On the other side of the sandy trail, grassy mounds funnel me to a single large boulder overlooking the river. A looming rock to hide behind while cloud shadows creep down the valley. A small grove of nearby cottonwoods fences me in against the wind starting to intensify closer to the ground. The whooshing of rushing rapids covers any noise I make while setting up my tent for the night, so the dark can come now—no person, nor even the expanding clouds, will be able to find me.

Early morning sunlight frosts the mountain peaks visible through the cedar trees on the other side of the river. Since bad weather is in store, however, I quickly pack up everything to stuff into the rental car before day-hiking up the Copper Canyon Trail to find a morning view.

As noon approaches, the wind picks up, at first a tender breeze around my shoulders, tickling my neck and face. Then, a jab of force against my chest as if to provoke me. Over the distant peaks to the west, gray clouds commence— heavy, agitated, mocking. Steadily advancing towards me, they quickly turn to black.

I adjust the straps tighter on my daypack and lean into the force of the wind, will against will. Yet, I know this strategy doesn't work all that often in other areas of my life—like men and family. My attempts at pushing back just yield frustration. I pause to check out the clouds, now looking bloated with moisture.

"Puff up good," I say out loud to them, glad that no one else is on the trail this morning. "Give me your nastiest show, your darkest underbelly. Throw those bolts! Rock the skies! See if I care."

As the clouds thicken and broaden over the Sierra, my disappointment festers in my mood. I quicken my descent to the car, grab my extra food out of the bear locker at the trailhead, and drive back along the King's Highway to find a high-elevation overlook, but the storm is slow moving even though it looks ready to explode.

"Come on, I want the tumult. The tempest. The turbulent," I scream at the sky through the safety of the windshield. No immediate rain comes, but in my imagination, horrific lightning strikes each of my projected backcountry camp spots along the Rae Lakes loop.

CAGIAN SYMPHONY

"Any options at all for an overnight in the backcountry that might actually be nearby, so I can get my permit *here*?" I ask the ranger as I pick at a fingernail. "Otherwise, I'll have to drive forty miles, then backtrack fifteen to the trail I *really* want."

She hovers over the park map under glass on the counter, then points to Redwood Canyon and shrugs. She's just doing her job; she has no control over trail openings on still-snowy closed roads, inclement weather, or the permitting process in general. Her finger lingers on the map while she talks, somewhat rehearsed: "Redwood Canyon meanders through a forest section containing the *largest* stand of old-growth trees in Sequoia National Park."

She's trying to placate me and I'm not happy about it. Okay . . . the huge trees are magnificent, like the grandfather redwood in the park: the General Sherman Tree at thirty-two hundred years old and a hundred and three feet in circumference at the ground. I actually touched it. It's still continuing to dig in its roots as a testament to longevity.

But a gentle walk in the forest? Down a canyon along a stream, according to the trail description. *What about a spectacular view?* Not wanting to spend more time driving than I have to, I fill out the permit form at the ranger station, find the trailhead for Redwood Canyon, and start hiking down the trail. A parched stream bed parallels the uninspiring dirt path. *Great. No water either.*

Farther along the route, I think I hear a trickle from somewhere. With newfound hope, I trod down the slope and check for flowing water, but find the stream bed dried up. Backtracking, I find the trickling I *thought* I heard, if one could even call a seep a "trickle."

Feeling this might be the only water source en route to the end of the trail, I explore a grove of nearby redwoods that offers a canopy under which I carve out a place for my tent, out of sight from the trail, and close to the seep. Remnants from an old song from the late 1960s roll around in my head while I set up camp—something about not getting what you want, but getting what you need. Trying to willfully shift my cranky attitude, I hold that thought as I cook my garlic vegetable ramen soup for dinner in the remaining daylight before the sun starts its setting trajectory. At least the rains have finally stopped.

The tallest trees in the world, these redwood timbers rise above this mixed-conifer forest canopy, some possibly reaching over three hundred and seventy feet. Based on the trunk circumference at the base, these cinnamon-hued giants have survived in this location somewhere between five hundred and two thousand years, a life span hard to fathom for me. Since they've lived such an enduring span, I secretly plead to these elders for their wisdom, *Why is it so hard for me to let go? Weather, views, men . . .*

As a past performer of twentieth-century classical music, I fell in with such great composing minds as John Cage. My chamber group had fun "playing" his famed, totally silent piece, 4'x33". The environment's sounds contained in that amount of time comprised the performance. Out of their comfort zone, audiences would squirm, cough, rustle their programs, stare out the window.

Cage, along with other experimental artists of the 1950s, explored the nature of random influence, and perhaps even the random influence of nature. They asked, "What music is around us when we think there is none?"

They felt that a symphony exists around us all the time. Even in those old vacuum chamber studies of complete silence, the ears could hear the pumping of blood through one's veins and the beating of one's heart. For those of us who have the ongoing, but taken for granted, gift of hearing, there really is a constant performance—if only we could quiet our minds enough to notice.

In my Sequoian forest camp spot, the six to seven a.m. time slot, for example, holds a Cagian birdfest. As I stretch within my sleeping bag while still groggy, I imagine the birds waking into their day, checking the current composer text:

Location "A": 6 a.m. Sing your best spring song.
By 7 a.m., move to location "B".
Use random intervals of time between song phrases. Have fun . . . the trees and,
at least, Gail are listening this morning.

Chirpy trills punctuate warbles, and croaky grunts pulse to woodpeckery thrusts. Cage would have been pleased by this echoing display of avian song acrobatics. And now, the birds echo down Redwood Canyon, and I barely hear their traveling show. A few remain behind, perhaps unable, or unwilling, to join the glamorous traveling life.

It's not just sound. Daylight filters into the clearing through my open tent door, the sun shifting through random variables like clouds, spring leafing of deciduous trees, dogwood flowers shifting in a slight breeze. Each morning, the sun paints a new random shading of light, and I wonder if these old, gnarly trees look down on the forest below and smile about their favorite new sun-painting.

I think about the idea of random influence during my walk along the Redwood Canyon Trail yesterday, noticing tiny wildflowers, the lack of poison oak, and even a few mushrooms despite a low snow year here in the California drought. By chance, I even ran into a USDA soil study person for a brief human conversation.

Choosing a random place to pitch my tent out of trail view but within access to the small section of spring-fed seeping water, I found that others have camped in this very spot. Even though natural fires have fled through this forest, leaving burnt memories on bark and twig, a ring of stones and charred wood proudly showcases past human presence. A peaceful breeze slithers through the redwoods' needles, or is it the trees finally whispering answers to me? As two squirrels race through my camp, circle around a tree, then stop to look in my direction before scampering up the hill, I wonder if this is spring mating, morning play, or even territorial aggression . . . maybe even their version of a Shakespearean stage act . . .

Or—just perhaps, one small part of a great Cagian Symphony.

BYOT (Bring Your Own Tent)

Merced, California

As he handed me his card back at Camp 4 in Yosemite, Jay threw out the invitation to rendezvous with him in California's Nevada County. My original plan was to head north, rent another car, and hike in Lassen Volcanic National Park. But the plan shifted because of trail closings in both Yosemite and Sequoia/ Kings Canyon. Since Lassen is farther north than here, I've checked online and most of the park hasn't opened yet for the season, so I need to re-think my timing.

Nevada County, west of Reno, is in Lassen's direction. If I decide not to keep heading north, it would be a gateway to heading east around the Sierra through Reno, or in some other direction.

While I waited for the weather to shift and my knee to heal in Yosemite, Jay and I attended several of the same evening ranger talks and chatted while walking back to our Camp 4 tenting spots. Part of his offer was for paid help. If I can't be out hiking the way I want, I might as well make some cash. The other part of the offer, I sensed, was for checking me out as potential girlfriend material. I'm skittish after my experience with Jeff in Santa Cruz, but I'm also trying to stay open. I send Jay a phone text to say I want to visit and ask if he can pick me up at the bus stop in nearby Auburn.

"BYOT," his return text says. "We'll be staying in the barn."

Jay is currently a nomadic llama shearer, traveling to his customers in the western states. Shearing and shots are easier with another set of hands. I have no background with llamas; all I know is that they are fuzzy camel-like creatures from South America with long necks.

But *I* will be the llama assistant. I book a Greyhound ticket to llama-world for two weeks. And . . . I've got my own personal tent.

My own tent is ready to go, having been used many times in the National Parks. Here it is during zone camping in Big Bend National Park, when all was well with the tent.

When camping in Camp 4 at Yosemite National Park, I was offered some paid work in Nevada County/Grass Valley, California helping out a nomadic llama shearer. Here is one of my favorite llama "girls."

Chapter 23
Llama Tales

Nevada County, California • May 2015

I bump the gate open with my hip and the metal latch clicks behind me. While scratchy hay flakes balance in my arms, all the "girls" nudge their way out of the upper barn and pause outside the open door and window, muzzles turned away. Furry llama butts huddle en masse next to the building.

"Be that way," I say to them as I toss the flakes into the feed bins. Jay tosses others over the outside fence and onto the ground until the cart is empty. Moist hay dust floats back down onto the strewn flakes as I hold my breath to avoid sucking the dust up into my nostrils.

Through the large, open barn window, I notice that the llama girls have corkscrewed their necks around to observe me. Their lips purse over their teeth, creamy eyelashes lower half mast over coal black eyes, feathery hair drapes over the edges of their perky ears. Trying for closer connection with them, I step towards the open window, but, as if in some capricious choreographed synchronicity, they turn again to look out over the fenced-in fields of disturbed dirt and struggling wildflowers. Llama butts once again find their place in the chorus line. So I rest my arm on the concrete window sill and let my hand dangle out over the wall. One after another, heads swivel back around in curiosity before looking away once again.

The black one on the end, however, only slightly taller than my own five-foot-two height, twists around even closer to sniff the air, lips pursed almost into a smile. She ogles me straight on, just for a flirtatious second or two, then turns back into the fickle llama line-up.

Blue tarps drape over the fence penning in the llama males along a field near the lower barn just down a path from the main house. The tarps hide the nearby females' field from view, keeping the males from pushing over the fence with their drive for sex. Spring llama mating has a specific calendar, I'm told—no primal urges can be fulfilled whenever these males just want to. What they can't see, they can't hump.

Once inside the lower barn, gated stalls line both sides of the dirt walkway where Jay and I set up our tents for the night. No breeze moves through this air, so we linger in the density of that special atmospheric blend that is uniquely "barn"—hay, llama urine, dirt.

We are joined by one of the males, confined for aggressive behavior, who defiantly positions himself at the edge of one of the gated stalls in front of us. Llama time-out. He's snorting and spitting, a way to prove dominance in the pecking order. Without other llamas in the barn, he picks a fight with us, trying to move up the llama ladder. I stare him down, then move my tent farther away from the stall to avoid any spray of llama spit.

In another stall closer to the barn door, Jay has placed a portable plastic chemical toilet behind a wall of boxes, along with toilet paper and peat moss. Peeing is done outside, so this is just for the other. The toilet is a new addition to Jay's nomadic lifestyle, allowing him bathroom ease wherever he needs it.

But peacocks have limboed their way under the door to the stall and procured a corner nesting spot. My challenge is to sync my bodily needs with the peacocks leaving the nest to head out into their peacock day. Their high-pitched shrieks are disturbing, echoing down the barn and shredding my nervous system. I'd prefer to avoid altercations with them since I've heard their sharp spurs are like razor blades.

Tired of the spitting and the peacocks, we carry our sleeping stuff across the field containing the llama males, jump over a trickling stream, and climb up a small knoll within a cozy grove of oaks. The grove has few mosquitoes and offers an overhang of leaves to umbrella the tents from the hot daily sun.

Each night, with headlamps on, we unlatch one gate to enter the field, hug the path along the electric fence, and exit through another latched gate to sleep under the stars. In the mornings, Jay shoos the peacocks from the toilet stall, then we get to feeding and watering the llamas and chickens. Every day, we wait on medicinal llama supplies that never seem to come.

Nevada County has a history of eager gold miners hoping to strike it rich. I, too, was eager to make a quick and easy cash windfall, but this daily waiting isn't offering me much profit.

Near the upper barn, the male peacocks' multicolored feather "eyes" fan out to expose the downy fluff at their bottoms as they puff up to impress the nonchalant females. Like a nightclub revue, the males embark on dazzling the peahens with their fan-dance, shaking their fluffy tush, then zipping around with shimmying plumage. When no peahens rush to the call, the cocks fold up their fans like sorry poker hands and head for the tree branches to soothe their egos.

I've watched Jay closely in his own puffing behavior since I arrived—exaggerating his self-importance about being the perfect hired caretaker. Following the peahens lead, without any romantic leanings towards him, I join the ranks of the nonchalant females.

Up from the grove, Jay gives a wide berth to the strutting peacocks guarding their territory while he opens the back of his sedan. He pulls out his almost-new, handed-down, two-burner Coleman stove to heat up some water for coffee, tea, and morning freshening up. While I get out my breakfast granola, Jay hangs a camel bag of warm water onto the car door and starts shaving in front of the side view mirror. He stops mid-scrape when a car accelerates from down the dirt road, and even though there are bushes between us and the street, Jay quickly herds me behind the horse trailer he uses for his llama tools and personal storage, where I give him a confused look.

"I'm homeless," he whispers, so even I can hardly hear him. "I live out of my vehicle, and not everyone understands that." He peeks around the back of the trailer to see if the car is nearing yet.

"But don't the neighbors know you are here temporarily to do seasonal work without any housing provided?" I say at full volume. The car driver, still having not reached us, certainly can't hear us. Jay's ongoing caretaking position had ended back in Nevada and his knowledge of llamas is keeping him nomadically afloat while he researches other options.

"People think that everyone should be living in a house or apartment," he says, "they don't understand."

"But this is a choice not to own property or rent while awaiting the right kind of opportunity. I would think there is nothing to hide about it."

I've been on the road now since last September and many opinions and judgements from those not understanding a nomadic life have come my way too—they seem to want everyone else to live the way they do. I get what he's saying. But for me, a creative life means pushing through those comfort zones.

Back in Arizona last fall, I danced with a San Diego man who had chosen to live out of his car while writing a book.

"I'm actually homeless," he shamefully explained while he shifted his gaze away from mine at the refreshment table at a tango event.

"I'm not sure I would say that you are homeless," I had said to him. "You've chosen to live out of your car while you work on your writing. Lifestyle choice, really. Like mine to travel for a year by buses and trains."

I mean, who really judges us? Do the neighbors really look at Jay through the line of trees while driving by and think something is wrong with him? Do people think someone is destitute because they've bought themselves a year of creative work by living out of their vehicle? Does this kind of misguided shame keep us all from our intellectual and creative potential?

The car finally moves by. Jay returns to shaving and I to my breakfast, when I think about my "bad beat," my quickly losing poker hand, and about freedom from expectations, judgements, consensus . . .

. . . and Jay.

Since there is no public transportation in this area, I catch a ride with Jay whenever he drives into Nevada City, where the Madelyn Helling Library is one of our destinations.

Jay is working on funding to re-instate a science research facility in the Nevada desert with the hope of caretaking it in the future. I'm working on a blog post. I can access the platform app on my iPad with internet, but the software works better on an actual computer.

"Would you like a PC or a Mac?" the friendly librarian asks me.

I peruse the signs tacked on the walls above the available computers: J.K. Rowling, Henry David Thoreau, Ernest Hemingway, Shakespeare . . .

"I'll use the Hemingway Mac today," I answer. I love that I have a choice. I've been to dozens of public libraries all across the country, but not all libraries are accommodating; some charge me to use the internet as a guest, and some insist only on thirty-minute sessions, if that. To my delight, this Hemingway Mac keeps extending my time in fifteen-minute increments. So far, this is my favorite library in the whole country, although I would feel the same way about any library that extends my time in fifteen-minute increments.

Once done there, while Jay picks up llama supplies in town, I hang out at

The Curly Wolf Espresso House. My drink of choice, of course, is hot chocolate. The Curly Wolf offers a unique blend of white and dark, steamed milk, and a wedge of block chocolate to melt slowly in the hot mug. Back in my element, with warm chocolate lingering on my tongue, I research, write, and put feelers out into the future. Right now, I don't think I'll be waiting for the llama medications to arrive. After two weeks, with only a few extra dollars in my pocket, it's time I pack up my bags and move on. Jay will have to shear and give shots to all those llamas on his own. Without better cash—or romance—I fold in my poker hand, forcing him to do the same.

Betting on the Cash

Amtrak Bus
Grass Valley to Sacramento, California

I shift in my window seat and re-cross my legs. The bus is full and there is no room to spread out, and all I can do is fidget. Out the bus window, the Sierra Nevada mountains recede but the snow-frosted high peaks still posture themselves up into the California sky.

Since I left llama-land prematurely, I have time to kill before my scheduled flight leaves from Oakland for Portland next week. Sacramento, for Memorial Day weekend, should offer me some transitional solitude for a few days before I fly.

Once the peaks are gone from view, I try to settle in to read some historical fun facts about Portland on my iPad, but the words don't stick. I reposition my body in the seat again and stare out the window.

Getting myself to Sacramento from Grass Valley hasn't been easy. Greyhound doesn't travel this route, Amtrak schedules a way-too-early departure out of Auburn, outside of Grass Valley, and the local bus from Grass Valley to Auburn's bus depot doesn't even run early enough to get a weary traveler to the transfer point in time.

Actually, the local bus doesn't run at all on weekends or holidays. Leaving Grass Valley on those days without a vehicle is impossible. Perhaps this entrapment goes way back to the golden days, when pan-handlers gave up on panning for gold, but just couldn't leave. Even after the folded poker hand, I had to grovel with the llama guru for a ride to Auburn where I was able to catch the Amtrak bus. I sure didn't want to be like those pan-handlers of old, stuck in Grass Valley with no way out.

But once again, I got backed into a corner—the "can't book it from here" thing with public transportation; Amtrak doesn't allow anyone to take their bus from Auburn to Sacramento without booking the bus in conjunction with a train portion of the journey.

Really? I mean, Sacramento is the capital of California. I had to pretend to book the bus/train combo to Davis, west of Sacramento, for an extra two dollars to be able to get the hell out of llama-land, but it doesn't mean I actually have to get on the train when I arrive in the capital city.

Finally on my way to freedom and looking forward to a rendezvous with my Vermont friend Anne as she explores the possibility of moving back to Portland, I open up my iPad to start reading again in preparation for my visit.

It was 1843 when Tennessee drifter William Overton and Massachusetts lawyer Asa Lovejoy beached their canoe on the banks of the Willamette River. Overton saw great potential for the timber-rich land, but his problem was that he lacked the twenty-five cents needed to file a land claim. He struck a bargain with Lovejoy: in return for a quarter, Overton would share his claim to the 640-acre site then known as "the clearing."

Soon bored with clearing trees and building roads, Overton drifted on, selling his half of the claim to Francis Pettygrove from Maine. The new partners, Lovejoy and Pettygrove, couldn't decide on a name for their budding township, so they decided to flip a penny to settle the argument. Pettygrove won on two tosses out of three, the clearing was named after his home town of Portland, Maine, and the coin toss was remembered forevermore as "The Portland Penny."

Gazing out the bus window at the flat grasslands of the Sacramento Valley, I find myself wondering about Overton, his choice to move on, and where he ended up. Due to his drifting nature, he knew when it was time to go. I ponder whether he would have regretted his decision if he had known what Portland eventually would become. But all we can do is make the best choice we can for ourselves in the moment. We have to trust what we feel and what we know in the here and now. I could have stayed longer with the llamas, eventually making the money I originally expected to make—but I knew it was time to depart. Money isn't everything, and Overton knew it, too, on some level.

This skill set emerges in me more easily these days—trusting when it's time to move on, to where, and why. Something murmurs in my gut, and there it is—I just know.

Overton's story morphs into Anne's Portland stories, told along our hikes in Vermont, from her time previously living in Oregon years ago. Relieved to be away from the llamas and Jay, I envision seeing Mount Hood and eating at food trucks in tiny neighborhood villages.

I hop a plane from California to Oregon, and rendezvous with a dear Vermont friend planning on moving back to Portland soon. We visit the Lan Su Chinese Garden surrounded by the modern city.

Chapter 24
Buckwheat Farmer

Portland, Oregon • June 2015

"Most cherished in this mundane world is a place without traffic, truly in the midst of a city there can be a mountain and a forest." —Wen Zhengming (1470–1559)

Some cities haven't been welcoming for me. I send out couchsurfing requests, usually five in the first round, wait a few days, then send out more, then wait. When no responses come through, I make alternate plans. But some locations have multiple hosts that offer hospitality to me, like San Antonio, San Luis Obispo, and here in Portland.

My first hostess insists on picking me up at the airport since she lives only seven minutes away and whisks me off to her home and my travel-trailer nest in her driveway. My hospitality stays can range from a living room couch to a spare bedroom all my own, to this, my own trailer.

She sets me up with keys and wifi password. She works for the city transit system and has maps of the bus stops and MAX subway stations, so I head off to explore my current world for the week. Anne will be staying with another friend of hers when she arrives in a couple of days.

Three nights are the most I request; two or three seem to be what most hosts say feels right. After three nights in the trailer, I move over to another house, into a basement room filled with art supplies. While we sip rich, red wine, my second hostess, her partner, and I share questions, travel stories, philosophies. Our words and images swirl around us like smoke rings off a slow, nurtured cigar, and we feel as if we've been friends for a really long time.

FOOD CART SHORTS

I walk around the whole block between 9th and 10th streets, and then along Washington Street looking for just the right food that will inspire me.

Many versions of gyros are advertised on signs, as are Thai dishes. I have no interest in burgers, or lamb, or any kind of schnitzel. I'm intrigued by the idea of Egyptian food but pass by. I ponder a crepe, but don't like the prices. The periphery of the block is lined with food cart after food cart, windows open, vendors waiting. I finally decide on one.

"Thank you," I say as I take my six-piece plate of potato and cabbage pierogi from the Polish food cart window. "I'll compare them to the ones my grandmother made when I was a a child."

With eyes now alert, the vendor leans out of the cart window and asks, "What did she put in *hers?*" I feel a competitive edge in the vendor's question, his pride on full display.

"Oh, potato and cabbage for sure. Cheese. Apple sometimes." He nods and remembers—maybe his own grandmother's special recipes.

I'm not sure that pierogi can be screwed up. They are what they are—doughy pockets stuffed with anything, really. This vendor advertises "buckwheat" flour for the dough, and I think back to my nephew's genealogical research into the Polish ancestry on my father's side of the family.

"Buckwheat," my brother had told me over the phone one year. "That's what he found out. Our last name translates to 'buckwheat farmer'. I tell people now to call me buckwheat." I remember rolling my eyes at that.

I know some names do originate by location or occupation. "Smith"—blacksmith? "Portland"—land of ports? "Grycel" —buckwheat farmer? *Hmm, I'm not buying it.*

A few days later, my friend Anne parks our car and pays the parking fee at the kiosk. Famished, we cross the street to circumnavigate the large lot lined around the block with food carts.

"This is the best lot of food trucks in the city," she tells me. "And close to downtown."

While in Vermont, she's mostly in blue jeans and tee shirts, even though her graphic design background inspires her towards more fashionable fabrics. Here in Portland, she's back into city-chic, her blonde-grey hair tied back into a pony tail. Over her black tights, her leopard skin print skirt swishes as she purposefully sashays along the row of carts. As we separate to place our orders at our preferred carts, I remember her finding that skirt at a consignment shop back in Vermont.

Gochujang sauce drips off the bamboo sprouts poking out of the end of my vegetarian bibimbap burrito from Bulkogi Fusion and Anne navigates through the crowd with her spring rolls from down the block at Thai Basil. Under some hanging branches, we rendezvous at a low cement wall, sitting there to watch long lines form at the windows of the more popular trucks.

"If I come back to Portland sometime," I say, "I'd like to try the Dump Truck cart for their specialty dumplings. Wait—or maybe the Egyptian food."

THE GARDEN OF AWAKENING ORCHIDS (LAN SU)

Our mild white tea steeps in delicate porcelain pots during our private tea ceremony in the Tower of Cosmic Reflections Teahouse at the Lan Su Chinese Garden tucked between city buildings in the northwest section of Portland, just a block over from the Willamette River. A warm breeze flows across us through the open windows on the second floor as we watch the timer pour sand granules through its narrow middle. First, five seconds, then ten, and so on, until our desired tea strength is achieved.

Beneath us on the first floor, quivering strings sing out a traditional Chinese melody played on the *erhu*, a two-stringed Chinese violin. Outside the building in the Courtyard of Tranquility, the five-bat motif on the drip tiles along the roofline symbolize the five blessings: long life, fortune, health, virtue, and painless passing.

I can't remember now when Anne and I first met. We seem to have different memories, and I suppose it doesn't matter now that years have gone by. I've built furniture for her and her husband, walked with her around her old Vermont family farm, free-form danced with a variety of her other friends during "girl parties." We've shared sadnesses, loss, frustrations, joy, and the exploration of life's questions. Why isn't friendship one of the five blessings?

It was she who housed me on my last night before leaving Vermont, she who drove me to the bus station in Bellows Falls and sat with me on the bench waiting. Hers was the last, long hug received by a friend as I stepped off into this journey. As steeped tea slips past our tongues, we continue catching up with each other's lives since we last saw each other in person back in Vermont.

Anne and I meander through the garden's varying ecosystems, where I share more about my travel adventures, and she tells me about her hope for a new beginning when she returns here to the Northwest.

Lake Tai's acidic and active waters erode stone into fantastic shapes back in China, some now transplanted here to Portland for the Knowing the Fish Pavilion. Along the edge of the pond, ripples lap up against rocks that evoke mountains and waterfalls depict cascading streams. Trees line the garden's edge along the fences holding out the city's chaos and traffic, allowing us an intimate moment with each other. A breeze following us shimmies a maple leaf overhead, and a bright red Rosa Sevillana petal, honoring Portland's "Rose City" name, brushes against my bare arm hooked through Anne's as we stroll down the tiled path.

PAVING THE ROAD FOR WOMEN

Prompted by a couchsurfing request on the hospitality website, I answer the call to participate in a questionnaire about traveling solo as a woman. By chance, Kit lives in Portland and we make a plan to meet at a local coffee shop for conversation about travel. Prior to meeting, she sends me a survey questionnaire to consider, with questions like: how do I pay my way, what's the last thing that blew my mind, what scares me, what's on my packing list, what is the best reason to talk to strangers, and how I am different while traveling.

In true Portland fashion, she rides up next to the coffee shop on her bicycle, removes her helmet, and enters. She orders a hot chocolate for me and a coffee for herself, then we get down to the business of travel stories. She's compiling profiles of women and their first-time road experiences for a new online site, including nitty gritty, practical travel info, as a way to inspire women and girls to find the courage to travel solo.

"I want women to know that they can do this, too," she tells me as she pushes wisps of blonde hair behind her ear. "No excuses. All is possible."

My version of empowering women and girls has been through the teaching of woodworking skills in workshops, courses, and summer camps. Through learning to problem-solve and use tools, I had gained enough self-confidence to eventually build furniture and cabinetry, then tackle the construction of my house, and I wanted to share what I had learned. I supported women in challenging old beliefs that women aren't capable of using tools, held their hands through overcoming their fears, and celebrated their wood creations—small tables, bookshelves, boxes—guiding them through their personal designs. This work has been the most rewarding I have ever done.

I admire Kit for her vision to offer encouragement to other women. At twenty-nine, she is already a seasoned solo traveler. We share tips and she is thrilled to learn something new from me—Post Office General Delivery will hold someone's packages for thirty days. I started doing this in California when I didn't need my dancing shoes in the wilderness. Right now, my backpacking gear is in a box waiting for me at a post office near the airport in Oakland, California, since I didn't need it here. After her own personal online profile, mine becomes the second—with answers like:

I rent out my house to pay while I go, and I have skill sets to barter for room and board.

My snorting and sniffing bear incident in the Yosemite backcountry was the last thing that blew my mind.

I'm afraid I won't find a free, safe place to sleep each night.

My iPad Mini with Bluetooth keyboard, hiking gear, dancing shoes, flexibility, and a smile are on my packing list.

The simplest of hellos with strangers can open incredible conversations, serendipitous invitations, local information, shared food, rides, and protection.

"And, most important of all," I reiterate to Kit, "I feel like I'm expanding. That's how I'm different while traveling—I'm witnessing myself in all kinds of new ways." She nods while scanning through her own feelings of expansion as we sip lukewarm liquids from our cups.

Kit has already uploaded photos to my profile—me with llamas, me on top of Bell Rock in Sedona, me camping with foxes in California's Channel Islands, me in the Texas Big Bend desert.

Once again, it seems that teaching woodworking classes to women isn't the only way for me to offer empowerment anymore— me being me out in the world seems to be inspiring enough.

Get the Guy

Post Office, Oakland, California

I scribble the post office address for Merced, California, under my name and "General Delivery" on the cardboard box. I've exchanged my dancing clothes and shoes for backpacking gear to take with me on the bus to San Luis Obispo, then on to Yosemite for a second visit. The snow has diminished in the higher elevations, and Tioga Road is now open for the summer season. Merced is where I'll catch the bus to start heading east again after I finish hiking.

As I repack the gear into my traveling packs for the bus trip south, my phone buzzes with a text message, and I check to see who it's from.

I stare at the words on the screen: "Come back to Santa Cruz after you land in Oakland."

Ever since I left Santa Cruz, Jeff has texted me, almost on schedule, every few weeks. "Where are you? What are you up to?"

I would send back short, cryptic replies without any emotion at all. I type in, "Can't do. Plans made already for a return to SLO." I press "send."

No way am I going back to Santa Cruz. It has been a few months, but I've regularly replayed the scene in my memory—the shutdown, the silent treatment, the dismissal. But in some strange way, I'm curious about whether he will ever be able to explain what happened back then.

I follow with, "Kelly and I will be heading to Yosemite for a day hike, then I'm meeting up with another girlfriend after. If you want to see me, meet me there. I can check schedules and let you know what's left over."

This is a new tactic. Kelly and I batted around dating nightmare stories when I was last in SLO couchsurfing with her in late March. I had chanced upon Matthew Hussey's book *Get the Guy* in the local SLO Barnes and Noble, where I sat reading chapters in a leather armchair at the end of the row of books on dating advice. She and I had agreed that our individual dating experiences had been grim and we needed some new perspectives.

Hussey, who has *taught* lots of women how to understand how men think through his book, YouTube videos, and intensive workshops, feels men want to earn love and women need to make them jump through hoops so that they can work for it. I thought I would try it on for size with Jeff by offering low priority in my Yosemite schedule.

At no time did I really expect his answer. "Okay. How about we hike the Grand Canyon of the Tuolomne? Takes about four days. Just tell me when to show up."

Wow. That was easy.

Back in California from Portland, I meet up with the Santa Cruz guy for a four-day back-pack along the Grand Canyon of the Tuolumne in Yosemite National Park. I find solace in my heart at the Tuolumne River's edge.

Chapter 25
Yosemite Unraveling

Yosemite National Park • California, June 2015

The poor guy in the back seat of the car has been acquiescing to Kelly's Mt. Whitney lectures for the last two hours.

"I think he understands," I say to Kelly as she drives the car through the tunnel.

She obtained a Park Service lottery permit months ago for an upcoming date to hike Mt. Whitney, California's highest peak. It's no easy mountain to ascend—the elevation and distance of the trail need training, acclimating, respect. She wanted me to join her for the Whitney hike, but I need to start heading back east soon. At some point, she met the guy in the back seat, who was willing to train with her.

I can tell she's on edge, so I continue, "I know you're nervous about the hike."

Almost before I finish the sentiment, she shoots me a furrowed look. "No, I'm not," she snaps back.

I change the subject. "Once we get to the trailhead, I'll stuff my backpacking gear into a bear locker while we hike."

"Why not leave it in the car?" the young man asks.

"The black bears here have figured out how to pop trunk lids and break windows to get at whatever they think might be food, including what might be in backpacks. I saw video footage in the ranger station last time I was here."

Kelly flips out. "Now you tell me. I have gum wrappers and all kinds of things floating around inside my car."

"Not a problem. There are three of us, and it won't take long to gather stuff up."

"You're just putting out bad woo-joo. Why are you doing this to me?" She overturns the steering wheel and the car slides towards the outside of the curve. I grab onto the door handle as tightly as I can for safety, while the guy in the back plunges into the back of my seat. I offer her reassurance, but nothing seems to calms her down. She continues to yell at me until I can't stand it anymore.

"I need you to stop now," I say firmly, and turn my attention to the mountain scenery around us. As she swerves around another corner, I grab the handle again, and turn back to look at the young man, whose eyes seem to wonder how he got himself into this. I just shrug.

Once in the parking lot, it makes sense for me to let go of the hike. Instead, I repack my gear and walk over to the right side of the road to hitchhike down to the Valley. The young man waves to me with resignation as he and Kelly start up the trail. The third car I flag down picks me up, guaranteeing that I'll make the last hiker bus out of the valley to Tioga Road and Tuolumne Meadows.

Once in my tent at the Tuolumne backpackers' campground, I feel the tension of the day as I try to write under the light beam of my headlamp, but all I can think about is how I felt like Kelly and I had been forging a new friendship, but now . . .

Human inconsistencies sure do test and re-test my ability to find compassion for someone else's challenges. But I don't allow myself to dwell on it since I feel all questions end up the same for me now: *How do I wish to be in response to my world?*

I attempt to adjust my attitude by trying to put myself in her shoes, whether she feels nervous about the hike or not, then make my choice of response, and walk over to the Tuolumne Store to get some wifi. I send an email to Kelly: "Good luck for a safe and nourishing altitude hike and a clear summit view on Whitney. I'll be thinking of you that day."

I hear nothing back.

BACKCOUNTRY GIRL IN TRAINING

Hail bounces off the windshield of Linda's parked car at the trailhead. She asks if this is still a good idea, and I wonder if she's regretting giving up some tango for this adventure.

Each Sunday while in SLO, I had attended the tango practica at the glitzy Madonna Inn—red and pink flowery fountain sprays illuminated by rosy lights, massive chandeliers with bronze cherubs, and conversations with Linda while waiting for tango partners to offer the elusive *cabaceo* (invitation to dance).

I've wondered, before, if I'm drawn toward a specific place because there is a destined crossing of paths with someone there. I had wondered this very thing about Linda as I returned each Sunday to the Inn. Before I left SLO, she had invited me to lunch to exchange travel stories, ending with her request to meet me in Yosemite for her first backcountry camping overnight.

When people I've met while traveling have asked me what I do for work, I've recounted my career history, but it is the teaching and empowerment of women that I offer up as "the best thing I've done so far." So, of course, I agreed.

"Weather changes," I say, watching more hail bounce on the car hood. "We'll wait it out. We only have the backcountry permit for tonight."

In the meantime, we read the directions for setting up her new tent, directions she didn't take the time to read before she drove out here to pick me up. The hail slows down, the wind calms, and the sun starts filtering through the fast-moving clouds.

At five-thirty, I decide a half mile would be enough for this trial, and we head across the road to start our short trek. The trail start is clear, but then brush and downed trees hide any obvious trodden paths from view. We end up circling around and backtracking before chancing upon a narrow trail leading us down toward the Tuolumne River.

I can tell Linda is nervous, but this is my terrain, and I know all is fine. We have a clear trail now, we're out of sight of the road, and the hillside is covered with tall pine trees. About a half mile in, we scout out a flat area to pitch our tents for the night and make dinner. One doesn't have to hike lots of miles to experience wilderness.

"I never thought I'd ever be doing *this*," she says, returning from within the trees with her small roll of toilet paper and my small orange plastic shovel. She carries a Ziploc bag containing her used toilet paper. A "Leave No Trace" policy expects us to carry our trash back out to civilization, including used TP. Since California is in a drought, campfires aren't allowed without a permit, so no burning of the paper, which is the only other way to dispose of it. One has to let go of the *ick* factor.

We cook away from the tents, then pack all smelly items into my bear canister for the night and stuff it between two tree trunks at the edge of the clearing. As the dark descends on us, a tree branch falls nearby in the forest, most likely due to the winds earlier on, and Linda jumps.

"Is it a bear?" she asks nervously, inching her way towards her tent, as if the thin fabric will withstand bear claws.

"No, I don't think so," I say, trying to remember the first time I camped out in the wilderness. I stayed awake all night listening to each small twig crackling on the ground and each low growly sound of an animal off in the distance. Even now when I go out alone, adrenaline keeps me from sleeping well the first night. I still have to talk myself out of the very fears my mother carries inside of her about me being out here . . . animals, weather, injury, other humans . . . and by the second night, I feel safe and in my element. We all have to start somewhere.

In the morning, back at the car, Linda says, "I don't think I'll ever do this again. But thanks for taking me out to try it."

Just as I expected.

GRAND CANYON OF THE TUOLUMNE

A car pulls into the trailhead parking lot next to us and Jeff gets out. Not only did I get him to drive to Yosemite, I arranged for him to meet up with Linda and me as we came out from the trail. From here, we'll leave his car at the Tuolumne ranger station and catch the free hiker bus to White Wolf Trailhead to start our traverse back toward Tuolumne Meadows. When I was last in Yosemite, Tioga Road and the Meadows were snowed in, so I'm looking forward to being in this section of the national park.

While I wait at the bus stop for Jeff to park his car behind a line of other hiker cars on the side of the road, I hear "It's Gail, isn't it?"

I turn to see a man smiling at me.

"Ed?" I step over to give him a hug.

I always wonder how this can happen. This day. This month. This bus stop. Of all the people coming and going, I run into someone I know.

Jeff walks up to the stop and plunks down his pack.

"This is Ed. We shared campfire time up in the Little Yo camp back in May," I say as I introduce them. I picture Ed popping pain pills as the rest of us at Little Yo learned about the car accident he had been in. Ed gives me a quizzical look, questioning a possible romantic connection with Jeff, and I just grimace so Jeff can't see me. Ed just came off the trail and is catching the

Tuolumne Meadows at the end of the four-day hike, a welcome respite to the emotional tensions.

bus back to the valley. Synchronicities happen more often like this or at least I notice them more.

Once we're dropped off at our trailhead, Jeff and I hike in the sun and heat for only a few hours, since we had a late morning start. Going off trail toward a rock outcropping, we find a clearing to set up our *respective* tents on one of the grassy terraces lined with summer wildflowers that cascade down toward the Hetch Hetchy Reservoir.

The wind swirls through the sparse trees and wildflowers just enough to keep mosquitoes away. As the magenta-frosted clouds pass over us toward the setting sun, Jeff reaches over and touches my arm as a romantic gesture.

A tingling spreads quickly through my body and memories of sharing his bed before I left for Hawaii flood through as well. The yearning in his eyes comforting me, exciting me. The heat of his skin against mine. Pillow talk and laughing, punctuated with passionate kisses giving me hope for new romance and the re-opening of my heart.

Maybe his texts to me every few weeks meant something. Then, there was his invite to return to Santa Cruz before going on to SLO again. Maybe it was a case of being too early arriving the first time there. I know that timing is important—when and how we cross paths with another. Maybe now is the right time and maybe this is the right place to re-open that door . . .

. . . or maybe it's too late.

I pull my arm away from his hand and whisper to him, "I can't go there right now," hoping he'll actually say something about the shutdown in Santa Cruz. "I don't understand what happened for us."

I remind myself that I deserve better than how he treated me. What was I thinking meeting up with him here?

But he doesn't speak. Over the next few days, he hikes about ten minutes ahead of me, stopping only at trail intersections and camping spots for the night. Nothing else is tried or said between us about our time together after my return to California from Hawaii.

On the third evening, as I sit alone watching the sunset, the Tuolumne River flows over large, flat rocks on its way down the canyon, and I wonder why he even came out here to meet up with me for the hike. He must have had his own hope for reconnection, or why bother. By the time we finish our ascent on our last morning, I'm glad he's hiking way ahead of me back to the car. Any hope of resolution disintegrates underfoot as I walk the trail at my own pace.

After he buys me lunch in Merced, avoiding conversation or even looking at me, which confuses me even more, we stand awkwardly in the parking lot outside the restaurant.

"I don't know what to say," he says, looking down at the asphalt beneath our feet, his hands jammed into his hiking shorts pockets. I give him time to figure out some words . . . any words. He pulls his car keys out of one of his pockets and fingers the key to unlock the truck door, then hesitates for a moment.

"I know," is all I can respond as he turns to leave, and I watch him saunter toward his car, never once looking back at me. All I can feel is his pain, but I know there is still nothing I can do for him, so I pick up my packs and walk over to the post office to retrieve the General Delivery box containing the rest of my belongings since I have a bus to catch.

Hostages to Time Uncontrolled

Greyhound Bus
Merced, California, to Denver, Colorado

Three-quarters of us are smokers and we crave the tension relief of that familiar drag. The other portion of us separates from the smokers and finds solidarity in small groups. Together, we try to let go of control and find our way to accepting all of the scheduling delays.

Our bus driver stops every couple of hours to allow us—hostages to time uncontrolled—breaks. We leave the bus to stretch our cramped legs, find a gentler bathroom experience than the bus restroom, and nourish ourselves with food and drink as best as we can.

We will miss connections, we will overnight at the bus station, we will lose even more sleep. A couple of us hold tight to any control possible through blame. "Five hours late? That woman back in Salt Lake will pay for this. I'm going to make sure she loses her job," says one woman who will continue on to St. Louis.

A young man who lost his ticket back in Salt Lake, but who found the itinerary with his name on it, allowing him to board the bus, remarks, "This bus company screws everyone over. This is not the first time for me, I've taken this route before. This driver doesn't know where the hell the stops are. We'll never get to Denver."

I watch, in witness, the quirks, emotions, and dramas that we all embody under stress. For me, I'm exhausted due to lack of sleep. My thirty-two-hour train/bus/bus/layover/bus trip slowly turns into a two-day nightmare of train/bus/bus/layover/bus/unscheduled-layover-waiting-for-a-driver/bus/change-of-driver/overnight-in-the-station/bus/bus.

I eventually stop struggling, stop counting. By midnight, I hope we will be in Denver and I will sleep on the floor as best I can. Others might make their connections, most of us won't.

I observe us, though, with fascination. Some of us, like me, let go. Some of us can't and continue to blame and complain. Some of us wear down and smoke yet another cigarette at each break. Some of us are preoccupied with other dramas.

The young woman wearing the black-and-white checked coat, for instance, mumbles something about having a fever while disembarking the bus. She keeps to herself on the sidelines, her black framed glasses shielding her eyes from the rest of us. Long, black, curly hair cascades out from under a wool hat and down her back as she shuffles off the bus and into whatever market is at the parking lot.

The man sitting behind me is negotiating a marriage separation. Phone calls get more frequent as the hours add up. He leaves messages for his wife, pleads for a different outcome, sugar coats his words. By phone, he pats the backs of friends for being there for him. He paces the parking lots and puffs cigarettes as if the very act of sucking in the smoke will change the course of his divorce.

The two teenage boys document everything as the driver winds the bus around bends in the road, where hills, cows, and uninhabited expanses ooze out to undercut the horizon. As the road leads us around highway curves, the boys make phone calls in response to the topography. "Hey . . . we've just passed a sign for the town of Dinosaur, so we're definitely in Colorado now. Yeah, we'll keep ya posted." A half hour later, they call with an update.

I stand outside on another break and chat with a woman who drives vehicles across the country. From Macon, Georgia, she drives to a destination and then takes Greyhound to a different city to pick up another vehicle. "Small Dawg Travel doesn't have the greatest track record. I take 'em all the time, and do I ever have stories," she tells me as we huddle next to the bus, the sun starting to set over Steamboat Springs as we wait for our new driver to arrive.

"I'm accumulating some myself," I say.

We change drivers in Steamboat Springs. Our recent fill-in driver settles into the front row of seats behind the new driver. We're confused about the change of driver and we wonder if drivers are allowed to drive only so many hours in a row. The last one has been with us now for eleven. Number two driver is fresh and knows these roads, even after the sun has settled itself behind the horizon.

Some of us hold on tight through the darkness while the bus leans around shadowy shapes on either side of the road. Some of us are able to sleep, sending out beacons of deep breathing and snorts. We pull into the Denver Greyhound station near midnight.

My ticket destination is across the city center at the Amtrak/Union Station, but the driver is in no mood to keep driving and makes it clear that this bus station is the end of the line for all of us.

Needing to start my trajectory back east, I stop in the town of Conifer outside of Denver, Colorado, to visit a man I met on the Big Island in Hawaii and who offered me housing if in the area. Here I am taking a break along a hike into the Chicago Lakes region of the Rocky Mountains.

Chapter 26

TEA, Anyone?

Denver, Colorado • June 2015

If you are lucky enough to be in the mountains, then you are lucky enough, states the carved sign on the wall above my sleeping couch in Conifer, a small town outside of Denver. Actually, I'll feel luckier engaged in some deep sleep after the last few days and the bus saga of getting to Denver from California. Having had too short a cat nap on the terminal floor during the wee hours of this morning, I would have thought I would fall asleep quickly tonight. Instead, I lie awake, staring up at the wooden sign, preoccupied with thoughts of my March visit to Hawaii.

While recovering from fever, not to mention the dregs of the poison oak, blisters, and arm slice, at a hostel in Kona on the Big Island, torrents of spring rain, the very rain I thought I had escaped from in Hilo, took an early evening pause. Stuck in the hostel all afternoon, travelers hunkered in with books while others watched the skies for freedom. Once the downpours started to peter out, Ron and I fled the hostel with umbrellas toward the nearest beach. Ron had come to the island for a relative's wedding, opting for cheap lodging at the youth hostel.

Sitting upon a sea wall that buffered the Pacific waves, he and I philosophically swam down the rabbit hole of metaphysics and quantum theories around the concept of infinity. Maybe it was the act of debate between Ron and me or maybe it was infinity itself placing crumbs of endless possibilities in front of me at that point in my travels, but the next morning as I checked out of the hostel, the front desk attendee handed me a note: "Sorry to miss you. If you come through Colorado, you're welcome to stay for as long as you'd like," with Ron's email address scribbled below the message. I had stuffed the note in my pack for future options.

At that time, I hadn't yet decided which route I would take east back

215

across the country once ready to move in that direction. So much depended on whether I would be going back to Santa Cruz. Look how that turned out.

Greyhound and Amtrak routes follow three east/west trajectories—one along the northern route through Montana, the Dakotas, and Minnesota; one along the south through Texas and Louisiana; and one slicing the United States in two halves horizontally through the grasslands of the Midwest. Once I decided to stop in Oklahoma en route, I emailed Ron about a possible visit in Colorado while I traversed the middle of the country. As my memories of Hawaii start to fade, sleep is what I decide to put my attention to, and I finally drift off into dreamland.

WHO AM I IF I AM NOT ALWAYS WHO I AM?

Hills frame the state highway that flows southwest out of Denver, "ever-green" with cool air wrapping itself around quaking aspens and lavender columbine, the state flower of Colorado. Mt. Evans raises its capped peak into the cloudy sky along Squaw Pass Road near Echo Lake, and the cascading series of Chicago Lakes peer down the valley between the lilting stems of yellow-petaled balsam root.

I drop my daypack on the grass, and sit down for a rest while Ron explores the upper Chicago Lake edge. I inhale as much oxygen as I can breathe in to offset the thinner altitude pushing on my lungs, and contemplate who I am becoming. Last night's weekly discussion with Ron's metaphysically thinking friends sparked an exploration into the evolution of a more humane world by some tipping point that brings us all together in sustainable connectedness. I love the archeological digging into human nature—I basked in my element. Of course, the momentum of our daily lives drags us back down into the ruts of the familiar and expected. At this point in my travels, I had hoped that my own ruts would have filled themselves in completely, with lots of new patterns emerging, and staying *fluid* while I dance with what comes at me—another Bruce-ism, as I've come to think about his travel wisdom.

But, every time I say something like, *"This is just who I am,"* the rut gets harder to climb out of. Here I am back at the beginning of my circle of questions about old patterns, ruts, and feeling stuck. Is it that I'm not willing to budge? Or budge enough? Back home, I succumb to the path of least resistance—efficient and familiar routines needed for navigating the everyday life of work schedules, finances, dances. Even though I still have certain routines as I travel—like public transportation schedules, places to stay, things to do—things feels different. I know I can make endless choices while traveling, sometimes on a whim, and I can change my mind more easily, leave a place earlier than originally planned, and walk away from drama. Something *is* indeed shifting in me. Who I am, I know, is anything I put my attention to and wish to be—infinite possibilities, really —isn't that the point of living a full life?

I ponder more about infinity as I watch Ron walk around the far side of the uppermost small lake and wonder about the synchronicity of our crossed paths over in Hawaii. Perhaps even that I needed to be here in Colorado for some reason. It was just one of the infinite number of paths that would lead me to be thinking about ruts, actively choosing to be out of my element, and inviting more of Bruce's take on life's mysteries and miracles.

Eventually Ron strolls through the balsam root to join me on the slope overlooking the other Chicago Lakes.

"It's all about TEA," he says as he plops down next to me.

"TEA?" I ask.

"Time . . . Effort . . . Attention."

"Hmmm," I mumble.

"It's what we choose to put our energy into and what we get out of it because of those efforts," he says.

"Isn't that what we all do, all the time? Choose where to put our TEA?" I lay down to photograph the yellow flower heads close up against the background of peaks lining the valley.

"Well," he continues, "like today's hike. We've taken advantage of a beautiful day before the rain comes. But, more and more, I'm not willing to give energy to those things, or people, or experiences that don't feed me the way I want them to."

"But how do you know if you don't give them, whatever they are, a chance to evolve?"

"Thinking about something too much ahead of time is just not worth my TEA," he says, digging into his own solidly formed ruts.

I just nod, but I don't really agree as I rethink the recent dishwasher incident at his house. Almost as soon as I arrived there, one of his housemates took me aside and told me to wash my dishes by hand, rather than put them in the dishwasher. Since that made no sense to me, I put a cereal bowl and spoon in the appliance. Later on, upon opening it, Ron flipped out. I had put the bowl in the wrong section of the tray. *What does it matter?* I wondered. *The items will still get washed.*

Perhaps my synchronistic intersection with Ron in Kona gave me the opportunity to remember just how many choices I do have to reinvent myself—or to let my experiences blossom into being worthy of *my* TEA. It's just too easy to dismiss something or someone due to unrealistic projections, or the desire to control every little thing. I think relationships are more important than the control—and that is something totally worth my *TEA*.

IDENTITY CRISIS

Cornered beneath the dart board, a red drum kit reflects off the back window. Behind the glass, a waterfall trickle descends over the rocky hill leaning onto the backside of the Sit-N-Bull Saloon in Indian Hills, near the town of Evergreen.

Graffiti-carved ceiling joists hang low over the crowded stage filled with guitars and microphones. Country rock vibrates through the bar where Joan, one of Ron's friends, wishes to expose me to local culture, and I shimmy between crowded tables to free-form dance. The Trubelos are Joan's personal friends and her favorite local band.

The singer's words, about first hearing the call of the highway, spill from the mic. Unknown to the band, I feel like they are playing my song already. Then the guitarist leans into his mic and croons about belonging somewhere else along the road, and I remember when I first felt the urge to leave home. By the age of four, I was trying to pack up and get out of my family already. My parental units were not worthy of my childhood TEA. Resigned, due to a lack of money, flashlight, and a plan, I had no choice but to pull my brown paper bag back into the house and suck up, oh . . . another fourteen years or so. Other times, I just daydreamed about leaving.

Bar stools jostle against the side wall where listeners dangle cigarette ash into bottle caps and bandanas wrap the heads of blue-jeaned and leather-vested drinkers. Tattoos bleed down bare arms and across the shoulders of those having a special relationship with the "road" as they search for their own version of living *true*. This is something we have in common.

Joan shoots me a grin and her hips wiggle to a guitar lick punctuating lyrics about searching out new zip codes, and walking a straight line. That pretty much says it all—mostly, I feel like I've been walking a pretty damn straight line through my whole life, even with some job shifts and regional location changes for love relationships. I've been cautious, over-achieving, always trying to do the right thing by everyone else's opinions. I flail my arms around in the air, but feel foolish with my stiff dance movements. Joan and I are the only ones dancing, and I pull my arms back down to try to blend into the surroundings without drawing even more attention to myself. As I pulse to the beat, a cigar is lit nearby, and I suck in my breath, trying to get my mind off the smell by returning to my thoughts about the lyrics.

No one believed I would take the risk, rent out my house, and leave like I did last September . . . or that I would still be out here zig-zagging around the country. Looking over at Joan, I start to gag from the cigar smoke and motion to her that I need to get out of the thick of it.

"It's considered an open-air establishment, so they can smoke inside," Joan screams at me as we maneuver through the crowd and increasing band volume to the front deck. The day's heat falls flat around the saloon, and as we writhe between two picnic tables to create our own slight breeze, more rings of smoke encircle us from those also in search of cooler air.

The chorus comes back around in the song, and I sing along under my breath—something about feeling like I'm running out of time. Yes, I think, life keeps getting shorter, and I wonder if I'm just in some middle-age crisis. I shoot Joan another desperate glance and head for the stairs down to the dirt parking lot.

And so it is we perform our line dance with the chrome- and leather-adorned Harleys strung like Christmas lights along the front of the saloon. "Right," I scream to Joan. "This is a biker bar. Ya know . . . I'm not . . . really . . . a biker bar kinda girl."

Groups start to gather around the bikes too, cigarettes dangling from fingers and mouths, conversations increasing in volume and now drowning out the band.

"It's smokier than usual," Joan bemoans as she pulls me out of line with the motorcycles. "Let's get outta here." Well, I certainly know who I am *not*.

NO HUSBAND, AGAIN?

I leave Conifer and move over to Littleton to stay with Joan. After our biker-bar-bonding experience, and enough TEA for now at Ron's, her place allows me some girl time and easy bus access to downtown Denver.

Littleton into Denver takes one and a half hours by two public buses. I accept these terms in order to arrive at the Denver Turnverein in time for the Tuesday night Argentine Tango practica. Built in 1921, the previously named Coronado Club, velour-draped and crystal-chandeliered, had been a glorified gymnasium. Gilt-framed photos of women swinging Indian clubs or thwacking volleyballs cover the foyer walls. By 2008, broken chandeliers had been fixed to illuminate the nightly cultural dances blocked into the hall's schedule.

Mike, my first dance partner, once done dancing me around the ballroom, pimps my evening for me. As soon I sit down to rest, another man's eye catches mine with the customary *cabeceo*. One man after another saying, "I hear you're from Vermont?"

But, in true Cinderella form, the clock strikes for me to leave early to catch my pumpkin coach (well, city bus) for the long ride via three buses back to Littleton before the routes end for the night.

Heels shift to walking shoes, and I nudge my way through the late night crowd waiting to enter an event at the Fillmore next door on Colfax St. I find my #15 bus stop and plop down on the bench to wait. Streetlights cast shadows onto establishments lining the street still open for business, and I ignore the two bars just behind and up the block from the bus stop bench.

"So, when did he leave?"

I turn my head to the right to see a man slowly sit on the other end of my bench, his dark skin glowing from the streetlight above, as he places a coffee cup on the ground next to the bench and takes a drag on his cigarette.

I'm the only other person on the bench, so I ask "When did who leave?"

"Your husband," he clarifies.

There would have been a time when I would have just ignored a question like that, but I feel relatively safe on this busy street, so I banter back, "No husband. Never had one."

"Are you gay?" he then asks.

"No. Just never interested in getting married." Then, I jab back, "Where's your wife?"

"Right here on the bench," he says as he looks me up and down, and I give him a look that says, "In your dreams, buddy . . ."

"Ya know you're cute, and that's why ya don't have a husband."

I just shrug and give him another look. "I'm leaving town soon. No kind of wife you want."

"Well, we can have fun rockin' and rollin' until you leave," he says as his eyes undress me right there under the streetlights. I hold back laughter at this ridiculous exchange and turn to the left to see if the #15 is coming up Colfax yet.

"I'm too old for you," I smile at him. "I'm actually eighty-two."

He swigs another sip from his coffee cup now back in his hand, looks me straight on. "Damn, you look good for your age." I give him another dismissive look.

I hear the bus coming up the block, stand up, smile, and shrug when the bus slows to a stop and the door opens. I climb on, drop in my fare, and shoot him one last glance.

Maybe it was all that sexy tango energy following me back to Joan's from the Turnverein. Cinderella and the glass shoe with the prince and all that. Maybe I'm letting another hidden facet shine through—I mean, who am I if I'm exuding sexuality?

Ha, I think I always have. So who am I just being the same as usual? Obviously, damn cute! At least to the guy on the bench. Regardless, at fifty-eight, it sure feels great to have a man come on to me, even though he never stood a chance at "rock 'n' rolling with me until l leave town."

I settle into the mostly empty bus with my transfer in hand. Now only about an hour and a half to go before my ball gown turns to rags.

Golden Haze on the Meadow

Greyhound Bus
Denver, Colorado, to Bartlesville, Oklahoma

Albeit only in my thoughts, I keep breaking into show tunes—"Surrey with the Fringe on Top," "Oh, What a Beautiful Morning," "Oklahoma" —the tunes that live forever in the 1960s psyche of one who grew up watching musicals, and then later on, in pit orchestras, playing them. I can't help it.

As the Greyhound bus moves along Highway 40 toward Oklahoma City, the outstretched landscape shifts between green grass surrounding sporadic small trees and bushes and expansive farm fields with brown dirt. Without mountains edging the cloud-puffed blue sky, I scan the horizon for other kinds of natural beauty—perhaps a *bright golden haze on the meadow,* or *corn as high as an elephant's eye.* Neither enter my view.

Since the bus wifi is actually working, I search for the highest elevation point in Oklahoma: Black Mesa summit, elevation 4,973 feet, is in the westernmost corner of the panhandle, and surprisingly towers over the Sooner State. While napping, I had totally missed it as we drove out of Colorado and through the Oklahoma panhandle. I stuff my iPad back into my bag on the floor by my feet, and consider my obsession with mountains.

Sometime during my early adult years, I climbed my first peak—it was a college date that I originally thought was lame. I grew up in suburbia, and a date meant a movie, or if my date could afford it, dinner and a movie. *But climb a mountain?*

From that date summit of Mt. Chocorua in New Hampshire, after begrudgingly pulling myself up the trail, my whole perspective changed. I stood in awe of the panoramic view of granite-laced mountain ridges and low, lush valleys. I felt small and inconsequential. Yet, simultaneously, I felt part of something larger than myself—an unforgiving, primal environment. I had never felt so alive.

Through the bus window, I watch the vast expanse of grassy prairie flow by. My mountain memory is soon interrupted by the frustrated young Oklahoman sitting next to me and rambling on about the state. According to him, the main economy of the state is its prisons. I take this with a grain of wheat, or maybe hemp. He is just returning from the big city of Denver, with its legalized marijuana, into the conservative mindset that supports the arrest of anyone in possession of a single joint.

He mumbles under his breath, "I hate it here in Oklahoma."

"Why are you coming back?" I ask.

"I'm homesick."

From his many phone conversations to arrange rides, since the bus is, of course, late, I know that he has a sweetie in the home state. Hard to shake those hometown roots, I guess. He dials his phone yet again, so I scan back to other times in my life, and land in Deming, New Mexico. I had flown, years ago, to visit my Vermont friend Laurie, who wintered there. Over dinner one evening with Laurie and a local Deming friend of hers, the local woman suggested I find a more interesting place to visit next time I go somewhere. Later, in private, I said to Laurie, "But doesn't every place have its story, its history, and its people? I would think that one just needs to stay open."

On that trip, I learned the story of Pancho Villa at a museum near the border with Mexico. My friend's neighbor took me into the Chihuahuan Desert to see my first petroglyphs. He also taught me to carry a stick to flush out rattlesnakes—continually striking the ground ahead of me as I walked to alert them I was nearby. There was plenty to explore and encounter.

And so, celebrating lessons learned in Deming, I remind myself to stay open to new experiences here in Oklahoma. From the bus window, I can see that the grasses continue all the way to the horizon—nothing like New England, which is thick with trees and underbrush. I suppose there could be a different kind of beauty out there in all that openness—if I look for it.

Off the phone, my bus neighbor tells me that he looked for a possible job while in Denver, and I suppose, if he had found one, he would have loaded up that surrey, fringe or not, and scooped up his beloved for the trek to higher mountains. A change of scenery, maybe perspective.

Does one always need a high summit, or can any panorama shift one's perspective? As I ponder the question, I take another look out the window at a large expanse of half-grown corn stalks. I smile to myself, wondering how high they would need to be to reach the height of an elephant's eye. Besides, when else, where else, could I nostalgically sing fun old show tunes in the actual state that inspired them?

Don't need a mountain for all that!

In Bartlesville, Oklahoma, to see another couchsurfing friend, I stand in front of Price Tower, one of Frank Lloyd Wright's designs built during the rise of oil in the area.

Chapter 27

Oklahoma Prairie Gathering

Bartlesville, Oklahoma • July 2015

After my arrival on July 4th at Cindy's mom's house where we are all staying, we do our part for patriotism—eat homemade blueberry-rhubarb pie with vanilla ice cream. After all, it's important to remember my American heritage through the celebration of real American desserts. I reach for a second slice.

"It's great to see you again," Cindy says. "I can't believe it was last September." Having grown up here in Oklahoma, she has that farm-girl physique—girthy and strong. She passes me the pie plate for easier second-helping access.

While I was traveling through Georgia early in the trip, I met up with Cindy not that far from where my brother and his family live. Cindy was wrapping up her father's estate after he passed away a couple of years earlier. She came back to Bartlesville to help her mother convalesce after a surgery and plans to stay.

We first met when she couchsurfed with me in Vermont while attending a week-long painting workshop up the road from my house. A couchsurfing veteran, she helped me find housing when I went to New Orleans and again in Austin. She knows a lot of people, everywhere.

With bellies full of pie and with canvas chairs from the garage hanging from our arms, Cindy and I eventually stroll through the neighborhood towards downtown Bartlesville to the Freedom Festival at Sooner Park.

Cutting our arrival close to dusk, we stake out our sitting turf, then wander about the festivities honoring veterans and active servicemen and women. Overspray from the dousing of bathing-suited children by the fire department cools us down as we stroll the main street of vendors en route to the bandstand. An army rock band's electrified guitar licks penetrate the crowd gathering around the stage. Although the band spokesperson announces that the band plays country tunes as well, all of their songs sound the same, clearly rooted in a screaming rock and roll rut.

225

Fourth of July is our very own American holiday, and I would imagine, from up high above the planet, one would see fireworks flare, sparkle, burst, sizzle, pop, and dazzle. Like the "wave" in a ball game's bleachers, these pageants would slowly move across the country, from east to west, as time zone boundaries silently fall away. Since we have come for the fireworks, we return to our seats for the pomp and pageant of sky-filled pizazz.

OIL: THAR SHE BLOWS

I acknowledge my hypocrisy—my New England liberal attitude about greedy oil companies raping the planet of core elements, like crude oil. And yet, until an electric pick-up truck with four-wheel-drive is available, or solar-powered, or wind-run with huge sails, or even pulled by a harnessed group of strong and fast-running squirrels, I have no choice but to keep stuffing my truck with gasoline and oil. I'd be more excited to learn about alternative energy resources in Oklahoma history, but that isn't the history that happened here. I try to channel another Bruce-ism about expecting nothing and staying open to life's surprises.

Instead, I delve into Bartlesville's pioneering story where folks' paths had crossed over to the west side of the Mississippi waters to search out a more adventurous life for those with a wandering drive.

Most passed through these prairies, heading to farther points west, but not New York–born Nelson Carr, who migrated west in 1859, stopping in Oklahoma to marry a quarter-blood Cherokee woman, and establishing a small trading post along the Osage Indian trail to the northwest of Bartlesville. Unbeknownst to anyone at the time, while Jacob Bartles was buying a corn grist mill on a narrow neck of Carr's land, both men would soon become rich.

As Cindy and I stroll through Bartlesville's Johnstone Park, the region's oil history comes alive around us.

"Ah, but lurking across the river from Bartles' mill, that new oil rig, called the Nellie Johnstone No. 1, was bubbling towards a future of fuel wars," I say out loud as Cindy reads the kiosk text over my shoulder. A large wooden reproduction of the oil rig looms above us, and casts shadows across the kiosk.

She picks up from where I left off. "The first commercial oil well in Oklahoma blew in during March, 1897. Hmm, I've forgotten some of these facts that I had to learn in school," she says.

"How could Carr and Bartles have known what oil would do to this town?" I ask. "Or this country? This world? This planet?"

She just nods—she grew up here, and oil is in her history. When the oil boom struck, Carr developed over one hundred producing wells on his family's farm. The city, by 1907, was a forest of derricks. I study an old black and white photo of the derricks as we continue to forge our way through the oil chronicles that changed Oklahoman grazing lands forever.

Then, we have Frank Phillips, who arrived in Bartlesville around the same time all those derricks were taking over the landscape. He and his brother opened a variety of banks and oil companies, and within a decade, the brothers had founded the Phillips Petroleum Company, which eventually dominated the whole town. Frank also bought up an additional 3,700 acres that he named Woolaroc. About fifteen miles out of downtown Bartlesville, Woolaroc became his personal wildlife preserve and country ranch.

"Phillips brought in all kinds of exotic and native animals and birds here to Woolaroc," Cindy tells me as we get out of the car at the Reserve. "As a kid, we'd come here often on family outings."

As we walk from the parking lot toward the Woolaroc Museum, horned goats rest high up on engineered rock outcroppings, paying no attention to us down below. I suppose this was an early version of a theme park and I feel sorry for the exotic animals brought in. At least they ran wild, rather than being housed in zoo cages. I scan the grounds around the museum, expecting to see zebras or rhinos, but all is quiet out there.

The ranch and lodge were used as a place for Frank to close business deals, reciprocate the hospitality of wealthy East Coast investors, share his friendship with local Native American tribal leaders, and rub elbows with local outlaws, bank bandits, and train robbers.

One whole museum room is dedicated to his annual gathering called "The Cow Thieves and Outlaws Reunion." I learn that Frank would leave instructions at the gate, like: "Welcome in any American Legion boys in uniform, any cowboy on horseback, and any full-blooded Indian in costume."

Reunion ground rules were simple: All guns, knives, and grudges had to be checked at the gate. After the festivities, the lawmen had to give the outlaws time to nurse their hangovers and get a twenty-four-hour head start. The gathering ensured that Phillips' lands and cattle would be left alone. The strategy worked. *Now, we're talking about something interesting!*

I like his self-preservation savvy—throw a party once a year, so no one tries to destroy you. I'll have to remember this tactic for the future, or, at least, until Disney buys up Woolaroc to make it into a *proper* theme park.

In the next room, we learn that in 1927, aviation history was made with a race to Honolulu—thanks to a revolutionary new petroleum product: Phillips Nu-Aviation Gasoline.

Eight airplanes had prepared for takeoff before a crowd of more than 50,000 at the Oakland Airport in California. Arthur Goebel Jr., a veteran barnstormer—one of those fly-over-your-home-for-a-few-dollars pilots who flew in and out of farm fields at that time—and Hollywood stunt pilot, joined seven other aircraft in the race just three months after Lindbergh's historic flight. The young pilot found a sponsor and friend in Frank Phillips and his Travelair won first place flying to Hawaii with Phillips 77 aviation fuel.

The plane, of course named *Woolaroc*, arrived after 27 hours, 17 minutes, and 33 seconds in flight. The only other finisher, a monoplane named Aloha, landed just over two hours later—with only four gallons of fuel remaining in its tanks. I ask Cindy what happened to the other six planes, but she doesn't remember. We read placard after placard in the Travelair room to look for the answer, but find nothing about survivors from those planes not finishing the flight.

Bright orange wings span the museum ceiling with large black letters spelling NX 8 on their undersides. Like butterfly appendages, the span dwarfs the small blue plane body that propelled Goebel across the Pacific to his Hawaiian victory. I'm amazed by those who dismiss danger like this, choosing to face the possibility of death with this kind of attempt. Those who failed the flight were forgotten; they deserve better than this. At least, they should have placards with their names here in a museum.

"Bartlesville was quite the happening place," I say to Cindy as we head towards the museum exit, surprised by all the history.

ESCAPING THE FOREST

"We're on a mission to visit every Frank Lloyd Wright building open to the public," a couple from England tells us in the Price Tower elevator. The woman shows me her checklist with buildings checked off and notes scribbled in the margins. "This building has a museum, a bar/café, and a library for architecture students. We're actually staying in one of the rentable rooms."

Though the rooms weren't designed by Wright, there can be little doubt when you step into one that they were done with his design aesthetic in mind: clean lines, sharp angles, and plenty of natural light.

"Who knew Bartlesville was an architecture destination?" I whisper to Cindy as she peeks out the room window to see if she can see her mom's house from here. Then, we squeeze into the tiny elevator to go up to the fifteenth-floor café, with its lofty view of greater Bartlesville, to buy a cup of tea.

Nicknamed "the tree that escaped the crowded forest," the Price Tower is supported by a central "trunk" of four elevator shafts, which are anchored in place by a deep central foundation, as a tree is by its taproot. The floors of the building are cantilevered from this central core, like the branches of a tree. Paintings of large green olives adorn the wall behind the bar. We park ourselves with our cups of tea at a small round table nested underneath a large Art Deco copper chandelier.

"Pretty cool, huh?" Cindy says.

"Honestly, I didn't think there would be much to see in Bartlesville. I was coming just to see you. There's certainly lots of history, and this is the first Frank Lloyd Wright building I've visited in person." As a woodworker and designer, I've always loved Wright's house designs. Now, I want to get a checklist of my own to see where his other structures are located.

Over tea, Cindy and I read more info from the brochure—how the design was meant for construction in New York City in the 1930s, and how H. C. Price asked Wright for two stories for his corporate headquarters, but, when it was finally built in 1956, got nineteen instead.

Seemingly out of place, the tower looms tall over the flattened prairie and the winding Caney River flowing through the city. I gaze out the nearby window to the west and look for thick forested landscapes among the suburban neighborhoods and beyond onto the grazing fields. But, in true competitive fashion, in 1963, the Phillips family went higher up, adding an additional hundred feet to *its* nineteen floors. One view shows several higher buildings that dwarf Price Tower, now ranking fourth in height in Bartlesville.

Yet, I'm still looking for some kind of golden haze out on a meadow. Down on the ground in front of the tower is a huge, orange Phillips 66 gas station sign sculpture, easily seen from the window. No haze anywhere.

"No thick forests here for a tree to escape from," I say to Cindy. She just laughs, knowing that clusters of oil derricks have been the closest thing to a forest in her native Oklahoma.

Bus Wisdom

Greyhound Bus Terminal • Tulsa, Oklahoma

A tattered, brown suitcase mysteriously appears in front of the glass door we will walk through to board the bus. Not that I've been staring at the door continually from my seat, but I didn't see anyone place it there.

I glance at the clock on the wall to check the time. When I look back at the door, a large red backpack roosts next to the first piece of luggage.

Tulsa's terminal is worn and weathered and hot. The air conditioning isn't working. I pull a bandana out of my bag to wipe away the sweat dripping from my temples.

I watch an older woman sitting across the aisle stuff her fleece blanket into her travel bag. If the AC is working on our bus, she'll need the blanket, then it'll feel like we're in a freezer. She catches me watching her and nods to the growing line of luggage by the door.

"Better get your stuff over there," she says in a low, husky voice.

She cradles a pillow in her folded arms, so I know she's giving me a gift of her experience. I nod back at her as I plop my belongings down in line, adjust my sundress, and return to my seat to wait the remaining time until the bus shows up.

It could be on time, but most likely not. Over the past ten months, I've learned to let go of rigid agendas. I've invited conversations with strangers both in terminals and on the buses themselves. I've gotten efficient at bookings and getting seats. I learned to trust that everything will come out okay in the end.

Periodically, I look to see how far the baggage line extends. She's good. I can see my large backpack near the front of the expanding piles.

With about fifteen minutes to go before our scheduled departure, I go sit on my pack and pull out my ticket just as the bus pulls into the bay. *What? It's actually on time?*

The first few passengers, including me, move through the open door as the driver scribbles check marks onto his clipboard. I hand him my ticket and ID, then deposit my large pack next to the open cargo doors under the bus seats. Getting onto the bus quickly allows me to choose a free seat among those folks already on the bus.

I slip into a window seat, charging cord already in hand, and check the charging outlet, which isn't working. I scoot across the aisle to another window seat to try the outlet there. I've learned that one whole side of the bus is usually on a single circuit and the other side is on a different circuit. I find an outlet that actually works before more people get on and plug in my device.

One young woman in front of me is snuggled across two seats, breathing low in a sleepy daze, fleece blanket half draped over her body. I try to look friendly and inviting as the remaining passengers board. Once all of the passengers are on and seated and the bus begins to move, the sleepy woman in front of me pops right up and starts scrolling over her phone.

Since no one sits next to me, I spread out over my own two seats. In isolation, I open my device and write as we power south toward Louisiana. Last November, my new Cajun friend Doug made it clear: "Do not come to Louisiana after May. Too hot and humid."

The bus AC dries the salt coating my skin and I wonder how much worse the humidity could possibly be in Lafayette compared to Oklahoma these last couple of days. As I pull out a long-sleeved shirt from my travel bag, I also wonder why I haven't picked up a small fleece blanket of my own.

Since I didn't get enough of zydeco dancing while I was in Louisiana, I return for another round of partying, and enjoy the beaded necklace remnants of past Mardi Gras' lingering in trees and on fences around downtown Lafayette.

Chapter 28
Pockets of Lafayette

Lafayette, Louisiana • July 2015

Doug was right.

Returning to the heartland, the heartbeat, my love affair with Cajun music and dance forms, I wonder who, in their right mind, would come here in July? A suffocating wall of Louisiana humidity hits me as soon as I descend the bus stairs at the station, where I find Doug waiting in the air-conditioned terminal building. After we toss my packs into his pick up truck, he transports me to the Blue Moon, one of those places that nostalgically wraps itself around my whole being.

My "Miss Gail" memories flush up to the surface as I check in, pay my key deposit, and receive hugs from staff and old friends. The Blue Moon only offered plug-in fans last fall when I first came for the dance scene at Festivals Acadiens et Creoles. But now, in this baking summer heat, the Moon envelops me in a cooler air-conditioned pocket for lounging and sleeping comfort. As I change out of my drenched clothes before the evening show, I get ready to wear as little as possible in this bayou-baked heat. Lafayette is filled with pockets of cool comfort to balance the baking—except the stage at the Blue Moon, that open air sardine can/dance floor.

Moving once again to Zydeco rhythms, I wipe away the salt flowing from my contact-lensed eyes, and my glisten turns to a dripped, dipped, dunked salt bath. Embraced in partners' sweaty arms, I dance away my sleep deprivation from the bus ride until I can't dance any more. My body swoons and my legs sway to the energy of the live music on stage at the Blue Moon while young dancers flock to hear up-and-coming Lafayette-based jam band Zydeco Radio. Pulling influences from a variety of genres for a Zydeco fusion mix, the band leader, Billy McDonald, rocks it out with his duet of vocals and accordion riffs featuring the hits of Beau Jocque, Boozoo Chavis and other Zydeco greats.

Packed tight, the dancers pull into small territorial floor spaces while others hold the perimeter back, beer bottles and cups jostling to the bass and beat under the large green Henderson Swamp sign tacked up on the wall next to the stage.

SUNDAY HARD-CORE DANCE MARATHON

Opened in 1990 as a Folklife Heritage Center, Vermillionville not only exhibits Acadien history, but hosts, in their Performance Center, a weekly Sunday afternoon dance series. Today is award-winning Kevin Naquin and the Ossun Playboys. Up on the old wooden stage, Kevin's accordion blasts out a Cajun groove, bellows squeezing out the celebration of Cajun breath, while his fingers punctuate the instrument's buttons, conjunct with the song's French syllables. Dancers two-step clockwise around the dance floor, turning again and again into the flow of traffic. Large corner barn doors are slid open to offset the rising temperatures within the hall, and some of the dancers flee to the outside and the breeze coming off the Bayou Teche river running through the historic property. Doug grew up on the bayou and these are his people. He introduces me to those who come to shake his hand, and I obtain ongoing dance partners, as well as bump into other lingering festival goers from across the country.

I decline rides to Whiskey River Landing in Henderson, where Geno Delafose and his band, French Rockin' Boogie are due to play later this afternoon. I first heard Geno and his band play back in early 1990s at a festival in Rhode Island. While volunteering on the parking crew to offset the festival costs, I still had time to take in the shows and attend Cajun two-step and swing lessons.

Since I'm hungry, I decide to grab a shrimp po'boy sandwich downtown at Old Tyme Grocery instead and prove myself less hardy for the heat and beat in Henderson. Old Tyme Grocery positions me close to the Feed and Seed Dance Hall where I've made plans to rendezvous with folks later, after I have refueled for the evening dances.

The Feed and Seed dance hall on the other side of train the tracks is where some of the hard-core Sunday dancers mix with those who come to dance to the local Western Swing band, Stop the Clock. This country-swinging gathering clears my Cajun palette as I gladly shift my groove to a six-count move with boot-sliding, Texas two-stepping partners, although other dancers settle into swing or Zydeco.

Without air conditioning, the hall fans work double-time to cool down that bayou heat and keep rhythm with the fast-swinging cowboy tunes. The swollen floorboards underfoot vibrate to the triple fiddle's harmonies riding over the twang of the pedal steel guitar in this old agricultural retail building-turned-dance-hall just a couple of blocks from downtown Lafayette.

But times have changed around the downtown grid. The woman taking money at the door tells me, "Please don't walk across the tracks. It's not safe now that it's dark."

Aware of my vulnerability, I solicit a ride to the Moon for the later show, and learn about the drug deals that go down within those two blocks before arriving at the safer part of Jefferson Street.

Unlike Friday night's Zydeco Radio blast at the Moon, Sunday evening's dual CD release party embraces an intimate group who has room to work the whole dance floor. Lisa Trahan of L'Esprit Cadien sings out her heritage in Acadien French. Doug and I are often the only ones dancing.

Neon beer brand signs slice a rainbow of colors onto those dancing on the crammed wood floor, while a few non-dancers bounce along to the beat while sitting along the worn bench traversing the length of the entrance ramp. The bright yellow sticker I stuck onto the Henderson Swamp sign next to the stage last fall sits among other new stickers crowding a plethora of bullet holes.

The crowd doubles in size for Nashville-based band Runner of the Woods, a new incarnation of the Doc Marshalls band out of New York City. Nick Beaudoing, the band's leader, explains, "I like to call our sound 'countrygaze' because it inhabits that middle ground between Indie rock and hazy, introspective country."

The pronunciation of Beaudoing's last name shows his heritage and Cajun is still a big part of who he is. The blazing fiddles and Zydeco rhythms were an integral part of the Doc Marshalls sound as well. At the Blue Moon tonight, they throw in some old flavor Cajun, too.

POCKETS WITHIN POCKETS

Doug waits to turn at the traffic light while I pray for a breeze to enter the truck's cab where I am slowly roasting. There should be a law stating that all motor vehicles residing in Louisiana need to have working air conditioning. I watch the cars streaming by in both directions and my dream state of small-town Lafayette streams by as well.

Like bees buzzing around their hive, these cars buzz around the hub of the city, and like bee wings flapping, these cars generate city-heat that adds to the bayou-heat already in the air. Doug finally turns the truck into the traffic flow, and I lean into the mild wind now lifting strands of drippy hair off my cheek as it blows in through the window. I watch the box stores whizz by and fast food chains wave their signs at me. Luckily, we are headed to the Blue Moon, a pocket of Lafayette untouched by modern mayhem.

Once we arrive, I leave Doug to work his shift and walk over to another cool comfort container, the public library on Congress Street, to work on a blog post. After the library, I stroll back down Jefferson Street to Carpe Diem, where anything can happen, for pomegranate gelato. Just the other day, after Doug, another friend, and I partook in eating Wednesday Happy Hour two-dollar fish tacos at the Jefferson Street Pub, we landed at Carpe Diem to sit out front and listen to Wilson Savoy of the Pine Leaf Boys play the outside upright piano. Not just Zydeco, for which the band is famed, but everything from blues to show tunes.

Today, I rendezvous with Doug now that his shift is done at the Moon, and find Wilson back at the piano, a fresh cup of coffee sitting on the piano's top. Doug informs Wilson that I also play the piano.

"I'd love to hear ya play," Wilson says to me, his Cajun French accent surfacing through his English words.

"No, actually you don't," I say as I give Doug a look of panic. My keyboard skills are nowhere near Wilson's. In the Carpe Diem restroom, an instructional Italian language tape plays through a speaker in the ceiling.

At Artmosphere, along the block between Carpe Diem and the Blue Moon, we take in the early show: Sabra Guzman and the Get Rights are on stage with Sabra already singing her country vocals.

Wilson follows us over, now there to listen and support the band. One of the Carpe Diem gelato servers arrives and while passing by, shakes Doug's hand and kisses the back of mine. Amidst the hubbub of the buzzing city, these people are the pocket of this community—hidden gems walking around town within the folds of sprawling population growth and industry.

My dancing pal Burt arrives and we two-step around tables, chairs, and those dancers just moving about the floor as Sabra's twangy vocals weave through the hooting and nannying from the crowd.

Later, back at the Blue Moon, I chat with Will who works the front gate. He artistically writes out the evening show band names onto white cardboard with his new neon markers and passes the sign under the blue light hanging near the front of his table to check the intensity of the neon. His cat, Fourteen, curls up on top of the wristband box near where Will is working. Will swipes a lock of sweaty hair across his forehead just under the cap he is wearing.

We all walk around in a southern glisten state—97% humidity today. Will tells me that the owner is renovating a larger facility over across from the Feed and Seed that will be available for larger named acts during festival times. A large dance floor and air conditioning. But not today. Today, we snuggle into the intimacy of what makes the Blue Moon what it is. This is the Lafayette I will remember. I don't know when I'll be back, but it is certain I will return to the bayou, walk down the streets while looking up at shiny strings of Mardi Gras beads hanging in the trees, learn more Italian words at Carpe Diem, dance in even more dance halls, and of course, bunk down at the Blue Moon.

Communication Carryover

Greyhound Bus Terminal
Winston-Salem, North Carolina

Several transfers get me to Winston-Salem by 7:30 in the morning, where I pick up my three small bags on the bus floor at my feet and attempt to climb over the man sleeping next to me. The early day's light brightens up the sky outside, but the aisle of the full bus is still in shadow. After I pull myself over the man's thick legs, I shuffle off the bus and collect my larger pack from the compartment underneath. Without any new passengers boarding, the bus doors close quickly and it moves on, hoping to make up some lost time in its late schedule. I drag my bags into the transit center to wait for the regional bus leaving for Wilkesboro in about an hour and rummage through my purse for my cell phone, eventually dumping all the contents out onto the floor around my feet. I had agreed to call my Workaway host once I got to the transit center to let him know I was on time with my connection to catch the regional bus.

No phone.

I do the same with my small backpack and the green bag I put miscellaneous items and travel food into. No phone anywhere.

Did it fall out of my purse as I climbed over my seat neighbor? Perhaps it's on the bus floor or seat or between the seat and the window panel?

I swallow my breath in panic, turn to look for anyone looking at all official, but no Greyhound agent is at the ticket window. Instead, attached next to the closed window is a piece of paper with a phone number to call for help or info. I toss my belongings back into my bags and packs, then jot down the number in my small notebook.

As I look around the terminal, I spot three pay phones mounted on a wall along a narrow hallway leading to the public bathrooms, dig out all of my coins from my wallet and head over to the phones. But I don't have enough cash for the phone call to my host, never mind Greyhound.

An older couple sits in the middle of the waiting area, and I exchange a dollar bill with them for more coins, then try the phones again. But none of the phones are working. Seeing my frustration, the man from the couple comes over to offer his cell phone for me to use. I make a quick call to my host, but don't feel right about multiple calls on the man's phone.

Back in Lafayette, I had a glitch with my phone—but, after turning it on and off a few times, it finally worked again. The phone isn't that new, and I had wondered if I should just buy a new one while in Louisiana. But, no, I chose not to bother. I just kept dancing.

Clearly the phone was trying to tell me something. Why was I not paying attention? I hear my friend Bruce's voice in my head now: "Perhaps, Gail, it's time to give up on old ways of communicating and embrace a new one." He loves the symbolism around experiences that are out of our control. Internally, I just roll my eyes, then fixate on the future annoyance of having to get a different phone number and inform friends, family, banks, and credit cards.

Bruce's words keep swirling around in my head, but I know that I've already embraced new ways of communicating over the last year. I've managed to gather up enough courage to ask for what I've needed and gotten back much more than I expected—rides, food, company, rooms to stay in, and just this morning, a phone to use. I've learned to walk around with the body language of a non-victim—a signal to those who might think I'm lost in some way and therefore someone easily duped. Regardless of whether they think I should have a *husband* . . . or not.

Through my blogging, I've come to have a new relationship with language, words, concepts, and the old ways seem outdated now. There is much more nakedness to the telling of my story—less fear of being exposed and seen for who I am. Through chatting with other travelers, on buses and in hostels, I've learned that all travelers lose something once in awhile. We have to pay some dues as we navigate through the loss to the other side. It's not the end of the world, even if it feels like it in the moment.

Back in 2010 when I was traveling with Bruce in New Zealand, I left my wallet on a bus in Arthur's Pass on the South Island. As I wept, Bruce found the phone number for the bus company and called them on my behalf. They found my wallet, and the next morning as the bus came through in the other direction, I retrieved it, totally intact.

I try to hold tight to the hope of someone being able to check for my phone on the bus. But, based on runarounds I've gotten with Greyhound so far, both online and in person, I don't have much optimism. I double-check the info number I jotted down and stuff my notebook into a safe pocket in my pack. Don't want to lose that, too.

One of the many rooftop art statues along Winston-Salem's Trade Street near the Transportation Center.

Once at my destination, my host offers me his landline phone to call Greyhound to see if there is a way someone can search for my phone. But all I get is the usual runaround. I call the number I had jotted down, where I am told "you have to call Richmond." So I do, but no one answers.

I call Winston-Salem back and I'm given a number for customer service in Texas, where I am also told, "You have to call Richmond." The clerk gives me a different number for Richmond, which I try. No answer. I find a third number online for baggage loss and the shipping department. No answer. I call customer service again and ask if a message can be sent to the driver, since I assume that someone has the ability to contact drivers en route.

"No ma'am, we don't have any way to call or text out," I'm told.

"Do you have a supervisor that I can have call out?" I ask.

"No, ma'am, no one in the whole building can call out."

Throughout the day, I keep trying Richmond. The whole next morning I keep trying Richmond. Maybe the man next to me saw the phone and turned it in.

Fat chance, I think. It's probably stuck in the seat cushion for the duration of its life.

Over the next few days, I catch a ride with another Workawayer into Wilkesboro to buy a new phone.

Leaving the summer heat of Louisiana, I bus to Wilkes County, North Carolina for a three-week work exchange through the online Workaway organization. Besides offering my woodworking skill sets, I help with farm chores in exchange for room and board. The poison ivy rashes are an unwanted bonus!

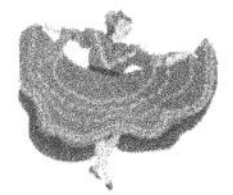

Chapter 29
Blue Ridge Napping Institute

Wilkes County, North Carolina • July 2015

My Workaway host Tim loves a good conversation, debate, or philosophical discussion. After dinner, all four of us workawayers gather in the living room of the main house to join him in front of the television.

The two young women who have been here for a couple of weeks are staying in the old schoolhouse up the path near the pond. There is a woman in her forties from Montreal, Canada staying in the small A-frame near the main house, and me—I've taken the other room in the schoolhouse for now. Tim and his two dogs are in the main house where we eat and where work is doled out. For our room and board, we're expected to work about twenty-five hours per week.

We're sent into the large garden for harvesting veggies and feeding chickens, told to grab baskets for wild mushroom gathering, and set to tasks in the kitchen for food preparation. There's a building project on the burner and time left over for whatever we want to offer, such as art projects. The two young women are currently painting a mural of a tree in the bunk room of the schoolhouse before they leave.

Every day after our communal lunch, Tim takes an hour nap and we're expected to leave the main house and allow him quiet time. When he first contacted me last January, I was intrigued by the name "Blue Ridge Napping Institute," and decided to stop here for a couple of weeks while en route back to Vermont to see what the napping was all about.

Tonight we gather in the living room to watch a documentary on homeopathy.

"Woo woo," Tim says as he puts the DVD into the player. "This film proves it." He shoots me a skeptical glance over the top of his reading glasses, his thick white hair falling onto his forehead. I happened to mention traveling with a homeopathic first aid kit.

I just smile back at him. "Tim, I doubt this will change anything for me. But I'm open to see what will be presented." I politely watch, even though I've heard all the poo-poo arguments before, about science studies proving homeopathy doesn't work.

I have my first-hand experiences and that's all I need for proof. Like the time I was laid up on my living room couch with a severe sinus headache advancing into infection. I would get those headaches now and then, probably from inhaling wood dust, then obtain a script from my physician for an antibiotic, which would make it better only until the infection could take hold again, causing me agony for a couple of weeks. A neighborhood homeopath taking my woodworking for women class at the time had offered barter to offset the class cost, so I picked up the phone rather than contact my doctor. After lengthy questioning, based on my answers, she drove over a remedy for me to try and told me to call her after an hour. By the time I rang her, the headache was completely gone. There are those who might claim "placebo," but I really did not care what cured me of the infection. Later, she helped me form my small travel kit of remedies for possible hiking concerns.

In the coming days, we watch films on fake gurus, the debunking of frauds from magicians to psychics to evangelists, the case that we don't actually have free will, and for lighter fare, the history of music recording in Muscle Shoals, Alabama. Lively discussion ensues each time.

BE CAREFUL OF WOO LURKING

As we pull down vines from the side of the house, we toss the debris into a pile nearby. Tim is excited to start in on the last section of decking construction. We are just about finished when he comes by to see our progress.

"On no, here's a poison ivy vine with the rest," he says. "I thought I had removed all of it."

I look over at the hairy vine that I had just ripped down. I hadn't recognized it since the leaves were so far above me. As the vine fell, it brushed bare skin—mine.

Within two days, the rash pops up all over my body. I try Oil of Oregano that another workawayer, Marie, brought from Canada with her, jewelweed juice dabbed onto the worst areas of the rash, and home remedies found online. Nothing helps, the rash keeps spreading down my chest, arms, and legs.

"Woo woo didn't work," Tim says one day. "We need to get you to a clinic for a steroid shot."

The cheapest walk-in clinic is in North Wilkesboro and Marie offers to drive me there. After the shot, the doctor hands me three prescriptions. I don't mind the two that cost about twenty dollars each. But the steroid cream, even the generic brand—$360. I buy the jumbo tube of hydrocortisone cream instead and hope for the best.

Part of this year's journey has been to understand more deeply the attitudes, fears, and worries that get in my way. Money is always one of them. Workaway exchanges are meant for me to save money, not spend more of it, especially on poison ivy remedies. Having to buy a new phone seems like nothing now.

I dab more cream on the red, inflamed rash and join the others on the deck project, trying to ignore the itching as I work. At least it's only one annoying thing. I flash back to Hawaii with my poison oak, sunburn, blisters, lava-sliced arm cut, fever, and sinus infection simultaneously. I quickly put my agony into perspective. Maybe a shift in perspective is the lesson I need to relearn while here at the Institute.

"Not everyone likes to stay up at the schoolhouse alone," Tim told the group early on, but I like the solitude now that the two young women have left. I have a battery to power a late night lamp for pre-sleep reading, a small sink with rinsing water from an outside gravity-fed barrel, and my very own outhouse. Once the cicadas quiet down at night, the silence has been blanketing me while I sleep.

But not lately.

It is as if the ivy toxins, stopped short of their external ooze by shot and pill, turn inward. I wallow in murky fluidity, dreamscapes refusing to release me, my feet stuck in the organic humus of Jungian images. I dream deep.

Every few hours, my bladder wakes me up, and I groggily reach for my headlamp, glasses, and a rag. I refuse to go all the way to the outhouse. Instead, I walk off the deck and pee in the dirt.

While I pee, I wonder if the drugs are what is affecting my sleep, or maybe it is the aborted ooze wanting to seep through the rashes' pores, but instead, is forced into the bloodstream, and then into the urine. Maybe my body is trying to release what it no longer wishes to hold onto—some mystery fear or attitude that never got vomited out back in Arizona early in the trip. Tim would accuse me here of more woo woo, but I don't care. At the least, my internal toxins are giving nutrients to the earth for even more prolific ivy cycles.

I return to the schoolhouse bed for another few hours, though I know my bladder pattern will reach a strong arm down into the muck and pull me out again too soon—rip from me another toxin. I close my eyes for now, pulling the sheet over me and sink back down into the organic matter of my last night's sleep here at the Institute.

This morning I say goodbye to my napping nest. As I drive the electric golf cart with dirty sheets and my travel bags back to the main house, I feel like a breeze kissing a morning-lit leaf. After my night's dance with urine and ooze, I'm feeling ageless and light. Something got ripped out of me last night and I'm not sure what it was. Once again, I check my palm for any messages left there by a raven and sense that the real message is that no one else can teach me the lessons I need to learn. I have to experience what is necessary for my evolution, then look back at the answers following me.

At the main house, Marie is fluttering around the kitchen making a farewell breakfast of crepes filled with blueberries and banana, honey dripping over them on the plates.

"Well, bon appétit," she says in her Quebecois accent as she brings the plates over to the table. "Remember I am not cooking so good. I am no housewife." She came here to practice her English.

Tim has taken matters into his own hands, though, to prep her for kitchen-hood and marriage. We take pictures of her working in the kitchen and laugh.

"I'll be sending out energies to attract a husband for you, Marie," he says.

"Tim . . . be now careful," she says, shaking a finger at him. "This is very *woo woo* of you."

He graciously takes what he's been doling out all along.

The crepes are golden and filled with heart. Memories of our debates, conversations, and explorations bubble up through the dough, lifting blueberries onto tiny pedestals.

Little Dog pushes his wet nose up my arm as if to say, "no, you can't leave yet, there is so much more love I need from you." The other dog, Stella, snores on the floor over by the fireplace. I pat Little Dog on the head again, Marie invites me to visit her in Montreal and I've made a new friend in Tim. Nothing up for debate here—these things are real.

Before Tim drives me to catch the regional bus heading back to the Winston-Salem transit center, he heads upstairs for a short nap.

An Albino Horse and a Crazy Goat

Greyhound Bus Terminal
Wytheville, Virginia

A forties-ish, scraggly looking man picks up his two bags from the Greyhound bus ticket agent, then walks over to sit near me on the single bench outside the tiny terminal located along the backside of the parking lot.

Something is off and I turn to look into his brown eyes that are shaded from the overhead lights by his baseball cap. *Do I smell alcohol?* No, I don't.

I've learned, as I travel, to be open to experience, but hold an attitude of not being a victim, so I pay close attention.

He understands how people see him and looks right at me while he tells me about his career as an underwater welder outside of Boston and the car accident he had been in.

"I'm David," he says.

I give him my name. He turns and looks out over the parking lot as he struggles to pull up the next words he wants to put forth.

"I don't know why they let me live. I was in a coma for six months. Now my doctors want me to take all of these pills three times a day." He opens his satchel to show me the plastic Ziploc bags. Each bag has a printed label with the item listed and specific instructions. There must be at least twenty-five bags in there.

His brown eyes flash in the moonlight streaming down on us as David lifts his baseball cap to rearrange his long brown hair away from his face. I zip up my jacket to ward off the chill from the dropping temperature.

"They're using me as a guinea pig," he continues. "I died about fifteen times. I just want to rest now. At one point, I tried a gun to my head and it wouldn't go off." He gestures with a fake gun pointed at his head, then points it at the ground and tells me it would fire in that position.

David looks over at me in frustration, his hands clenching, then lightly touches his head where he has had some brain injury. I look away. I don't know the right thing to say. "Not your time to go," is the best I can offer, then change the subject. "Where are you headed?"

The city of Whyteville nests within Virginia's rolling hills and Blue Ridge mountains as they cascade their way south to the Smoky Mountains.

"Caribou, Maine, to see my mother, but couldn't get a ticket there from here. They told me I'll need to buy another ticket in Richmond, and again in Washington D.C., New York, and Boston. Today is a good day though, I've talked to two good people."

"Tell me about your mother?" I ask.

"She's dead," he says, and I don't understand. "She's going to Boston in a couple of weeks for cancer treatment."

David looks up at the moon now moving behind a cloud.

"Oh," I say. I assume that he means that she could be dying rather than dead. He opens his phone and shows me pictures of his three children and tells me his wife took them away after the accident.

"They're beautiful, David," I whisper as I close my teary eyes.

"I'd like to get a cow," he moves on. "I already have an albino horse, a crazy goat, and some chickens back in West Virginia." He shows me a photo of the albino horse. "When do you think the bus will come?"

I look at his ticket—we're waiting for the same bus, which is late, as usual. According to his ticket itinerary details, he'll be fine with this ticket until D.C.

Buses fill up fast over the summer though, and he'll have a hard time getting a seat when he gets there. I head over to use the wifi at the nearby McDonald's to research ticket options for him and find several tickets available from D.C. all the way to Bangor, Maine. I go back to the terminal, which has re-opened, to negotiate a ticket in David's behalf. If he has to keep buying tickets along the way, it'll take him all week to get to Maine.

"He's challenged with communication. Why can't you sell him all of what he needs?" I plead as I show the agent what I found online.

Annoyed, the agent makes an excuse and then issues the rest of the transfers David needs to get to Bangor. I return to the outside bench and David heads over to the McD's. When he gets back, he places a bag and a cup next to me.

"Thank you for your help," he shyly says to me, then sits down beside me again.

I look into the bag and see the hamburgers I don't eat. The cup holds coffee I won't drink. But I know he needs me to accept his gift.

I look in the bag again and see the fries, then look over and into his eyes, smile, and tell him that the fries will be just perfect, but I don't eat meat.

"My sister is a vegetarian as well," he informs me. I'm not really one, but I just nod in agreement.

Once the fries are gone, I take the bag inside to offer the rest to the ticket agent, who just points to the trash barrel. I toss it in, then head back outside to thank David on the ticket agent's behalf.

It's getting late, but I remain present, since I can't imagine that many people are willing to just be witness to who David is. This is one of the lessons I've learned on the road this past year—just *be* with strangers and I might be surprised. I watch him open the bags of herbal pills and prescription drugs and one by one, swallow them, washing them down with a bottle of whiskey.

Up in the sky and free of the clouds now, the moon seems to look down on us with gentle compassion. I wish I could go to Bangor with him to make sure he actually gets there. But I will get off in Roanoke, as planned, and hope the bus drivers get him safely on the right transfers. The bus, now two hours late, comes and we get on. I find a seat near the front and David heads farther back.

Silently, I wish him a safe journey, hope he finds peace, sees his children someday, gets a cow, and spends time with his mother before she dies. I lean my head back against the bus seat, and relieved to be in the darkness, I finally allow myself to weep.

Coming full circle, I stop in Roanoke, Virginia en route back to Vermont to see my couch-surfing friends once again. While there, we walk this labyrinth, and I meditate on the year of travel behind me.

Chapter 30

The Labyrinth

Roanoke, Virginia • August 2015

"I've been writing more since I saw you last," Brian says while pulling items out of the fridge for the usual morning smoothie, just like when I was last here, and places them on the counter. "You've inspired me. I have stories to tell, too."

I remember how he told me he always says *yes* when someone asks him to do something. This is how he's found himself in compromising situations, on buses in third-world countries, ducking gunfire from Russian guards—he has plenty of stories he likes to tell again and again.

Not unlike the individual pieces of fruit he drops into the blender—each of our stories, with their specific flavor and texture, swirls around within each of us.

I can see Brian, along with our other friend Ellen, couchsurfing at my home in Vermont on their way to Montreal several years ago. Unknown to each of us at that time, we would stay in touch. I would start and end my year of travel with them.

"I'd love to hear more of your stories," I tell Brian as he cuts up slices of banana to add into the mix.

"You've acquired a lot now, too," he says with respect, pulling back his long gray hair and adjusting his wire-rimmed glasses. "You should write a book about your travels."

"Perhaps . . ."

While the blender whirs, I re-study Brian's artwork along the wall in his living room—his large colorful geometric paintings, some he hasn't quite finished since I was here last September.

I chance upon the collage with the mummified Barbie dolls leaning against the wall by the brick fireplace. When I first saw the Barbie collage, I felt both saddened and outraged by them—seeing in them how, throughout my life, I

My dear friend Bill Saari (named Brian for the sake of this book) with his artwork at the Alexander-Heath Contemporary Art Gallery in Roanoke, Virginia during a show in 2019. *Photo courtesy of Ed Hettig, curator/founder of the gallery.*

had limited myself by caution, afraid of any exposure that would humiliate me. This year of travel has allowed me to unwrap myself from all that caution—to expose myself, expand, reinvent. As I unwrapped more and more each month, I learned that being fully open isn't an invitation for getting hurt, but, instead, for deeper connection.

Maybe physical freedom away from Vermont is what I needed in order to find enough courage to show myself fully. In the end, what is important is how I view myself. Maybe I had to leave home to remember other parts of *me*, lying dormant, and trust in them, exploring what had not yet evolved, and learn that if I change how I see myself, others might see me differently, too.

Photo courtesy of Ed Hettig, curator/founder of the gallery.

Brian and I sit down at the kitchen table with our smoothies in hand to share more stories of adventure with each other, both of us understanding what it means to say *yes*.

"Will you tell me the story of the Russian guards again?" I ask.

LABYRINTH

Soapy film hangs in suspension within the bubble wand. I can't tell if I am awake or not. The wand readies itself to be blown in either direction, rainbow iridescence clinging to the bubble surface. I wipe the soap slightly away from the plastic stick holder and try to peek through, but no reality exists clearly within the soapy sphere. Each color sheen seems to open a window into a different blurred landscape, into a faceted maze of options and choices. Bright sunlight shines onto my face through the window. Clearly awake, I turn over to keep the glare out of my sleepy eyes.

This is how I slowly woke up this morning, just in time to get ready to accompany Ellen, with her violin, and her friend Jill, with her guitar, to their paid music gig at the Unity Church. Normally, I don't remember dreams, but lately, they're too vivid to forget. There are so many experiences from the past year floating around in my psyche.

Now that the service is over, the three of us walk the labyrinth behind the church. Low to the ground, rusty metal edges and smooth stones mark the labyrinth's way as we pass each other along the many turns. At any time, any one of us can step over the edge and leave the labyrinth for the familiar grass.

But we don't.

We keep going with the meditation, contemplate the importance of the steps needing to be taken, allow ourselves to just *be,* walking our individual paces. Here, physically, I can see the end of the matrix, but in the bigger picture of life, I cannot—the journey is complicated. Over this past year, I've often heard my friend Bruce's voice in my ear: *You have to trust your path*. This hasn't been easy at times.

I used to believe that I always needed to have a destination in mind, a goal to achieve. Before I set out on this journey, I felt as if I was walking in circles, circles that I myself had created, circles feeling stagnant, lacking purpose.

But here along the labyrinth, the winding maze suits me more. The unexpected twists and turns need presence, attention, mindfulness, like the Buddha-like surfers waiting patiently on their boards on the Pacific ocean near San Diego, California. I like the challenge to be alert, to listen, to invite life's mysteries.

Not unlike the soapy film buoyant in the bubble wand in my dream, I feel suspended through each step, trying to trust that each turn will lead me toward new perspectives and new choices. Ellen and Jill are focused inwardly on their own thoughts as I pass by them going in a different direction. We catch each other's gaze, but each of us is deep within our own experience.

What was the highlight of the year? is the thought that surfaces while I walk. Tim asked it while I was at the Napping Institute. Brian asked it just yesterday. I'm constantly pondering the question and offer whatever answer emerges in the moment.

Memory flashes with each mindful step I take, celebrating the people, places, and experiences from over the year. Like a stream of bubbles floating around me, as soon as I remember an image, the bubble pops and a new memory takes its place.

I linger on a scene from Ellen's lawn last September, listening to the music of Coyote Joe as he sang about daring to recreate himself, daring to risk *living true.* I used to think that freedom came from letting go of old beliefs and attitudes. Now, I realize that letting go of anything is unnecessary. Brian is right— say *yes* to experiences that are offered— and see what changes us. A year ago I couldn't imagine *who* I would be traveling out there *on* the road. Now, I can't imagine who I will be *off* the road.

In my dream, I had slowly stepped up onto the rim of the bubble wand and ran my hand over the facets of the soapy film. I readied myself to go through, but knew not into which reality. I couldn't find my way through the maze of colors and light. This is how it has to be now—continuing to walk along with the unknown.

Back on the grass, the three of us say nothing, but silently walk back to the car. There isn't anything for us to say. Yet, I feel I say everything by my choices and decisions; I say everything by what I expose *of* myself, and trust *within* myself.

I return back to my straw-bale home in southern Vermont.

Vermont Return: What Empties Must Fill
(Tao de Ching)

Westminster, Vermont • August 2015

Having retrieved my truck, I park in my carport and ascend the stairs onto the cedar deck. When I slowly open the door into my kitchen, silence permeates the empty house, and I hesitate. This silence is filled with bittersweet memories: the arduous house building, my handcrafted cabinetry work for clients, the music shared with friends, the heartaches and painful heartbreaks. These memories, like ghosts of what has already come and gone, now seem like a lifetime ago.

I'm not ready to pick up from where I left off a year ago. As I round the corner by the stairs, the sun shines through the living room window and across the tile floor in front of the couch I left behind for my renters to use, the only piece of furniture waiting for me. Next to the couch is the empty, clean, cat food dispenser and litter box left by my renters for my return, and my heart fills with sadness about the loss of my feline pal.

I lower myself onto the tired cushions and close my eyes to allow snapshots from the year to surface again: Louisiana alligators, then a young girl dancing to Mariachi music in a chapel in San Antonio, Half Dome towering over Yosemite Valley, Channel Island foxes tumbling in the grass. But those are from the past now, too. I've gotten used to living in the moment, looking for the beauty that exists in each different place.

The light of the late afternoon shifts to illuminate the landline phone blinking with messages and I wonder if they are all from my mother. I hope they are from dear friends, like Nan, welcoming me home to the end of the year's circle. Or is it the center?

I don't get up to listen to the calls but linger in my heart rather than in my head. I bask in the warm sunlight, focus on my breathing… feeling this is both my sanctuary *and* my belonging.

Who have I become over this last year?

My transformation might seem subtle. Many won't even see it in me at all—my need to empty what no longer works for me, to fill up again with what has evolved while traveling paths and passages, false starts and dead ends.

When I return to routines, my challenge will be to stay *fluid*, to keep dancing unabashedly in the chapel aisle to Mariachi music, living as *true* as the young girl in the ruffled skirt.

And when the next journey beckons me back out onto the road, I want to be ready with an open heart and Bruce's wisdom packed away in my head: *keep inviting life's mysteries, grit, and miracles . . .*

At a tea ceremony at the Lan Su Japanese Garden in Portland, Oregon.

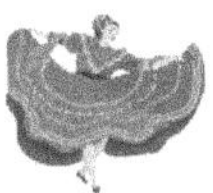

Acknowledgments

I can't even thank my writers group enough for their relentless, and I mean relentless, feedback, encouragement, and support in this book getting published: Sandy, Susan, Barbara, Mary, Roger, Mia, Eric, Nick, Dave and Sue, along with others who popped into the story and out again over the last few years.

Through the online peer-critique site Scribophile, several peer authors stuck with me through the reading of my chapters, offering me valuable insights and comments on my writing, storytelling, and more. I especially want to thank authors Veronica, AR, and Mitchell.

Who knew, in the summer of 2016, on top of a mountain in Maine, I would meet Nancy E. Randolph, whose publishing and editing expertise would give me support once this book was ready to move from my hands into the world. Her consulting generosity has been over and beyond that seed of synchronicity while meeting during our individual backpacking trips along the Appalachian Trail in Maine's Bigelow Preserve.

Then there is my long-time nomadic friend Bruce Margarido, who has offered guidance, wisdom, and perspective throughout all of my travels.

I would also like to thank my dear friend Sarah West for her photography of my biography photo, and Nahid Razon and Kotha Redwana from Bangladesh for their illustration talents.

But it all started with Brenda Beardsley, my writing instructor back in 2013, when I took her five-week writing class on a whim. Because of her enthusiastic support, I continued along my trajectory with creative writing.

Thanks also to my editor, Rachael Cohen for her generosity of time and expertise with content feedback and copyedits.